IS THERE A JEWISH PHILOSOPHY?

THE LITTMAN LIBRARY OF
JEWISH CIVILIZATION

Dedicated to the memory of
LOUIS THOMAS SIDNEY LITTMAN
*who founded the Littman Library for the love of God
and as an act of charity in memory of his father*
JOSEPH AARON LITTMAN
and to the memory of
ROBERT JOSEPH LITTMAN
who continued what his father Louis had begun
יהא זכרם ברוך

'*Get wisdom, get understanding:
Forsake her not and she shall preserve thee*'

PROV. 4:5

*The Littman Library of Jewish Civilization is a registered UK charity
Registered charity no. 1000784*

Is There a Jewish Philosophy?

Rethinking Fundamentals

❧

LEON ROTH

London
The Littman Library of Jewish Civilization
in association with Liverpool University Press

The Littman Library of Jewish Civilization
Registered office: 4th floor, 7–10 Chandos Street, London WIG 9DQ

in association with Liverpool University Press
4 Cambridge Street, Liverpool L69 7ZU, UK
www.liverpooluniversitypress.co.uk/littman

Managing Editor: Connie Webber

Distributed in North America by
Oxford University Press Inc., 198 Madison Avenue,
New York, NY 10016, USA

First published in paperback 1999

Catalogue records for this book are available from the
British Library and the Library of Congress

ISBN 978–1–874774–55–6

Publishing co-ordinator: Janet Moth
Proof-reading: Lindsey Taylor-Guthartz
Design: Pete Russell, Faringdon, Oxon.
Typeset by Footnote Graphics, Warminster, Wilts.

Printed and bound in Great Britain by
CPI Group (UK) Ltd., Croydon, CR0 4YY

Dedicated to the memory of

JOSEPH ROTH (1866–1924)
who migrated from Poland to England in 1885,
successfully established himself in London,
married Etty Jacobs, and became the father of

DAVID ROTH 1893–1958
DANIEL ROTH 1894–1959
LEON ROTH 1896–1963
CECIL ROTH 1899–1970

1896–1963

Contents

Publisher's Note

LEON ROTH was the first Professor of Philosophy at the Hebrew University in Jerusalem, where he taught from 1928 to 1951. The purpose of this volume is to make known to a new generation Roth's writings and teachings on Judaism, ethics, and philosophy and their interrelationships.

Thanks are due to Gabriel and Helena Roth, to Rabbi Albert Friedlander, and to all others who helped to assemble this collection and make it available to the Littman Library. We are particularly grateful to Edward Ullendorff for his encouragement, and for preparing the Foreword, and to Raphael Loewe, who generously undertook the translation of '*Imitatio Dei*', an article previously available only in Hebrew, provided the bibliography of Leon Roth's writings, and resolved various questions that arose in the process of preparing the book for publication.

The Library is also grateful to the institutions who have kindly agreed to the inclusion of previously published essays in this collection; full acknowledgement of these sources appears at the start of each essay.

Foreword

EDWARD ULLENDORFF

LEON ROTH was the first Professor of Philosophy in the Hebrew University of Jerusalem. He was an ornament to that seat of learning in its early and heroic days. He served as Dean of the Faculty of Humanities and as Rector, the academic head of the university, in the crucial period of 1940 to 1943. He was for twenty-three years, virtually his entire active career, one of the three or four most influential men in the shaping of the academic structure and ethos of the university. With J. L. Magnes, the President of the university, Martin Buber, and Gershom Scholem he stood for an Arab–Jewish partnership, for forbearance, disavowal of violence, and for genuinely civilized values. He was, to the best of my knowledge, the only scholar to be elected a Fellow of the British Academy whose working life had been spent abroad. He was an inspiring teacher, a true friend, and a man of uncompromising honesty. He did not suffer fools gladly. He could be impatient with those in positions of power, but he was uniformly kind and considerate to those who sought or needed his help or advice. He possessed wisdom, wit, and charm in equal measure. He was self-effacing (anything else would have appeared vulgar to him) but was endowed with an entirely natural and unself-conscious authority of a quite unusual order. He had exceptional courage, both physical and moral: in the worst days of the Palestine troubles he would insist on seeing me home, late at night, to a remote district of Jerusalem—pretending that his constitutional took him there in any event.

Roth was born in London in 1896 to an observant Jewish family. Both his parents were descended from rabbinical families in Poland. His father, Joseph Roth, emigrated to England from Poland in 1885 and was successful in developing a glass and building materials business. Joseph engaged as a teacher for his four sons Rabbi Moshe Vilenski, who was not only a brilliant rabbinical scholar but also steeped in general philosophy. Thus, the Roth boys (the youngest of whom was Cecil, later to become a historian and Reader in Jewish Studies at Oxford University) were brought up not only as orthodox Jews but were exposed from an early age to classical European literature and values.

Roth won a scholarship to the City of London School, with its fine classical tradition, which eventually took him to Exeter College Oxford, with a scholarship in Classics. But his studies were interrupted by the First World War when Roth, like many of his contemporaries, volunteered to join the army and saw active service in France. In 1917 he was commissioned and transferred to the newly formed Jewish Battalion of the Royal Fusiliers but, to his regret, was not sent to Palestine. His sergeant in the Jewish Battalion was David Ben-Gurion.

One of his reported accomplishments in the Jewish Battalion was his successful defence of Jacob Epstein when the sculptor was court-martialled for allegedly infringing army regulations. Roth argued before the court that it was wrong for a man of Epstein's talents to spend his time peeling potatoes. The argument won the day, and Epstein was moved to a drawing office.

On his return to the university Roth won two of the most prestigious scholarships in very disparate disciplines, the John Locke in Mental Philosophy and the James Mew in Hebrew. These scholarships laid the foundation of his work on Spinoza, Descartes, and Maimonides. In 1923 the philosopher Samuel Alexander called him to Manchester to join his department as lecturer in philosophy.

Many years afterwards, in the late 1950s and early 1960s, I would occasionally invite Leon Roth to lecture at Manchester University when I was serving there as Professor of Semitic Languages. He would then take me to the large entrance hall of the Faculty of Arts building to stand for a few moments in reverence before the bust of the great Samuel Alexander.

Between these two events—his first appointment to an academic post at Manchester in 1923, and his homage to Samuel Alexander thirty-six years later—lies a career of quite exceptional significance. A visit by him to Jerusalem in 1925 to represent Manchester University at the opening of the Hebrew University on Mount Scopus quickened his interest in the idea of such a university, which expressed the Hebrew renaissance in Palestine. In 1927 the renowned Hebrew essayist and philosopher Ahad Ha'am died in Tel Aviv, and the university at Jerusalem resolved to establish a Chair of Philosophy bearing his name. I do not know what the field of candidates was in 1927–8, but in retrospect the choice of Leon Roth as the first occupant of that Chair seems so obvious and natural that it is quite impossible now to envisage any other person in the foundation Chair of Philosophy at Jerusalem.

Thus in 1928, at the age of 32, Leon Roth came to Jerusalem to initiate the teaching of philosophy and to supervise research in it. He turned out

to be the most mythopoeic of men. His mannerisms, conscious or un-
conscious, were numerous. They ranged from such trivia as the hand-
kerchief, carefully lodged in his left jacket sleeve[1] and occasionally withdrawn during his lectures and then meticulously returned to that (to us
unfamiliar) habitat, to his exceptionally beautiful, yet simple, Hebrew
that was produced and modulated in an English voice and accent which,
at any rate at first, were quite startling. There was, of course, no reason to
suppose that, say, Isaiah or Jeremiah would have considered the usual
Russian or Polish accent of Hebrew more authentic than Roth's English
pronunciation, but in those days the Anglo-Saxon lilt was virtually unknown, and most certainly in conjunction with Hebrew. It was, in fact,
confined to the Englishman Leon Roth and, to a much lesser extent, to
the American J. L. Magnes. It must again be emphasized that, curiously
enough, English in Palestine was an incidental result of the Second
World War and came in when the British administration went out.

Roth was philosopher, teacher, and educator *par excellence* (certainly
not educationist or educationalist—expressions that were anathema to
him). He taught and educated, in the widest possible sense, successive
generations of students at Jerusalem who sat spellbound at his feet. His
classes were by far the largest; at a time when there were some 500–600
students inscribed in all the faculties, about 150 of that total number
would regularly attend his lectures. He would insist that students should
be punctual and be seated in their places when he entered the lecture hall.
He disliked the discourtesy of latecomers and the disturbance they
caused to concentration on complex subjects. At some stage he decided
to lock the lecture hall after he had arrived and put the key into his
pocket. This measure certainly deterred the stragglers. On one occasion a
student fainted during his lecture, and some of her friends ran forward to
obtain the key from the professor, who reluctantly parted with it and
exclaimed in his inimitable Hebrew: 'Is it conceivable that anyone can be
ready for life at a university if that is what my philosophy does to him?'

At first I used to be astonished when Roth said, as he frequently did in
his lectures or in reply to questions, generally with a slightly mischievous
smile: 'I do not know' or 'I simply have no notion what this text could
possibly mean'. This was unheard of; most professors at Jerusalem at that

---

[1] Information from Helena Roth, Leon's daughter, that this was a habit picked up in
the army, which frowned on handkerchiefs being placed in jacket or trouser pockets. I am
greatly obliged to Gabriel Roth, Leon's son, for commenting on the Leon Roth chapter
in my *The Two Zions* (Oxford: Oxford University Press, 1988) and for giving me some
additional factual information.

period were products of the continental tradition where professorial omniscience was axiomatic. In later years Roth and I often spoke about this, and no piece of advice has been more useful in my own career: confessions of ignorance, real or alleged, were always applauded—certainly above any pretence to all-knowingness.

Apart from the strength and independence derived from his English background—a great asset under the British Mandate—Roth also had the reputation (I do not know whether it was justified or was an aspect of those mythopoeic qualities) of being sufficiently wealthy[2] not to draw his salary. In a country of such scarce financial resources as Palestine was in those days, the advantages, in terms of independence of mind and position, which such assurance conferred were considerable. Moreover, there was the ordered and tranquil background of a stable and untroubled country of origin, an inestimable benefit to the few immigrants from Britain and the United States. Roth also possessed a fine house and an extensive library; his immediate family and, as far as I know, more distant relations as well were safe and, unlike those of so many others from central and eastern Europe, out of Hitler's clutches.

Although as an undergraduate I was primarily concerned with oriental studies, I was naturally curious to see this famous professor and university character and to savour his personality at first hand. When, at the end of the first term, I presented my registration and attendance book to him for his signature, he pretended to be puzzled: 'Could you have mixed up philology (which you are supposed to be studying) with philosophy, the "love of words" with the "love of wisdom"? I was saved [he added] from philology by the First World War, for when I returned to Oxford after the war I had enough sense to turn to philosophy.' I enjoyed his teasing and the twinkle in his eye. During my first few weeks I had thought he was much too elementary and read Plato in Hebrew instead of in Greek, but that was just a mixture of ignorance and youthful arrogance on my part. The artistry of Roth's teaching method lay precisely in its simplicity, in his ability to make the most complex matters appear easy and clear. In his seminars (of which I attended only a few) he employed his Socratic maieutic skills (the art of the 'midwife') with consummate ability. Students may have feared him, for he could *appear* aloof, but most respected him greatly; and more than a few (among whom, even as an outsider, I numbered myself) revered him.

The fact that Plato or Aristotle, Leibniz or Hume could be read in

---

[2] I have since been informed that Roth was never what could correctly be termed 'wealthy'.

Hebrew was entirely thanks to Roth who, soon after his arrival at Jerusalem, set out to create a library of classical philosophical texts to be rendered into Hebrew. He shared this work of translation with some of his disciples, with whose collaboration he fashioned a vocabulary and syntactical receptivity in Hebrew which allowed this process to be pursued successfully. The student body who congregated in his classes had widely differing educational backgrounds and aptitudes (much more so than in the more narrowly defined disciplines), which made the creation by Roth of the library of philosophical classics in Hebrew such an essential requirement.

I would suppose that the 1930s and the period of his rectorship in the early years of the war were the best years of his professional career. His wife and children offered wonderful support to him; I have rarely seen such a united and contented family as his, over which he presided with quizzical humour and the true pedagogue's light touch.

During his rectorship, Ben-Gurion (then Chairman of the Jewish Agency) and Moshe Shertok (in charge of the Agency's foreign department and later, as Sharett, the second prime minister of Israel) came up to the Hebrew University to urge students to join the army. When war broke out it became clear that, under the rules of the Mandate, the British Administration had no legal powers to introduce conscription. At first this appeared to be an unimportant restriction, as, in a war against the Nazis, Jews could scarcely fail to do their duty. However, with some of the young men the memory of the 1939 White Paper, which seemed to have placed severe limits upon the development of the Jewish National Home in Palestine (the official designation in terms of the Balfour Declaration and the League of Nations Mandate), was still too fresh. So, when Ben-Gurion visited the university, he declared that we must fight the war as if there were no White Paper, and we must fight the White Paper as if there were no war. This was no doubt the right spirit, but a somewhat greater emphasis on the fundamental distinction between political disagreement and genocidal mania would have been welcome. Ben-Gurion spoke for about an hour and was then followed by Shertok with a much shorter peroration. I do not recall that either speaker made a great impact on the student body on that occasion.

The meeting was brought to a conclusion by a brief 'footnote' (as he put it) from the Rector, Leon Roth. I can remember his speech in every detail, not least because my principal talent as an undergraduate lay in an ability to imitate two of my teachers, of whom Roth was one. It is, alas, impossible to reproduce in English the flavour of his Hebrew, not being able to reflect on paper all the nuances and extra-linguistic concomitants of his brief address:

My brother and I were at Oxford during the First World War. Initially there was no conscription in England, and we thought to continue our studies. We thus found ourselves in much the same position as that in which you are now placed. But more and more of our fellow-students joined the forces, and we came to feel that we had to choose between being scholars or gentlemen. We chose to be gentlemen and not scholars. I know, of course, that all of you prefer to be scholars (*melummadim*) rather than gentlemen (*gentlemannim*).

It was powerful, humorous, and highly effective.

I recall another occasion, not long after the end of the war, when I briefly served in the academic secretariat of Jerusalem University and happened to see Leon Roth in action. It was, I think, December 1946, a dark period in the annals of Mandatary Palestine, with Jewish terrorist activities by Begin's IZL (National Military Organization) and by the Stern commandos at their height. The government would intercept illegal immigrant ships and send them to Cyprus. The Va'ad Le'umi (Jewish National Council) would then declare a general strike, usually from 10 to 12 in the morning. Roth often lectured from 9 to 11 a.m. At 10 o'clock the students would leave the lecture hall, while Roth continued with his discourse before a virtually empty hall. It was not that he lacked sympathy for the hapless victims of Nazi persecution who wished to find refuge and a home in Palestine, but he did not believe that either terrorism or strikes were the best—or indeed a defensible—means of achieving these aims. On the occasion on which I happened to be passing his lecture hall, with the students banging the door to disturb his teaching, I heard him call out to them:

Gentlemen, listen to me for one moment, and then you can continue with your highly cerebral activity of door-banging. Let me just ask you what you think is more likely to bring about the end of British rule in this country—your noisy door-banging or my philosophy? Surely no reasonable man can doubt that it is my philosophy that will achieve those ends!

By that time Leon Roth was deeply troubled and unhappy. Developments in Palestine towards the end of the war and the following period, culminating in the murder of Lord Moyne, the Minister Resident at Cairo, the bombing of the King David Hotel, and the assassination of Count Bernadotte in Jerusalem as well as other acts of terrorism perpetrated by Jewish paramilitary organizations, led to his profound disillusionment and to ethical, moral, and ideological doubts which could no longer be suppressed. This was not how he and his colleagues, Magnes first and foremost, had envisaged the building of a Jewish commonwealth in Palestine. No doubt there was also some conflict of loyalties between his English birth and upbringing and his devotion to the Jewish National Home and its university which he had helped to create and to perfect.

So after twenty-three years of service, at the age of 55, he took his leave of Jerusalem, resigned his Chair, and returned to England. It was a profoundly traumatic decision, arrived at after prolonged heart-searching. It was said that the university was 'more than reluctant to accept his resignation' and that 'strenuous efforts were made to persuade him to remain in Israel', for the 'Government of Israel . . . appreciated what an asset to the country he was'. It was also reported that 'he was offered the Presidency of the University' and that 'his appointment as Minister of Education was mooted'.[3]

Typically, Roth made no public statement of his intention to resign. He broke the news by passing a handwritten note to his colleague and fellow Professor of Philosophy S. H. Bergmann, in the middle of an academic meeting. According to Bergmann,[4] the note was to the effect that Roth had decided to leave his teaching post and Chair; that he had given to the university all that he could and did not wish to repeat himself *ad infinitum*; and that man has a duty to move to other tasks while still able to undertake them. In reporting this, Bergmann suggested that the incident that triggered Roth's resignation was the massacre, in April 1948, of over 250 Arabs in the village of Deir Yassin by members of two Jewish terrorist groups. Though not a pacifist, Roth abhorred violence and detested hypocrisy.

Another colleague, Ernst Simon, reported a farewell walk and conversation with Roth: 'I said to him "I think I know why you are going to leave us." He replied with his customary irony: "Really? Tell me, I would like to know it, too." I answered: "Because you prefer to be a stranger among strangers rather than being a stranger among your own people." He stopped in his tracks and said: "You are right." '[5]

Although Roth left Israel, he did not leave the Hebrew University, to which he had given so much of his spirit and genius, without a parting gift

[3] R. Loewe (ed.), *Studies in Rationalism, Judaism and Universalism in Memory of Leon Roth* (London: Routledge, 1966), 5.

[4] In an obituary article in the newspaper *Ha'aretz*, 11 Apr. 1963.

[5] *Ha'aretz*, 11 Apr. 1963.

of some 10,000 of his books. Many of these treasures of his library testified to his expertise in Jewish texts and to his love of the Bible. He liked to travel with a *tikkun* and to read the weekly *parashah* in the synagogues he visited. He was a deeply observant Jew, but never ostentatiously so, for he shrank from all forms of ostentation; at the same time, he had a remarkable knowledge of English literature. His administrative abilities were manifested in his pioneering work as Rector and Dean of the Hebrew University, whose system of studies he influenced in many fundamental ways. It would be impossible to offer an adequate portrait of Roth the man without referring to his love of walking. He had ample opportunity to indulge in this hobby in Jerusalem and at Cambridge, as well as the many other places he visited: the West Country of England, St Andrews in Scotland, Switzerland, and, finally, New Zealand, where he died.

As an undergraduate and only occasional student of his, my personal acquaintance with Roth was fairly superficial. I admired him from a distance. When I served in Eritrea–Ethiopia during the war we had some occasional correspondence, and it was then that I came to develop the greatest respect for his pithy epistolary style, characteristically forceful writing, and sage counsel. During my brief service in the academic secretariat of the Hebrew University I saw a great deal of Roth, as I was associated with him, in a junior capacity, in the preparation of an international congress in Jerusalem. I observed him in his dealings with his Jerusalem colleagues and his confrères all over the world, his stewardship of the university press, and his relationship, always self-assured as well as humorous, with the leaders of the Jewish community in Palestine, particularly with the upright Yitshak Ben-Zvi, the head of the Jewish National Council and, later, the second president of the State of Israel.

But I saw most of Leon Roth, and at close quarters, during the last ten years of his life, between 1953 and 1963, in London, Cambridge, Brighton, Manchester, and St Andrews. I was then teaching Semitic languages at St Andrews University, and he and Mrs Roth would come in the autumn for a week's visit to Scotland to savour the academic atmosphere of a small and ancient university city. During this last phase of his life, perhaps mellower and sadder, yet ever stimulating, wise, and witty, he would travel all over the world with his wife, lecture occasionally, and write books devoted to an interpretation of Judaism that was rational and humane.

When I was at St Andrews, and later at Manchester, he came to give a lecture that was entitled 'Some Observations on Useless Knowledge'. It was a *tour de force* and greatly enjoyed by all who listened to it. It was a typical piece of Rothian wit and wisdom. Alas, it was hard to persuade him to consider another teaching post. Perhaps professional philosophy had become too insular and inbred, or perhaps he was too much out of sympathy with current fashions in the subject to feel sufficiently comfortable in a Chair of Philosophy.

To one particular suggestion by me to consider another university appointment he replied in characteristic terms:

I can claim acquaintance, I think, with the major trends of the philosophical tradition in the modern world, and, while not a Greek specialist, I have learned both to feel and to win respect for the thought of Plato and Aristotle. On the other hand, I know nothing about mathematical logic; I have doubts as to the final value of 'analysis', and I see no cause to believe that salvation is of the sciences. While having been faced from so near with so much wanton killing and destruction, I am more disturbed by the problem of evil than by that of induction.

In a sense, this letter embodies much of Roth's credo and also affords a glimpse of his style and personality, as well as of his approach to ethics and philosophy. He was a very practical, down-to-earth person, far removed from the stereotype of the absent-minded professor. He did not have much use for ideas that were not related to serious problems. For example, his insistence that morality should be based on absolute values, an issue on which he differed from Ahad Ha'am, arose from the fear that, if it were based on such concepts as 'the social good', it would open the door to the horrors of totalitarianism. Roth was interested in the process of good government and regarded biblical ethics as a major element in its development.

Leon Roth was a truly singular personality; when he died, suddenly and painlessly, at the age of 67, I felt bereft and desolate. Now, more than thirty-five years since his death, I still mourn his premature passing. For so long he had been at the very centre of Jerusalem life and letters; and when he departed from that environment, which he had graced so elegantly, his moral stature still shone brightly—but something of his *joie de vivre* had departed. Present generations of students at Jerusalem have hardly heard of him; many of his own students have gone by now. And when I think of his fame and power and central position half a century ago, I am more conscious than ever of the inexorable truth of *sic transit gloria mundi*.

Note

PROFESSOR ULLENDORFF has graciously allowed me to append a few words to his own admirable sketch of the life and personality of Leon Roth. I, too, remain acutely conscious of the void which he left at his relatively early death, and regret that, to the present generation, his is but the name (coupled with that of his brother Cecil) of a square in a suburb of Jerusalem. But it is at least a matter of satisfaction that in 1997 a doctorate was conferred by the Hebrew University on Jan David Katzew for a thesis, written in English, entitled 'Leon Roth: His Life and Thought. The Place of Ethics in Jewish Education'.

It may serve some purpose to record here where obituary notices and tributes appeared at the time of his death: *The Times*, 5 April 1963, supplemented by E. Ullendorff, 8 April; the *Jewish Chronicle*, 5 April; the *Jerusalem Post* (Norman Bentwich), and *Ha'aretz* (S. H. Bergmann), 4 April; the *New York Times*, 5 April; *Molad*, 21 (1963) (Ruth Kleinberger); the *Proceedings* of the British Academy, 50 (1965) (T. E. Jessop). The Magnes Press of the Hebrew University published a memorial brochure with contributions by S. H. Bergmann, M. Sternberg, and N. Rothenstreich, and a brief memoir by myself appeared in a memorial volume edited by me, and entitled *Studies in Rationalism, Judaism and Universalism* (London: Routledge, 1966).

Professor Ullendorff (p. xv) records Hugo Bergmann's surmise that the incident that made Roth decide to leave Israel was the massacre, in April 1948, of many Arabs at Deir Yassin by members of Jewish terrorist groups. In this connection, it is pertinent to reprint here a letter which he published in the *Jewish Chronicle* (4 December 1953) in reply to one from Dr Abraham Cohen in the aftermath of the Qibya raid. Cohen, writing apologetically, had conceded that the Israeli action deserved censure, but claimed that such Jewish protests as it had evoked were merely inspired by sensitivity to gentile recrimination. Roth rejoined as follows:

Problems of morals are notoriously complicated, and I have no wish to add to the difficulties raised by what is now called the Qibya incident. Dr Cohen's summing-up is clear. The Israelis, he says, are censurable, but most of the censurers should have remained silent.

So far so good. Two of the factors involved (the Israelis on the one hand and the rest of the world on the other) have been satisfactorily dealt with. But there are other factors to be considered as well. There is, for example, the religion, or the system of thought, called Judaism. And there are, too, the non-Israeli Jews considered either in themselves or in so far as they represent, or profess, Judaism. The problem is whether either Judaism or Jewry can acquiesce in this incident. It is the type of action which we have been accustomed to say that Judaism taught the world to condemn and from which Jewry itself has so often suffered. If we identify ourselves with it now or condemn its condemners, where will Jewry be the next time it itself is the victim, and what will Jews be able to say the next time Judaism is attacked?

Shall we still be able to say that we demand one law for all and that we do not do to others what we do not wish others to do to us? That the *lex talionis* is not Jewish; that we abhor the spilling of blood, even of animals; that we are commanded in the Pentateuch to care for the non-Jew ('love the stranger'), as was noted by the rabbis of another day, thirty-six times? Shall we still be able to say that institution of properly constituted courts or the investigation of crime is one of the fundamental moral requirements of Judaism; that the Torah bans private revenge and insists on due process of law; that fathers should not be killed for the sins of children nor children for the sins of fathers, but each man should suffer for his own acts; that responsibility before both God and man is in Jewish eyes personal?

Dare we repeat the old commonplace of which we were once so proud that Jewish courts were so careful to avoid the shedding of blood that they disallowed all circumstantial evidence and in practice all but abolished the death penalty? If kindness to animals is the essence of *sheḥitah* and we resent any breath of denigration of that venerable institution can we cry out against honest and liberal-minded men, even of other religions and types of thought, who on the grounds taught by Judaism recognise an Israeli action for what it is?

The real tragedy is of course for the Israelis. And it does not lie in the political deterioration of their borders. It lies in the moral deterioration of their souls. What manner of men are these who could contrive this action, or what persons could carry it out? And what manner of men are those who, arrogantly dismissing the moral issue, bemuse themselves and us with their *realpolitik*? Where terrorism is used as an instrument of policy the worst consequences fall on those who use it.

And here I should refer again to Dr Cohen's letter. Dr Cohen says that we have no right to object to the drastic action taken by Israelis at Qibya unless we could conscientiously assert that in the circumstances we would not have done the same thing ourselves. I think that the detail of the formulation of the facts of the case could be questioned: but is Dr Cohen's general principle sound? It is surely a truism that the very meaning of morality is the correction of feeling by judgement. Judgement to be judgement must be external to the facts; indeed, else why the institution of independent witnesses and courts of law? Dr Cohen's principle is perilously near that of the jungle, according to which there is no real judge at all since each man is his own judge. To do only what is right in one's own eyes is the Bible's very definition of wrong.

Further, is Dr Cohen really sure, as he says, that Jewish condemners of the

Qibya incident probably condemned it for fear of 'what the Gentiles might say'? Should he not credit his fellow-Jews with a normal share of human feeling, and is it unreasonable for men to think that babies and unarmed women are human beings although they happen to live over a border? But even assuming his suspicion to be true, is it indeed so wrong to take into account, and even to be guided by, other people's judgements? Is not that the way in which moral ideas are in fact inculcated and spread? I can quite conceive a Jew saying 'I cannot judge this matter myself. I have been taught that Judaism is a religion of justice and love. And I have been told that the new State of Israel was founded on justice and love. Let me hear what the world says before I condemn my people and my religion. Perhaps I am too obtuse: or too sensitive.'

Such a Jew (and there must be many of them) would, I fear, search in vain for even the half-hearted approval of the Qibya incident. He would have probably heard it condemned in the same terms as the 'incidents' of Lidice and Oradea. And I am afraid it is no use our saying: 'Look what is being done by their own people in this place or that. Why don't Jews raise their voices there? Why just against us?' In the first place two wrongs do not make one right. And secondly, is it not perhaps a compliment to Jews and Judaism that our friends say to us: 'We expected better of *you*'.

In closing, I venture to repeat, in abbreviated form, what I wrote at the end of my memoir listed above. Jewish tradition makes quite frequent use of military metaphors for the enunciation of its own truths, such as the struggle against the evil inclination; and the cut and thrust of talmudic debate, which aims at achieving halakhic decisions that shall be both socially workable and ethically defendable, is itself sometimes called 'the Torah's war'. In Aeschylus' play the *Seven against Thebes* the emblems on the shields of the seven heroes are described. The shield of the sixth assailant, Amphiareus the prophet, bore no device, for

> Not to seem great he seeketh, but to be.
> The fruit of a deep furrow reapeth he
> In a rich heart, whence his good counsels rise.
> O, find a valiant champion and a wise
> To meet him. Great is he who feareth God.

LINES 592–6
GILBERT MURRAY'S TRANSLATION

Plutarch records that when the play was first performed at Athens, these lines made the audience turn instinctively towards Aristides, known as 'the just' (*Aristides* 3. 253z). And as an epitaph for Leon Roth they are no less fitting.

RAPHAEL LOEWE

Is there a Jewish Philosophy?

I The Problem

I TAKE my text from the concluding words of Husik's standard work on the history of Jewish medieval philosophy:[1] 'There are Jews now and there are philosophers: but there are no Jewish philosophers and there is no Jewish philosophy.'

Let me read that again: 'There are no Jewish philosophers and there is no Jewish philosophy.' You will note that he is talking about the present ('There are Jews *now* and there are philosophers'), with the implication (presumably) that the matter was not always so: after all he had just concluded a big volume on Jewish medieval philosophy himself. But even among the philosophers whom he describes there would seem to be some who would not merit the title *Jewish* philosophers even though they lived long ago. You may recall, for example, the remarks prefaced by the editor to the first edition (1560) of Gersonides' *Wars of the Lord*: 'His words seem to contradict our Torah and the wise men of our people. . . . But he has explained in his Introduction and the last chapter of his First Part that the Torah is one thing and philosophy another, and each occupies itself with its own affairs . . . '. Since the sixteenth-century editor does not seem to be shocked by this avowal of Gersonides, it would seem that in Renaissance Italy too it could be said that there are Jews now and there are philosophers, but that it does not follow from the fact that a philosopher happens to be a Jew and even writes in Hebrew that his philosophy is necessarily Jewish.

So the problem is fairly set. In what sense can we talk about Jewish philosophy, and what can we expect to find if we look for it?

This lecture was one of a series arranged by the Education Committee of the Hillel Foundation and delivered to the London Jewish Students Association in the autumn and winter of 1959/60. It was published in Raymond Goldwater (ed.), *Jewish Philosophy and Philosophers* (London: The B'nai B'rith Hillel Foundation, 1962), 1–19. Reprinted by permission of the B'nai B'rith Hillel Foundation.

[1] I. Husik, *A History of Medieval Jewish Philosophy* (Philadelphia, Pa.: Jewish Publication Society of America, 1916; pbk. edn. New York: Meridian, 1958).

II   The Meaning of Philosophy

And there is a further difficulty. I shall have to discuss with you not only the word Jewish but also the word Philosophy. As you all know, philosophy in our day and country has fallen into disrepute, and not so much in the mouth of the ordinary man as in the mouths of the philosophers themselves. Philosophers in England today seem to spend their time in pointing out how foolish previous philosophers were. They asked questions they should not have asked (we are told) and gave answers which are no answers; thus wasting their own and other people's time in the pursuit of a will-o'-the-wisp which does not exist. This is as may be; but as I am to talk about a traditional subject—or rather a small part of a traditional subject—I hope I shall be forgiven if I use traditional language. I shall explain first therefore what philosophy traditionally means.

If you take up, as I hope you will, Professor Salo Baron's monumental *Social and Religious History of the Jews*,[2] you will find, as the title of the fifth chapter of his first volume, the phrase 'Rethinking Fundamentals'. What Professor Baron meant by the phrase in its context is neither here nor there; but I propose adopting it in explanation of what I intend when I use the word philosophy. This is an old and respectable meaning of the word, and I choose Baron's phrase because it is handy. It also contains a compliment to ourselves. By saying *re*thinking, it flatters us with the suggestion that we have done some thinking already.

The phrase 'rethinking fundamentals' reminds us of two things which have always been characteristic of philosophy. The first is thinking, *thinking*, that is, as opposed to *feeling*. Whatever philosophy may be, it is at least a *reflective* activity. It is not the immediate sensation or feeling, or the recalling of an immediate sensation or feeling. It is a pondering on it, a considering of it, a weighing of it. If it were only a record or recall of an original experience, it would be history or possibly (you will remember Wordsworth) poetry. It would not be philosophy. To be philosophy it must be not only recalled but also reflected on, thought and rethought, until it is seen as part of a wider pattern fashioned by a host of other experiences as well as by itself.

But this too is not all. Philosophy is not just the activity of weighing experiences, *any* experiences. The experiences it weighs are of a certain dimension and importance. They may be, for example, those ubiquitous elements which seem to appear in all, or almost all, the things with which we come into contact—space, time, form, matter, or more abstractly and

[2] [2nd edn. (Philadelphia, Pa.: Jewish Publication Society of America, 1952–   ).]

more difficultly, causation. These are *fundamentals*, pervasive factors the removal or alteration of which would change the nature of things altogether.

So philosophy as the 'rethinking of fundamentals' is a very serious and responsible activity. It means thinking and rethinking, pondering and repondering, those elements in our lives, in history, in Nature, which would appear to be not incidental, transitory, casual, trivial, but basic. Philosophy is the search, through thought, for the permanent; and it is with this conception in our minds that I am going to ask you to consider with me the question: Is there a *Jewish* philosophy?

The first and obvious answer is: 'Of course. Are there not books on it? Are we not now starting a course on it?' Indeed we are; and I am proud to be allowed to introduce it. But it is as well to start by knowing what it is that we expect; and as I listen to myself articulating the words 'Jewish philosophy', I cannot help remembering how the analogous phrases 'Jewish physics', 'Jewish mathematics', used to strike so harshly on the ear in the bad old times of racist theory and genocide practice. Is there such a thing as a Jewish physics? Surely the answer is decidedly, No. There is indeed a subject of rational enquiry known as physics, and valuable work in it has indeed been done by men of Jewish parentage. But equally valuable work in it has been done by men of *non*-Jewish parentage, and in either case the result has been not Jewish or non-Jewish but physics. Is there a Jewish mathematics? Surely the answer is equally, No! There is mathematics and there are mathematicians, some of them Jews and some of them—believe it or not!—non-Jews. But whatever the mathematicians may be, the subject itself remains neither Jewish nor non-Jewish but mathematics. Why then should there be a Jewish philosophy? In philosophy as in mathematics, as in physics, as in philology and classical scholarship, as in botany and geology and physiology, Jews are found on most sides of most controversies, each speaking his mind and each speaking differently. In the United States of today both Oppenheimer and Strauss are Jews, but they seem to hold different opinions on the legitimate use to be made of recent discoveries. The Salk vaccine is—in part—the contribution of a Jew to medicine. It is not Jewish medicine.

III   The Nature of the Subject

The year 1933 saw, among other things, the publication of the last product in the direct line of the authentic Judaeo-German 'Science of Judaism'.

I refer to Julius Guttmann's *Philosophie des Judentums*.[3] Julius Guttmann was the distinguished son of a distinguished father. Guttmann the elder, Jacob Guttmann, rabbi of the community of Breslau, had gone patiently through the classical Jewish philosophers from Isaac Israeli to Abrabanel and summarized clearly both their own teachings and the influence they exerted on others; Guttmann the son, Julius, a student of economics as well as of philosophy, had started his career as a lecturer in general philosophy in the University of Breslau, and as Professor of Jewish Philosophy in the Jüdische Hochschule in Berlin he had by his comprehensive and independent studies of the whole field rounded off the results of his father's labours into one coherent and systematic whole. It was this which appeared in Munich in 1933, a Hebrew version with some additional chapters being published in Jerusalem after the author's death in 1951.

The significant thing about Julius Guttmann's volume was its title, *Die Philosophie des Judentums*, The Philosophy of Judaism. Earlier books on the subject, for example that of Moritz Eisler in German and of Husik in English, had all borne as their title or part of their title the words 'Jewish philosophy'. Some of them, indeed, taking advantage of the German partiality for compound terms, had squeezed in the word 'religious' before philosophy. The pioneer work of David Kauffmann, for example, on the attributes of God, and that of S. Horovitz on the psychology of man, are named specifically contributions to 'Jüdische *Religions*-philosophie', that is, the Jewish philosophy of religion. The great Munk, however, in his celebrated *Mélanges*, was content to speak of Jewish (and Arabic) philosophy; and in this he was followed by most students of his own time and indeed is so followed today. Some scholars ventured even further. The brilliant and original, if unconventional, David Neumark entitled his Hebrew edition of his German history the *History of Philosophy among the Jews*.[4]

The only book on the subject written originally in Hebrew, that of S. Bernfeld, adopted a different name altogether. Its title is *Da'at elohim*, The Knowledge of God; and whether or no Bernfeld's use of this phrase coincides with that of Hosea, it made a title of great interest. For it suggested at least that the philosophers with whom it dealt had something to communicate rather about the nature of God than about the universe in

[3] Munich: Ernst Reinhart, 1933; a revised and enlarged version of the Hebrew edition was published in 1953.

[4] *Toledot ha'ikarim beyisrael*, 2 vols. (Odessa: Moriah, 1912 and 1919); *Toledot hafilosofiyah beyisrael* (New York: Stybel, 1921).

general, and that that something was connected, in however distant a way, with the doctrine found in the Hebrew Scriptures.

IV Philosophical Interpretation of Judaism

So we have before us, reflected in these various titles, a variety of possibilities as to the nature of our subject. At the one extreme we may place Neumark with his *History of Philosophy among the Jews*, then Munk and the generality of students with their histories of Jewish philosophy. The intermediate position is occupied by the histories of the Jewish philosophy of religion. The other extreme is held by Bernfeld with his 'Knowledge of God' and, more explicitly, Julius Guttmann with his 'Philosophy of Judaism'. You will remember that, broadly speaking, the matter of all these books is the same. Even Neumark's highly suggestive, and highly controversial, writings cannot do more than cover the usual list of thinkers—Philo, Saadya, Maimonides and the rest; and one sees even with him a recognition of the fact that, even when we speak of the history of philosophy among the Jews, we are not really considering a series of attempts to rethink fundamentals in general and to give freely the results arrived at. We have, rather, the restricted interests commonly covered by religion and in particular by historical Judaism, and a series of attempts to work out, in the light of specific historical data, its basis and presuppositions. It is this fact which is recognized clearly by Guttmann and expressed in his title. The genuinely philosophical side of the so-called Jewish philosophers, he explains, is derived from without, that is, from the non-Jewish culture of their time. What they did was to select from that culture such ideas as would offer an account of Judaism which should be consonant with the spirit, or, if you like, the vocabulary, of the age.

We may perhaps put the matter thus. There is an old talmudic saying, made much of by medieval writers, that the Torah spoke in the language of men. Since the men in whose language the Torah spoke passed away long ago, it would seem to rest with each successive generation to provide the Torah with a new vehicle of expression. This, historically, was the task and achievement of the philosophers (or at least of most of them), and their work is therefore quite fairly described as the, or a, philosophy of Judaism; as indeed emerges clearly if they are considered soberly one by one, even Gersonides' *Wars of the Lord* which we noticed before being admissible, and admitted, under the rubric 'Wars *against* the Lord'.

It is this which is the subject of later lectures in this series, and I shall not attempt to anticipate them except in order to illustrate my present point. At the head of the long line of thinkers to be presented to you there is set generally the name of Philo, the Alexandrian Jew who lived in the early days of the Roman Empire and whose recorded public appearance was on the mission to Caligula in the years 39–40 of the Common Era. Philo was a great Jew and an original and interesting thinker, too; but he thought and breathed Plato and the Stoa, and it was his interpretation of Judaism in the light of these non-Jewish systems which constituted his 'philosophy'. True, he came to some surprising conclusions, and these conclusions led to conclusions yet more surprising; but they were the result not of thinking out the nature of things in general but of a Hellenized thinking on the nature of Judaism. The greatest figure we have is undoubtedly Maimonides, but he would be a rash man who would speak of a Maimonidean philosophy. For did not Maimonides himself state explicitly that so far as philosophy, that is, the wisdom of man, is concerned, we must all go back, as to a sole source, to Aristotle? True, as Philo used Plato, so Maimonides used Aristotle, in an original way with original results. But the originality consisted not in his philosophy, which was that of Aristotle (or rather, of the Arabized Aristotle), but in what resulted when he applied his Aristotelianism to Judaism. In the same way, the German Jewish philosopher Mendelssohn reflects the political thinkers of the seventeenth, and the theologians of the eighteenth, century; Lazarus and (in his own fashion) Hermann Cohen set out from the philosophical foundations laid down by Kant. The same holds true today. Students of contemporary Judaism in the United States know how influential a figure is Mordecai Kaplan. But Kaplan took his philosophical ideas from John Dewey; and he then proceeded, in the light of Dewey's ideas, to produce what can only be called, not a Jewish philosophy but a philosophy of Judaism. Similarly, the work of one of the all-too-few Jewish theologians of this country, Dr Ignaz Maybaum, is based on the thinking of the existentialists; but the result is an existentialist philosophy of Judaism, not a Jewish existentialism.

V   The Philosophy Offered by Judaism

At the risk of tiring you I shall push this contrast home as it is important. I spoke earlier of the analogy to Jewish philosophy presented by a hypothetical Jewish physics and Jewish mathematics, and I suggested to you that all such terms are nonsense. Let us consider now the further analogy offered by a phrase often heard recently, *Christian* philosophy. In the twenties or early thirties there was a grand debate on this phrase in the French Société de Philosophie. (The minutes were published in their Bulletin and make interesting reading.[5]) Many different views were expressed, from that of the extreme religionists that there is no genuine philosophy which is not Christian to that of the extreme secularists that philosophy and Christianity have no connection with one another whatsoever. The honours of the debate went to the secularists; but the religionists made the excellent point that religion poses certain fundamental problems which all philosophies must attempt to meet, and suggests certain answers. This was in essence Neumark's position in his *History*. There are, he said, specific problems like that of the origin of the world, of the constitution and destiny of man, of the nature of truth and right action; and on all of these, Neumark held, Judaism gave an intelligible and coherent answer which, implicitly or explicitly, in different stages of development, and in different degrees of conscious articulation, can be found in texts and documents throughout the course of Jewish literary history and more particularly in the writings of the philosophers and especially in those of Moses Maimonides. The world as such, Neumark would seem to be saying, poses its questions and Judaism, when properly understood, that is, as understood by Maimonides as understood by Neumark, gives the answers; just as the proponents of Christian philosophy would say that the world as such presents its questions and that the answers to them are given by Christianity as understood by, say, Thomas Aquinas.

Buddhists or Taoists could be forgiven if they were sceptical about these claims, although they might concede that any religious system might embody some truth or offer some persuasive account of some element in experience. And here, I think, we may leave the matter. We have seen enough to suggest that, however much we may use the term 'Jewish philosophy', the most we should intend by it is a philosophy of Judaism, that is, a discussion of the answers offered by Judaism to some of the general problems of life and thought; and we must recognize that this is not philosophy in the authentic historical sense of a *universal* curiosity and a *universal* questioning into the *widest* aspects of human experience. It is on the contrary a restricted study of certain historical ideas severely

---

[5] Since this lecture was delivered there has appeared the striking *Le Philosophe et la théologie* by the veteran historian of medieval thought, M. Étienne Gilson (Paris: Fayard, 1960). It is to be strongly recommended to any serious student of the issues involved in these topics, together with the same author's *L'Esprit de la philosophie médiévale* (Paris, 1932), also available in English translation.

limited in relevance and space and time. Now it may possibly be that these historical ideas are of a universal interest, even of a universal importance. But this is a matter of enquiry and discussion. It is not a self-evident truth.

VI   Jewish Philosophy: An Enquiry into Judaism

And we may have to go even further. The Neumarkian view is, as I have said, that the world poses its problems and Judaism offers the solutions, of course the right solutions. The philosophy of Judaism is therefore the philosophy *offered by* Judaism. 'Of' in this case is a possessive: the philosophy of Judaism is equivalent to Judaism's philosophy.

But are we sure we know what Judaism is? In our generation, a generation (I am afraid) of little learning and less understanding, it is just the nature of Judaism which we need to study and enquire into. So I suggest we take the term a little differently, rather after the model of the 'philosophy of science' than of that of the 'philosophy of Kant'. The philosophy of Kant is the philosophy *held by* Kant. The philosophy of science is the philosophical enquiry *into* science. Science is not the inventor but the object of the philosophy. Philosophy, as we saw at the outset, is the thinking and rethinking of fundamentals, and when an object is attached to it, the sphere of its application is restricted. The philosophy of science is the thinking and rethinking of the fundamentals of science. The philosophy of Judaism is the thinking and rethinking of the fundamentals of Judaism.

And that, I think, is the historical fact of the matter. When Philo faced the Jewish Hellenists, when Saadya argued against the Karaites, when Maimunists and anti-Maimunists excommunicated one another, when Jacob Sasportas fought his lonely battle against the followers of Shabbetai Zevi, when S. D. Luzzatto extolled Rashi and Yehudah Halevi as against Maimonides and Ibn Ezra—the object of discussion was not the nature of the world at large but the nature of Judaism.

So at long last we have found our proper subject. Jewish philosophy, or rather the philosophy of Judaism, is the thinking and rethinking of the fundamental ideas involved in Judaism and the attempt to see them fundamentally, that is, in coherent relation one with another so that they form one intelligible whole.

VII   Why Jewish Philosophy?

Now that we know what it is that we are concerned with, we can ask why we should be concerned with it. Why should we worry ourselves with the enquiry into the fundamentals of Judaism and the attempt to see them together as one intelligible whole?

Why indeed? But once you look into the material offered, you will, I am sure, fall under its fascination. Its variety and present relevance is astonishing. Begin with even the Jewish philosophers in the textbook and severely technical sense and you will find in them—true, disguised somewhat, but we are all detectives in these days and can see beneath the black spectacles—all our present hopes and fears, arguments and discussions, even our divisions and sectarian differences, writ small or large, and followed to their natural end, centuries and centuries ago. And this holds quite generally and outside the technical field as well. Are you interested in the phenomenon of what is now called assimilation? Read Philo on the Jews of Alexandria. You enjoy Hyde Park on a Sunday morning with its religious disputations? Study Nahmanides' accounts of his debate before the king of Castile in Barcelona. You are eloquent on the shortcomings of our learned men? You could not treat the subject with more acuteness than the Karaites. You follow the higher critics? So did Hivi of Balkh, and he was less respectful to authority than you would care to be. If you don't—as I don't—love the hasidim, read the sober first-hand accounts of them in the autobiography of Solomon Maimon or the satire (*Megaleh temirin*) of Joseph Perl. If you admire simple piety, take up Abraham's collection of Ethical Wills or the Memoirs of Glueckel or, best of all, the sayings of the Old Rabbis in the *Ethics of the Fathers*. These form an essential part of the background against which the philosophers need to be studied, and they amply repay attention.

When you turn to the philosophers themselves, those of us who care about serious thinking on serious subjects will still find matter to chew on in, say, Maimonides' theories of prophecy and immortality, his account of the good for man, his method of treating the Scriptures, his interest in anthropology, his approach to the difficulties of time, creation, divine omniscience. Most interesting of all is his attitude towards science and his basing of morality. I am not saying that his treatment of these and other topics is final or even satisfactory; but it is there, and can be discussed, and discussed not only in itself but in its historical reverberations. Maimonides was taken up by the Rabad, by Gersonides, by Hasdai Crescas, by Isaac Abrabanel, as well as, later, by Spinoza, Solomon Maimon, Hermann Cohen; and each thinker raised new points or removed old ones so that the implications of the original thought become gradually clearer and its significance more closely defined. There is here a real historical process, a prolonged sifting and a progressive elucidation, which in terms of length of time it would be difficult to match.

This is a oneness of continuity; but we may observe too a oneness of diversity. Let us consider, for example, the three luminaries of the Islamic period, Ibn Gabirol, Halevi and Maimonides. They are all difficult authors, and I should hesitate to suggest to a general audience that you should go home and sit down at once to the *Fons vitae*, the *Khuzari* and the *Guide for the Perplexed*. But however general the audience, I do suggest that when you go home you do sit down at once and read Gabirol's *Royal Crown* and Halevi's devotional poems and the first book of Maimonides' Code. These men were philosophers enough for the philosophy to overflow into their wider labours, and in these works we find not technical philosophy but something of even greater interest and importance, the quintessence of the thought of three master-minds all differing in outlook and yet all the same in the passion of their vision of what to them was truth. They were all members of diverse schools. The historians tell us that whereas Gabirol was a Platonist and went one way and Maimonides an Aristotelian and went another, Halevi cried a plague on both their houses and rejected Plato and Aristotle and indeed all philosophers alike. Yet he too was in our sense of the word a Jewish philosopher, thinking and rethinking the fundamentals of Judaism; and although a far less powerful thinker than either of the others, he was yet the vehicle of views which appeal to many today.

VIII   Philosophy an Antidote to Intolerance

I sometimes think that it is this diversity in unity, rather than the unity in diversity, which constitutes at least one great element in the importance for us today of the study of Jewish philosophy. It focuses our attention on the *important* rather than on the *accepted*. The last half-century has seen in the Jewries of the world a double growth of sinister significance. The one side of the growth is parochialism; the other—its natural accompaniment—sectarianism, dogmatism, intolerance. It may be that as a people we are naturally quarrelsome; it may be that with the break-up of the larger communities the natural love of power, starved of its proper outlet, resulted in 'parnass' politics and a vested interest in ideological fragmentation. In any case reason has been made a slave to passion and slogans are embraced as principles. A study of genuine principles reaching back to Moses and the Prophets and the Psalms, and proceeding through the long line of distinguished theorists about whom you are to learn in this series of lectures, is not a complete antidote to this degeneration of our living cells but it is, I fancy, the only one that exists.

I would ask you though to see to it that the study should be a study, not a mere casual attendance at a lecture: lectures are no substitute for study, only an indication of what you should look out for while studying. And keep in mind throughout that you are dealing with a living thing, however diverse its formulations and however distant in space and time. Gabirol, Halevi and Maimonides are not just faded words on a printed page. They are ideas, forceful and vivid today as they were eight and nine hundred years ago—but only if you make them so; and they are waiting so to be made.

I look forward then, as one result of your study of philosophy, to a certain ripening of the mind of Anglo-Jewry: a knocking off of corners; a mellowing, a sweetening, a more easy acceptance of other opinions; not, of course, indifferentism, the Hegelian night in which all cows are black, but a maturer outlook which appreciates the fact that although a man may go to another conventicle, or to none, he is yet a man, even a Jew, for all that. I look forward to a broadening of discussion. There are, I think, few theoretical opinions of any kind on religious or 'national' subjects precedent for which cannot be found in our classical literature, and it is salutary to learn that what we condemn now as heresy was maintained by men whom posterity holds in high honour. We are all too hidebound; too cribbed and confined. We all have articles of faith and will not see beyond them. O for the masterpiece (but it will have to be published not only anonymously but also posthumously) which will demonstrate to our formula-bound souls that there is no single one of the Thirteen Articles even of Maimonides' alleged creed which was not rejected, explicitly or implicitly, by leading lights in the history of Judaism, including, I fancy (but I only whisper the suspicion), no less a person than Maimonides himself. We should know this and be humble.

IX The Study of Jewish Philosophy a Necessity

I have tried so far to show that a study of Jewish philosophy is desirable. I suggest now that it is more than desirable. It is essential. We need a philosophy of Judaism today for the same reason as we need philosophy in general: in order to enable ourselves to escape the clutches of *bad* philosophy or *pseudo*-philosophy.

For it is a mistake to think of philosophy as a subject of study exactly like all other subjects, that is, as something you either learn or you do not. We either learn Chinese or we do not; but we are all philosophers. We all think about fundamentals. We all have views on the wider issues of life, that is, philosophies. The only difference between us on this score is that some of us philosophize a little better, some a little worse. The same is true in the sphere of the fine arts. We all pronounce judgement on pictures, on music, on poetry. We all know, as we say, what we like.

Yet it is surely true that in all these and kindred subjects some opinions are better than others. Skill is acquired and improved by practice. So is taste. So is any faculty of discrimination. Both the physical and the mental palate can be trained. Accustom the physical palate to good cooking and it will demand good cooking. Accustom the mental palate to good philosophy and it will demand good philosophy. And it will despise and reject the bad. To work through a first-class philosopher is like smoking first-class cigars or drinking first-class wine: we acquire a standard and cease to enjoy the inferior.

The value of a training in philosophy—the thinking and rethinking of fundamentals through the mind of a master—is thus not so much that it gives us a body of truth as that it helps to enable us to see through the sham and the false. If it gives us truth, too, so much the better; but what it gives is hardly likely to be Truth with a capital T, the final, the definitive, the incontrovertible. It will be a morsel, a fragment, a crumb; some small thing that one can cherish, and honour, and on occasion obey, but in no wise one massive, all-comprehensive, system. It will be an idea, or possibly only a suggestion of an idea, perhaps only a faint gleam of a suggestion of an idea—you see I am not promising you much from your study of philosophy in general or of Jewish philosophy in particular. But something, however little, you will assuredly get, and, more importantly, there is much you will get rid of: the easy answer, the dogmatic affirmation, the private revelation, the crushing Juggernaut of triumphant self-assertiveness which overrides all opposition and all argument and all good manners.

I retain a vivid memory of an episode in my first visit to Switzerland. I was at Zurich, and from the bridge over the river caught my first sight of the Alps. It was just a glimpse of the line of distant snow-mountains which I had the good fortune to see lit up for a passing moment by the setting sun.

I have been pursuing that glimmer ever since, and I hope that in your study of Jewish philosophy you will do the same. You might catch it in the *Royal Crown*, an awe-inspiring creation which is a kind of cross between Lucretius and Traherne. You might get it from the reading of some chapters of the *Guide*. You might get it from a poem of Halevi or a casual phrase of Abraham Ibn Ezra or an essay of Samuel David Luzzatto or a sermon of Philo or a queer piece of speculation by Abraham bar Hiyya or a majestic paragraph of Hermann Cohen; but once you get it, it becomes, as both Jeremiah and Plato noted, not a gleam without but a fire within.

X The Mystics

You will ask me why I have said nothing about the mystics, but in their regard I am incurably old-fashioned. Philosophy, whenever and wherever it appears and of whatsoever brand it might be, is a thinking and a re-thinking of fundamentals; and whatever mysticism may be, it is not *think-ing*, and its way is not the philosophical way of *discussion*. I am not here talking in terms of values. It may be that the way of the mystics is the right one and the way of the philosophers the wrong. But let us not confuse our minds and the issue. If we are talking about philosophy let us talk about philosophy; and if we remember that philosophy is a thinking and rethinking of fundamentals, we shall see that mysticism is irrelevant.

Now it is questionable—and I support myself in this on the great authority of Professor Zaehner—whether, in the accepted sense of the word, there is such a thing as Jewish mysticism at all. The notable characteristics of mysticism in the strict sense of the word seem to be lacking in our literature. As has been pointed out so often, there is hardly a trace in the kabbalah of the 'mystical union'; understandably, since the doctrine accords ill with Judaism's teaching about God. The fact is that kabbalistic theosophy, according to its latest and most sympathetic student[6] (and in this judgement he only reaffirms the opinion of the first great pioneer students of the movement in the past century), is nothing but a resus-citation, through devious and so far untraced channels, of Gnostic myth-ology.

The recognition of this fact adds point and justification to the judge-ment of Maimonides when in a famous responsum he said of the mystical classic *Shiur komah* that it is idolatrous and should be destroyed. It is a stern verdict, but it touches the quick of the modern predicament of Judaism. In the place of the second commandment we are offered alien myth and the worship of alien myth with the old cry: 'These are thy gods, O Israel!'

The argument is a recurring one. Moses had it with Aaron over the golden calf, Elijah had it with the prophets of Baal; Jacob Sasportas, alone in his generation, had it with the enthusiasts for Shabbetai Zevi. I myself

6 [The reference is to Gershom Scholem.]

find some comfort in recalling that masterpiece of *mis*interpretation found in the Talmud of the verse in Isaiah (49: 15): *eleh* ('*these* are thy gods') will be forgotten, but *anokhi* ('*I* am the Lord thy God') will not!

I am personally coming to the conclusion that if Judaism is to live—and it will live—it will have to be presented to us, and to the world at large, in the same way as it was, in the language of their time, by the classical Jewish *philosophers*. They joined Moses and the prophets in declaring Judaism to be the *war against myth* in all its shapes and forms, and they strove in every way to rise above myth, however popular it may have been and however much it endeared itself to the masses. We must learn again to see Judaism as the classic expression of plain monotheism with definite implications both for morality and for science.

This will not be done by feeling, only by thinking, that is, by philosophy; and I commend it to you who are starting on this course today, both as *our* need and as *your* task.

Imitatio Dei
and the Idea of Holiness

❧

IN the philosophy of religion the question of the relationship of God and man is central. It may be approached from two angles: either by asking how, and why, God created man, or by asking what difference it makes, for man, that he was created by God. If one adopts the second approach and seeks an explanation, we find the answer in the fact, or axiom, that it is from God that all man's ethical values flow—that is to say, his instinctive awareness of things that he should do, and of the way in which he should proceed. If we follow this up by enquiry into the nature of such awareness, we frequently encounter the notion that it is God who is the model for that ethical behaviour which it is incumbent upon us to adopt and to 'cleave' to—that is, in essence, the ethical obligation means 'to emulate God in all ways possible to us'.[1] Attempts have been made to introduce into Judaism the notion of the *imitatio Dei* as the basis of all ethical theory, or to discover its presence within the parameters defining Judaism. Although I shall not ignore the wider picture, it is within the framework of those parameters that I propose to consider the subject here.

I

At first sight, the question would seem to need no answer. As is well known, the notion of emulation of God finds expression in the Bible itself: 'Ye shall be holy: for I the Lord your God am holy' (Lev. 19: 2). And

Given as the second Ahad Ha'am Memorial Lecture ('Hahidamut la'el vere'ayon hakedushah'), delivered in Hebrew in 1931 and published in that year; it was subsequently republished in a collection of eight Ahad Ha'am lectures given from 1929 to 1937 (Jerusalem: Hebrew University Press, 1937). It is published here by permission of the Magnes Press. The English translation is by Raphael Loewe. Where biblical references differ from those in the Hebrew Bible the AV reference is given in brackets.

[1] So Plato, *Theaetetus* 176AB, ed. H. N. Flower, Loeb Classical Library (London, 1931), 128; cf. Aristotle, *Nichomachean Ethics* 10. 8. 1177b, ed. H. Rackham, Loeb Classical Library (London, 1926), 16. [But Aristotle did not, nor could he, introduce the idea of *emulation*. R.L.]

indeed, it is of interest to note that within tannaitic literature, in connection with this very verse, we find the word מחקה—the verb corresponding literally to the Latin *imitatio* which, rendering the Greek *mimesis*, has become the conventional term for the notion. However, it transpires that within that literary corpus this specific word occurs nowhere else, and that even here the text[2] is questionable; in place of מחקה, 'imitating', the medieval commentator read מחכה, which sounds the same but means 'waiting expectantly' (in the sense of watching and anticipating the object's moves). But even supposing the reading meaning 'imitating' to be substantiated, it is significant that the word occurs in a parable: 'Abba Saul said, "What is the royal retinue expected to do? It has to imitate the king."' In any case, there is no doubt whatsoever that the author of this apophthegm knew exactly what he meant, for it is none other than he who is cited as the authority for the well-known rabbinic exegesis of the words *zeh eli ve'anvehu* 'this is my God and I will glorify Him' (or, 'I will prepare Him an habitation' (Exod. 15: 2): 'just as He is merciful and gracious, so do you be merciful and gracious'.[3]

And so, the question stands. The difficulty is obvious enough. From many other passages of Scripture we learn that it is impossible to attribute any form whatsoever to the Creator, and there can be no question but that this view is of the very essence of Judaism. If that is the case, what can possibly be meant by 'ye shall be holy, for I am holy'? How is it possible for a created form to make itself like the one who fashioned it? '*I* am holy', and consequently, 'it is up to *you* to be holy, like me'; but the Bible says 'to whom will ye liken Me, or shall I be equal? saith the Holy One' (Isa. 40: 25).

Clearly, the nub of the question is the word 'holy' (*kadosh*), and we have to consider what it means. There are two possible avenues of approach. One is to follow Plato's method in a well-known dialogue, and to examine the notion of holiness in absolute terms, the other is to investigate it experimentally, by looking at case-histories, inasmuch as the concept is linked with certain known facts and incidents. If we follow the first, we shall find ourselves pointing to the logical conclusions that flow from the concept as such. To follow the second is to learn what we can from the material at our disposal, whether directly, that is to say, from personal experience, or indirectly, from the way it finds expression in the relevant literature. Let us begin our investigation along the latter lines, and turn to our ancient texts to see if they can help.

[2] Sifra, *Kedoshim* 1, ed. I. H. Weiss (1862), fo. 86ᵛ, col. i.

[3] *Mekhilta, Shirta* 3, ed. I. H. Weiss (1865), 44a; ed. J. Z. Lauterbach (1933), ii. 25.

We shall divide the material into two parts. The first comprises all that is linked to the notion of holiness in regard to both man and God, and the second with what concerns God alone. The first will touch directly on the idea of emulation, or *imitatio*; the second, on the nature of the God-head.[4]

II

In regard to the first, the relationship of God and man, I am emboldened to formulate the following principle: wherever in Scripture man is called upon to be holy in the way that God is holy, the substance of such summons is negative, and never positive. So let us turn to the texts, and in particular to the nineteenth chapter of Leviticus which, for present purposes, constitutes the *locus classicus*.

The chapter, after its initial summons to be holy, consists of a long list of cautions about what should not be done:

Turn not to idols, make no molten gods . . . do not wholly reap the corners of your field, glean your own vineyard or gather its every grape . . . do not steal . . . do not swear by my name falsely . . . do not oppress your neighbour . . . curse not the deaf . . . show no favour [in judgement] to the poor . . . go not about as a talebearer . . . hate not your brother in your heart . . . take no vengeance . . . do not cross-breed domestic beasts or sow your field mixing the seed . . . the first three years' fruit of a tree is not to be eaten . . . eat no [flesh] with the blood . . . round not off the corners of your sidelocks . . . do not make of your daughter a common whore . . . regard not familiar spirits . . . vex not the resident alien. (Lev. 19: 4–33)

The few apparently positive precepts mentioned in the chapter confirm this: 'Ye shall fear, every man of you, his mother, and his father, and keep my sabbaths' (Lev. 19: 3). *Tira'u*, 'fear', with negative implications, stands right at the head of the list, and to the observance of the sabbath commandment *shevitah* 'rest', or rather 'refraining', is integral: 'thou shalt do no work thereon' (Exod. 20: 10). In another passage the link is made quite explicit: 'If . . . thou wilt call the sabbath a delight, to be

---

[4] [Although Roth here wrote *be'etsem tiv ha'elohut*, it is clear from p. 26 that he distinguished semantically between *elohut*, which may reasonably be rendered by 'deity'— i.e. an abstract philosophical construct of what the notion of god must exclude and may include—and *elohim*, or *el* =[the reality of] God. The words *be'etsem tiv* anticipate his conclusions, and the whole phrase must refer to the latter concept. I consequently use the term 'Godhead' wherever it is clear that what Roth intended is something more than 'deity' as here explained. R.L.]

honoured as [dedicated] to the Holy One, the Lord, honouring it by not doing thy normal occupations . . .' (Isa. 58: 13). The Sabbath is a matter in which holiness is involved, and consequently its precepts are not positive, but those of separation, distance, negativity.

It is clear, then, from Scripture itself that the summons to emulate the Holy One here proclaimed is not intended to induce positive action. It is, on the contrary, a caution as to what is not to be done, warning us to distance ourselves from engaging in sundry specified activities.

Moreover, later Judaism has preserved the notion, as is clear from its ethical literature, regardless of the particular tradition that it represents. By way of example, we may cite the *Mesilat yesharim* of Moses Hayim Luzzatto (1707–46), or the *Avodat hakodesh* of Meir ibn Gabbai (1531); for each of them, as in earlier generations, the 'holy' always means separation and abstention, the only difference being that in their case the sphere of such abstention is limited to sexual conduct. There is, of course, some parallel tendency towards this view in older rabbinic literature: one recalls the soubriquet 'our holy master', bestowed on Rabbi Judah the Patriarch, and the explanation for it given in the Talmud,[5] that his eyes had never focused on his organ, and the assertion by Rabbi Judah b. Pazzi in the Midrash,[6] that wherever Scripture singles out for mention an individual's marked self-control in his sexual life, the context also refers to holiness. But even for the talmudic sages, such circumscription was not always operative. Thus, in a discussion of the nazirite's vow of abstention from wine,

Rabbi Eleazar *hakapar*, son of the rabbi [Bar Kappara] asked, 'Why does the text (Num. 6: 11), [in detailing the sacrificial ritual at the termination of the period of abstinence] use the expression "the priest . . . shall make atonement for him, arising from his having sinned against the soul" (*vekiper alav me'asher hata al hanefesh*)? Against what, or whose, soul has he sinned? The explanation is, that he has deprived himself—his own soul—of wine: if someone who has, by supererogatory abstinence, deprived himself of wine, is declared a sinner, how much more so one who subjects himself to general abstinence.' But Rabbi Eleazar (ben Pedat) said, 'A Nazirite is declared to be holy (6: 5), "holy shall he be, letting the locks of the hair of his head grow": and if someone who denies himself but one thing—wine—is declared holy, how much more so one who imposes general abstinence upon himself?'[7]

[5] *Shabbat* 118*b*.
[6] *Leviticus rabbah*, *Kedoshim* 24: 6, Vilna edn., fo. 34ᵛ, col. ii (foot). Similarly elsewhere, see Talmud, *Yevamot* 20*a*, *Isur mitsvah, isur kedushah*.
[7] Talmud, *Ta'anit* 11*a*.

It is quite clear that in this passage holiness is not limited to sexual matters. To take another example: 'And ye shall be holy men unto me' (Exod. 22: 30 (31)); Rabbi Ishmael said, 'so long as you are holy, you are mine'. Issi b. Judah said, 'whenever God introduces a new precept for Israel to observe, he increases their [opportunity to cultivate] holiness'. Issi b. Guria said, 'both in this text and at Deut. 14: 21 holiness is mentioned in reference to Israel—in each case the context concerning forbidden foodstuffs'.[8] Once again it is patent that holiness consists in distancing oneself from whatever is under discussion, and not merely (or especially) in sexual concerns. And if this holds good for the rabbis of the Talmud, it is *a fortiori* true for the very earliest authoritative texts. 'Thou shalt not wear [clothes of] mixed stuff, wool and linen together' (Deut. 22: 11) likewise refers to something with holy implications, being one of the items listed in Leviticus (19: 19) of required abstention from common practice. Indeed, the commandment enshrined in the previous verse, 'thou shalt love thy neighbour as thyself', falls within the same category; and it is worth remarking that Ahad Ha'am—apparently following the thirteenth-century Sefardi halakhist Solomon b. Adret—observed that, by virtue of its content, it really belongs with the negative precepts.[9]

Thus we find that in a chapter upon which, according to the early commentary Sifra,[10] 'many of the basic institutions and values of the Torah depend', holiness is essentially a negative concept. This is true of every text in which the details of a particular precept are set forth in connection with the word 'holy', as the following passages are sufficient to show:

every thing that creepeth on the earth is an abomination, not to be eaten . . . do not render yourselves abominable through anything that creepeth . . . for I am the Lord your God: but ye shall sanctify yourselves, and be holy, for I am holy. (Lev. 11: 41–4)

Ye shall therefore distinguish between clean and unclean beasts . . . and shall be holy unto Me, for I, the Lord, am holy. (Lev. 20: 25–6)

[The priests] shall take in marriage no harlot or profaned woman, nor take a woman divorced from her husband, for [the priest] is holy unto his God . . . for I, the Lord, who sanctify you, am holy. (Lev. 21: 7–8)

---

[8] *Mekhilta, Mishpatim* 20, ed. Weiss, fo. 103ᵛ; ed. Lauterbach, iii. 157.

[9] *Al parashat derakhim*, Berlin edn. (1921), iv. 48; see the important note on p. 49, referring to Solomon ben Adret, *Ḥidushei agadot*, on Talmud, *Shabbat* 31a (see Jacob ibn Habib, *Ein ya'akov, Shabbat* §17, Furth edn. (1766), i. fo. 63b (first of two folios numbered 63), col. i (at the foot).

[10] Sifra, *Kedoshim* 1, ed. Weiss, fo. 86ᵛ, col. i.

Similarly, even without explicit reference to God's own holiness:

thou shalt not intermarry with them, giving thy daughter to his son, or taking his daughter for thine own son . . . for thou art an holy people to the Lord thy God. (Deut. 7: 3–6)

ye shall not make [ritual] cuts in your [flesh] . . . for thou art an holy people to the Lord thy God. (Deut. 14: 1–2)

Ye shall not eat of any thing that dieth of itself, for thou art an holy people unto the Lord thy God. (Deut. 14: 21)

Or again:

and thy camp shall be holy, so that [God] shall see no unseemly thing amongst you. (Deut. 23: 15 (14))

thou shalt burn the remainder with fire; it shall not be eaten, because it is holy. (Exod. 29: 34)

Or again:

thou shalt not make [incense] like it, for it is holy . . . and as for the incense . . . ye shall not make any for yourselves: holy shall it be. (Exod. 30: 32, 37)

There is no need to multiply examples: wherever holiness is mentioned, there will also be found some cautionary injunction, either preceding it: 'Ye shall be holy men unto me, therefore 'ye shall not eat any flesh that is torn of beasts in the field' (Exod. 22: 30 (31)), or following: 'that ye go not about after your own heart and your own eyes . . . and be holy (Num. 15: 39–40).

III

Some might argue that what we have here is simply an instance of taboo: what is holy is, *ipso facto*, fraught with danger. J. G. Frazer observed, more than once, that amongst primitive peoples the holy is viewed as something like electric current, against contact with which one has to guard—an infectious disease, contact with which must be avoided, a force from whose sinister attack one must strive to escape. Whosoever touches something holy likewise contracts holiness, and is required to remain outside the social group.

I do not intend to enter into this question for the moment, although I hope to show that at least for our present purposes such a view is mistaken. But, for the sake of argument, let us for the moment suppose that holiness, whether that of the deity or of man, is nothing more than a taboo, a dangerous force involving the need for what Frazer likes to term 'insulation'. The facts to which, up to this point, we have drawn attention, speak for themselves. The question which we propounded was whether the concept of imitation can constitute the basis of a theory of ethics, and on the basis of the biblical material we have to answer that it does not. I am not here raising the general question as to whether or not ethics can be formulated on purely negative premisses, nor am I asking the question, pertinent to Judaism specifically, whether or not it is possible to discover any other basis for ethical theory in the Hebrew Bible. I am merely adverting to the facts that, first, it is not possible to extrapolate any positive theory of ethics from the notion of *imitatio Dei*, and second, judging from the import of the biblical texts themselves, no one has ever attempted so to do. And the reason is obvious. The God of Israel is a God who 'hides Himself' (Isa. 45: 15), whose name, according to the Talmud's perceptive interpretation[11] of Exodus 3: 15, is *le'olam*: not 'for ever', but 'must be hidden' (*le'alem*). What is hidden from us we can neither imitate nor emulate.

The significance of this stands out in high relief if we glance for a moment at a system of ethics which really is based on the notion of *imitatio*, and which calls on humanity saying, quite literally and with explicit detail, 'you are to do what God himself has done'. I refer, of course, to Christian doctrine as spelled out in the work, published in numerous editions, of Thomas à Kempis, *De imitatione Christi*, and before him by St Paul (Eph. 5: 1–2). When Thomas à Kempis would fain encourage his readers to experience the joy of fulfilling the divine imperative, or to accept tribulation ungrudgingly, he says 'remember what joy was his', or 'remember how he submitted to tribulation'. Quite clearly there is a world of difference between rallying-cries of this kind and what we find in Leviticus 19, even though both are, at first sight, founded on one and the same notion—emulation. The difference, of course, centres on the nature of the subject of imitation. Thomas à Kempis could point to a specific individual whose biography was known to himself and his readers from books regarded by them as trustworthy, in that they are inspired: a man who, according to those books, did certain things, sustained certain feelings, and behaved in a certain manner. What we have here is imitation, *mimesis*, as conceived in the thinking of the Greeks, with the following difference: in place of the gods in the poems of Homer and Hesiod, who act in a reprobate manner and who, according to the testimony of some

---

[11] *Pesaḥim* 50a.

of the best Greek minds, constitute but a type of moral corruption, and in place of the god of Aristotle, whose whole essence is pure thought, a god of whom to posit activity of any kind at all is a derogation, we are confronted by a man whose acts are known to us and are patient of being imitated in exact detail. 'Just as he did . . . so do you.' In other words, there must stand before us, as a prior condition for the construction of any positive ethical system on the basis of the notion of *imitatio*, a man—one whose humanity is on a par with our own, who thinks and behaves in the same way that we do ourselves.

IV

It is, moreover, quite certain that this was already appreciated in antiquity, for many a scholar has endeavoured to discover, from talmudic literature, the consequences of emulation, or, to use the conventional term, imitation, of God. But, as one of them has observed, the rabbis did not call upon people to imitate *all* the divine characteristics as they are described in the Hebrew Bible: and, from the philosophical point of view, this is the heart of the matter. We find no such summons as 'just as I am "jealous and vengeful" [cf. Nahum 1: 2] so be you likewise jealous and vengeful'. Here is proof that the essence of the whole concept, even when propounded according to the foregoing formula, is not simply imitation. There is a selectivity of the appropriate characteristics for emulation; and once this is granted, imitation, as such, is not the touchstone. One may gain insight into the whole problem from studying a wonderful parable in the Talmud:

A king of flesh and blood while travelling arrived at a toll-gate and commanded his servants to pay the toll to the collectors. They said, 'but all the toll belongs to you!' He replied, 'let all wayfarers learn from my example, and not try to avoid paying toll'.[12]

The king is under no obligation to pay the toll; on the contrary, all the toll revenue accrues to him. But he includes himself as subject to the general obligation to pay, so that from his behaviour others may learn. Just so is the situation regarding man's moral behaviour and God: whereas mankind is obliged to live in accordance with certain general principles, God is not. But precisely in order that the parable may act as deterrent and encouragement to its members, mankind subjects God, so to speak, to the same obligation. Nevertheless, this 'obligation' does not constitute

---

[12] *Sukkah* 30a.

either the basis or the essence of the ethic, but rather, if one may so put it, its window-dressing.

The early sages sensed this, and indeed were concerned to spell it out. In case anyone should suppose that the notion of *imitatio* is indeed the basic sanction of Jewish ethics (a supposition which, as we have suggested, would lead one far outside a Jewish mental universe), and that a peg for the notion might be found in the great verse 'ye shall be holy, for I, the Lord your God, am holy', they made the following comment on it—and their words are striking, no less for their clarity than for their delicate tuning of sensitivity:

' . . . for I am holy': meaning, 'if you make yourselves holy, I will consider it as if you have declared Me holy, but if you do not, I shall consider it as if you have failed to declare Me holy. And should anyone contend that, provided always you declare Me holy, I am, in virtue of such declaration, rendered holy, the text stated 'for I am holy': that is to say, my holiness inheres in Me, irrespective of whether or not you declare Me holy'.[13]

Here we have a clear assertion of the doctrine of transcendence—the utter qualitative difference between the nature of God and that of man.

V

As we have seen, some have identified holiness, as it appears in Jewish contexts, with taboo: can this view be accepted? In my opinion it cannot, for the following reason. In the Hebrew Bible the concept of holiness—which has, admittedly, something about it reminiscent of mere taboo[14]—is associated with another concept, from which taboo is absolutely distinct. And it is at this point that we reach the second section of our enquiry, namely that concerning the quality of holiness as relating to the deity alone. Here, too, it seems to be that a general principle may be established: wherever in the Bible we find mention of God's own inherent holiness (i.e. where the concept of *imitatio* is not present), we also find reference to the concept of righteousness—*tsedek*—either reference to righteousness in general, for the most part God's requiring that insults suffered by the poor shall be redressed, or reference to righteousness of more limited application, i.e. the deliverance of Israel in particular.

Once more, we have to deal with things as they are, and not as some

---

[13] Sifra, *Kedoshim* I, ed. Weiss, fo. 86ᵛ, col. i.
[14] See I Sam. 6: 20; but it is to be observed that the speakers are not Israelites, but the Philistines of Beth Shemesh.

might feel they should be. And we shall find that the sources substantiate the facts. Let me cite some typical passages.

And they shall know that I am the Lord through my executing judgments on [Zidon], and I shall be sanctified in her. (Ezek. 28: 22)

His sanctity is made palpable by his executing judgment, and it is by virtue of this that he is known to be God.

And I shall vindicate justice from him . . . and shall evince my greatness and evince my holiness, and will be known for what I am in the eyes of many nations. (Ezek. 38: 22–3)

Once again, the same linkage—judgment, holiness, deity. Similarly,

and the poor among men shall rejoice in the Holy One of Israel. (Isa. 29: 19)

thus saith the Holy One of Israel: because ye reject this word . . . [the consequences of] this iniquity shall be to you as a breach ready to fall, swelling out in a high wall, whose breaking cometh suddenly at an instant . . . for thus saith the Lord God, the Holy One of Israel, through returning and quietude shall ye be saved . . . and therefore will the Lord wait, that he may be gracious unto you, and therefore will He be exalted, that He may have mercy upon you: for the Lord is a God of judgment (Isa. 30: 12–18)

Once more—holiness, sin and its punishment, justice. And similarly everywhere: 'Hear this word, ye kine of Bashan . . . the Lord God hath sworn by his holiness, that lo, the days shall come upon you when . . .' (Amos 4: 1–2).

I have said that the effecting of justice linked to holiness may be general or particular. The title 'Holy One of Israel' is often repeated in connection with redemption, the time when God will 'lay bare his holy arm' (Isa. 52: 10), 'sits on his holy throne' (Ps. 47: 9 (8)), 'bestirs himself from his holy dwelling' (Zech. 2: 17 (13)), or 'his holy temple' (Micah 1: 2), and 'makes known his holy name to the nations' (Ezek. 39: 7). 'Our Redeemer' is, in the mouths of all the prophets, 'the Holy One of Israel' (Isa. 47: 4), 'the Holy One of Israel is thy deliverer' (Isa. 43: 3). There is no occasion here to question whether he delivers because he is righteous, or is righteous in virtue of the fact that he delivers—a question with the answer to which is bound up the value of Judaism as Israel's religion. He delivers because he is righteous; and the deliverance of Israel is but a particular instance of the over-arching principle of God's deliverance of the poor. For in connection with this general concern to deliver all the poor, whoever they are, we find precisely the same connection: 'for He hath looked down from the height of his holy place . . . to hear the groaning of the prisoner' (Ps. 102: 20–1 (19–20)). Albeit the prisoner referred to is apparently a Jewish prisoner, or at any rate one who subsequently comes 'to declare the name of the Lord in Zion, and his praise in Jerusalem' (Ps. 102: 22 (21)), this is not the case in other passages. It is the *holy* God who listens to all, without exception:

For thus saith the high and lofty One who inhabiteth eternity, whose name is holy, I dwell in the high and holy place, with him also that is of a contrite and humble spirit to revive the spirit of the humble, and to revive the heart of the contrite ones. For I will not contend for ever . . . (Isa. 57: 15–16)

Who else is 'the father of orphans and judge of widows' but 'God in his holy habitation' (Ps. 68: 6 (5))? Not of priests, Levites, or Israelites, but of widows and orphans. In short, Scripture attests that holiness is unthinkable as a quality in God without justice: and Isaiah seems almost to be formulating a definition when he says 'the Lord of hosts is exalted in judgment, and the holy God evinces his sanctity through righteousness' (Isa. 5: 16).

It is difficult—perhaps hazardous—to rely for support on mere words: but it would seem that this point—the interrelationship of holiness and justice—was not forgotten by later generations in Israel. If we look at the exposition of the Midrash on Leviticus 19: 2, which was our starting-point, this is what we read:

'Ye shall be holy, for I, the Lord your God, am holy'. Scripture elsewhere states: 'the Lord of hosts is exalted in judgment, and the holy God evinces his sanctity through righteousness'.[15]

The formula linking these quotations, literally, 'this is what is written', is the regular one for exegetical correlation of two texts; and the insight implied by such unelaborated juxtaposition is remarkable indeed. And it is not less surprising to find the same connection asserted by Plato, in a well-known passage of the *Theaetetus* where, in discussing the imitation of God, he says: 'our duty is to exert ourselves to escape thither [i.e. to the realm of the gods] hence with all possible speed, and such escape constitutes becoming like [*homoiosis*] God as best we may: to become like [Him] means to become righteous and holy'.[16]

VI

We have, so far, established two points on the basis of the clear evidence of the sources. First, that the concept of holiness trails negative consequences in its wake, and secondly, that it is associated with that of righteousness. The first of these depends, as we have seen, on the notion of

[15] *Leviticus rabbah, Kedoshim* 24: 6.   [16] *Theaetetus* 176AB.

God's transcendent separation from the created world; and it is my opinion that this applies likewise to the second.

The conventional view treats monotheism as a simple derivative of polytheism, the one God being the vanquisher of the many. According to this line of thinking, the difference between monotheism and polytheism is merely arithmetical—one king *vis-à-vis* many. In my view the case is otherwise. What is emphasized in the assertion of monotheism, in contrast to polytheism, is not God, but unity—we ought, perhaps, rather say uniquity: the significance lies in the concentration in one subject of that creative power which produced the cosmos. If that is so, because it is the case that he judges the whole world as one, it rests with him to do justice. There is no place for favouritism in one who, in his transcendence, is equally superior to all. He cannot be bribed, since the world and all that is in it belongs to him; nor can he be intimidated, seeing that his is an existence shared by none other. The entity whose righteousness is perfect has to be the Creator, and no one else; and he is perfectly righteous *by virtue of* his creatorship; precisely because, to use the traditional Jewish formula, 'He had but to speak, and the world came into existence', he is *tsadiko shel olam*, the one and only truly righteous being that the world knows.[17]

VII

It is worth pausing to consider this, as something of significance to all. The idea of the holy has figured large in recent research into the nature of religious thought, and in the view of a number of well-known scholars its source lies in the sense of dread and awe inspired in man by the cosmos—a feeling whence derive both religion and the notion of deity. According to this view, there is, in the world about us, something unique which arouses in us fear, indeed terror, and forces us into prostration towards a power the energy in which we do not understand, but can merely feel as present about us. The foundation of religion is thus a feeling within ourselves, stirred into life by an aspect, itself not understood by us, of our external world: a feeling of which typical expression is given by Jacob's exclamation 'How full of awe is this place!' (Gen. 28: 17). There was about the place a quality which he sensed, and was overwhelmed.

For myself, I am unable to accept this. I do not see how, logically, the

[17] The divine title 'He who but spoke . . . ' (*mi she'amar vehayah ha'olam*) occurs frequently, e.g. Talmud, *Sanhedrin* 76*b*, but it is best known from the early hymn *Barukh she'amar*, which occurs in the daily morning prayers. For the formula *tsadiko shel olam*, see *Genesis rabbah* 49: 9: Vilna edn., fo. 101ʳ, col. ii.

sense of being threatened can form the basis of religion, since something is missing—the notion of the Godhead itself. Even granted that nothing distinguishes deity from the sense of something inspiring fear—a view precluded by the evidence that we have assembled—it would follow from it that the Godhead is but an adjunct of the idea of deity. We know, so to speak, what is meant by deity: and from deity to God would seem to be but the smallest of steps. This seems to me to be topsy-turvy. Religion, I would hold, depends not on deity, but on the Godhead: and the secret at the heart of religion is to be found, not in Jacob's first words as quoted, 'how full of awe is this place', but in what follows—'this is none other but the house of God'. The crucial element is not the place, but whose place it is. God is not an adjunct of deity, but vice versa: deity depends on the existence of God. And the difference that it makes is palpable. If deity is prior, it can relate to all kinds of things and all kinds of people, since it is merely a quality associated with everything and extending through everything. If priority rests with God, he, not deity, has to be the beginning, inasmuch as nothing else exists save what is derived from, or, in Neoplatonic terminology, emanates from, him.

Let us, then, assume that it is the unique character of God, and not the awe-inspiring aspects of the cosmos, that is the notion lying at the centre of religious thought: and God is the (uniquely) holy One. It is by now clear what this epithet, 'holy', means—what is described as being holy is, as we have seen, separated, distinct, because the archetype of holiness whom rabbinic idiom calls the Holy One, blessed be He, is distinct, that is to say transcendentally separate from, the cosmos: not something embraced within it, no mere quality, but rather a unique entity, outside and not inside the world of our experience.

This notion makes it possible to understand the two general principles that stem from the subject of our discussion. The first is that in Judaism the idea of *imitatio Dei* does not introduce any kind of obligation, and the second, that the quality predicated uniquely of the concealed entity that we call God is righteousness. That being which is transcendentally separate from the cosmos is unique, in being utterly dissimilar from anything included within creation, the qualitative and not merely quantitative gulf separating them being the difference between creation and Creator. And, correspondingly, its relationship to each and every created entity is equal—as Job put it, referring to the after-life, 'The small and great are there, and the servant is free from his master' (Job 3: 19). It is because God is distant from all that he relates equally to all. His quality of righteousness springs directly out of his holiness.

Religion is not the product of metaphysical reflection, but rather of the instinctive feeling of common folk. An unsophisticated awareness of God establishes a relationship between God and man, a relationship of which the field is the creative process. God, as Creator, stands *vis-à-vis* mankind, the work of his hands. Secreted within the notion of God is that of creation, and Maimonides sensed, accurately, that this affirmation is an indispensable foundation of Judaism.[18] Since it is creation that constitutes the mystery of the utter distinction between God and the cosmos, it is likewise the mystery of holiness; and it is thus no surprise that holiness and righteousness are mentioned alongside creation in so many texts. The Holy One of Israel is 'He that made him' (Isa. 17: 7, 27: 11), 'his fashioner' (Isa. 45: 11), who proclaims that 'when they see . . . the work of mine hands in their midst, they shall sanctify my name' (Isa. 29: 23). When viewed from this angle, the essence of what is meant by divine righteousness finds expression where 'rich and poor meet together, the maker of them all being the Lord' (Prov. 22: 2). The uniquity, holiness, and righteousness of God are integrally bound up with his creatorship. The prophet asks 'To whom, then, will ye liken me, or shall I be equal? saith the Holy One' (Isa. 40: 25), and now we can see the point of the answer which immediately follows: 'Lift up your eyes on high, and see, who hath created these things . . .'.

VIII

Why should we concern ourselves with this sort of theological enquiry? Does it really matter to us that he who is supremely righteous, he who is, *par excellence*, the Holy One, and the Creator are one and the same, or if, in relationship with us, mankind, holiness is a negative factor? My reply is twofold. In so far as we are prepared to concern ourselves with speculative matters, it is a fact that the ethical values set forth in our ancient literature depend on the recognition of the absolute transcendence of God. For those of us, however, who live in Erets Yisra'el there is also another dimension to the subject. Here we are, living amongst our own people— the *holy* people—on our own soil—the *holy* land—and indeed in Jerusalem, the *holy* city, doing our best to speak the *holy* language. And it is right that we should pause for a moment over a word that we use, so often and so glibly, without properly understanding its implications.

---

[18] *Mishneh torah, Hilkhot yesodei torah* I. I. 8; Commentary on the Mishnah, *Sanhedrin*, ch. 10, first of the thirteen principles of Judaism.

Jewish Thought as a Factor in Civilization

꿔

I Introductory

1. The great bodies of constructive ideas on which modern Western civilization is built are conventionally traced back to Israel, Greece and Rome: morals and religion to Israel, the sciences and the plastic and literary arts to Greece, law and public administration to Rome. If this is true, it is true only roughly. No civilization can exist without possessing in some measure every one of these activities. Greece and Rome had religion and much of it survives today, just as Israel and Greece had, and bequeathed, law. Indeed, religion and art and science and law appear everywhere (howbeit in varying degrees) together. Further, there is much in modern Western civilization which is unique and original to it, and where the 'legacy' from the past is most apparent, it has been most modified in use.

This essay will make therefore no exclusive or pre-eminent claims. It will try to present Jewish thought as a coherent system of ideas; but it will be mindful of the fact that the truer the ideas, the more they may be expected to have appeared elsewhere. Nor will it insist on the connection between Jewish thought and the individuals known as Jews. In a sense, Milton's *Paradise Lost* or Handel's *Messiah* or Blake's *Illustrations to the Book of Job* are Jewish, although their authors were not. One may compare the connection of mathematical thought with its first inspiration in Greece, or of the Roman road with its original Roman builders. Roman roads were also built by other than Roman citizens; and mathematical thinking, although brought into the world with and by the Greeks and remaining (possibly) true to its Greek type, has produced results far beyond any Greek achievement. An old talmudic saying is helpful here. Why was the Law given in the wilderness? the rabbis ask, and answer: In order that no one country could claim proprietary rights to it.

Reprinted with permission from *Jewish Thought as a Factor in Civilization*, published in the series The Race Question and Modern Thought (Paris: UNESCO, 1954). © UNESCO 1954.

2. This is true of ideas of any kind. They are by nature universal. They arise, presumably, in individuals, and they develop their power through communities. But to speak of them in sole association with one person or community is to belie their character. Indeed, the more general they are, the more their character as ideas is manifested.

Further, they can be described only up to a point. They can never be described finally. They are only what they can be, and that cannot be known until they are. They may conceal within themselves at any one time what will reveal itself only at another.

For ideas are not dead things. They are alive and their life is their own. They may at times seem dead or asleep. But suspended life returns; sleepers awake. Like the dry bones in Ezekiel's vision they may breathe again and stand up.

3. Like everything living, ideas are active. They are not mere words to be manipulated at our convenience. Rather they manipulate us. They are charged with energy of their own. They possess, or are possessed by, their own power. Their action is therefore unpredictable. However casually they may be cast into the sea of events, they may cause a maelstrom not to be foreseen.

And we may add a last preliminary consideration. Like any other organic growth, ideas manifest themselves at different stages of development; but we can only appreciate the different stages of development in the light of the full and complete. It is only the perfected product which gives us the key to the understanding and interpretation of the imperfect.

4. When speaking then of the ideas behind Jewish thought we shall treat of their highest development. It is obvious that it is the lot of very few, men as well as ideas, to reach, or maintain, self-completion. But however we judge men, ideas should be taken and judged only at their best. The Jewish prophets dreamed of universal peace and clothed the dream in imperishable language. That idea remains, however much the prophets themselves may seem in other passages to forget it. We shall then ignore much which is, possibly, imperfect, and fasten our eyes on the high peaks.

II The Background

1. Each of the three great peoples on which Western civilization is generally held to rest conceived a distinct idea of itself as contrasted with others. The Greeks thought of themselves as masters of articulate speech as opposed to the uncultivated barbarians who could only mutter incoherent sounds. The Romans, leaving the arts and sciences to others, recognized their destiny in empire: *regere imperio populos.* The Jews, intensely conscious of God and his working in man, saw themselves as repudiators of idolatry.

This conception is enshrined, according to the traditional etymology, in the very word Hebrew which is the alternative name for Jew; and in order to appreciate its paramount importance it is worth while referring to the Jews' account of themselves as it is recorded for us in the Bible. The account may not be an exact recital of what actually occurred, but it is none the worse for that. Indeed, it is in such 'myths' that a people's character and aims are most intimately and profoundly reflected. But we must be careful to follow the story in its traditional form, not in the form which it has assumed as the result of critical examination. The traditional story will help us to understand the subject of our enquiry, the special character of Jewish thinking about the world. The revised critical version will only help us to understand the critics.

2. According to the traditional story the Jews (Judaei) are the men of Judah; and Judah was one of the children of Israel or Jacob, himself a son of Isaac who in his turn was a son of Abraham. Abraham came from a family which lived 'beyond the river'. 'Beyond the river' is in Hebrew *ever lanahar*; and from the word *ever* is derived, according to the tradition, the other name of the Jews, the Hebrews.

The Jews or Hebrews then are those who came from beyond the river; and they came for a reason which bit deep into the national consciousness and became to themselves the symbol of their being. Terah, Abraham's father, was an idolater. He worshipped 'other gods'. And Abraham, by divine command, left his family and homeland beyond the river in order to be able to worship the one true God. Thus Abraham in the consciousness of the Jewish people represents a fresh start in the history of humanity. He is 'chosen', and chosen for a purpose. He is appointed the 'father of a multitude of nations'. He is the 'friend of God', plucked from his old environment and set down in a new land in order to found a new family and a new people with a new way of life for the regeneration of mankind.

The universal significance of this act is emphasized from the first. Abraham is to be a name of blessing to all the families of the earth. Yet the difficulties were great and were not to be overcome by the mechanical application of any principle of heredity. Abraham's first-born was rejected in favour of Isaac, Isaac's first-born in favour of Jacob (afterwards called Israel), while of Jacob's own twelve sons the oldest were condemned either as weak, or as violent and treacherous, men. The leadership passed to Judah (whence finally the word 'Jew'); and the children of Israel went down into Egypt.

But again there was need of a fresh start. Egypt became a house of bondage and the children of Israel slaves. But they were brought out of it to a 'new domicile of freedom', and the covenant with their ancestors was reaffirmed. This time, however, it is not one individual with whom the pact was made, nor is the maker of the pact a local or family deity. The 'whole earth' is declared to be God's; and within it the children of Israel are to be a 'kingdom of priests and a holy nation'.

3. The secular history of the Jews began to take shape with King David and his son Solomon, and after many vicissitudes ceased with the destruction of the Second Temple by the Romans in AD 70. From that time they have lived not as a political nation with a territory of their own but as a separate community, or rather as a number of separate communities, more or less autonomous, scattered over the world and distinguished from the peoples among which they dwelt by various, and often varying, marks. Of these, religion, internal organization, social habit and (sometimes) language were the more prominent. Time and again members of these communities have come to the notice of the world: Philo, Avicebrol, Maimonides, Spinoza, or in the modern period, Mendelssohn, Heine, Ricardo, Disraeli, Karl Marx. Of the leaders of thought in our own century one recalls readily the names of Bergson, Husserl, Durkheim, and Freud; among the still living, of Einstein. Yet it would be difficult to determine in what degree, or whether at all, these thinkers owe their inspiration to the ancient covenant between God and Jewry, and it is to this that we must return.

4. The ancient covenant, reaffirmed many times—we are following, it will be remembered, the biblical account—is always of one tenor. It is the assertion, and acceptance, of the sovereignty of God and with it the obligation to abandon one way of life and to assume another. The phraseology is almost stereotyped: 'After the doings of the land of Egypt, wherein ye dwelt, shall ye *not* do: and after the doings of the land of Canaan, whither I bring you, shall ye *not* do ... *My* judgments shall ye do, and *My* statutes shall ye keep.' The repudiation of idolatry has thus a definite and forcible positive intention. It is no theoretical doctrine of the constitution of the universe or of the powers controlling the universe. It is a practical rejection of habits of living which are declared to be disgusting and abominable.

5. The new way of life is no secret. It is neither a priestly cult nor a Pythagorean rule for initiates alone. Nor is it a doctrine with varying shades of meaning adapted to different degrees of intelligence by means of esoteric formulae. In essence it is simple: 'to do justice and judgement'; to have 'clean hands and a pure heart'; to 'do justly and to love mercy and to walk humbly with God'. But as it is passionate in its insistence on what it knows as good, so it is uncompromising in its condemnation of what it knows as evil: sexual malpractice; human sacrifice; the breaking of troth; the grinding of the face of the poor. It is given through various channels but its message does not vary whether coming from legislator or prophet, psalmist or chronicler or priest. It is always plain-spoken, without mystery or metaphor. Nor is it given as advice or counsel of prudence. It is command: 'Thus saith the Lord.'

Its simplicity is elemental. The first murderer is seen as driven off the earth by the earth itself; the inhabitants of Canaan are 'vomited out' by their country for their abominable practices. There are actions which are unnatural; and the penalty for unnatural acts is expulsion from nature by nature itself.

The right way of life is thus not arbitrary or conventional. It is involved in the very make-up of the physical universe. It has its roots deep down in the nature of things and claims obedience from all the children of earth.

6. The Jewish Bible does not begin with the Jews. It begins with the Creation and the story of Adam. In Hebrew Adam means simply *man*, and the rabbis quote the verse in Genesis 5: 1 as: 'This is the book of the generations of *man*', remarking that it does not say 'of priest', 'of Levite', or 'of Jew', but 'of *man*'. The children of earth are envisaged as one family. They have one ancestor who is father of all. There is by nature no such thing as caste or class, no differentiation by blood or descent. Human equality is thus a primary fact: the pedigree of all men is the same. Again we may quote the rabbis. 'Why was man created one?', they ask— and answer: 'In order that no man should say to another, My father was greater than thine.'

What is true of human beings as individuals holds good also of the families, and the family of families, to which they belong. The races and nations and peoples are all seen as clusters on one genealogical tree. They are 'families of the earth', interconnected and of one origin.

The family structure is thus all-pervasive. Human life is inherently social. It is lived in community and disdains the anarchy of 'each man doing what is right in his own eyes'.

7. The right way of life is conceived of as the detail of the general principle of the love of God, and by it the love of God is preserved from becoming an empty formula or an abstract desiderium. The love of God is, as it were, translated from an article of belief to a method of living or a mode of behaviour. As such it can be taught. It was to be expounded, therefore, on set occasions in public, and it was to be the constant subject of home study and private meditation: 'taught to your children with all care, talked of when you are at rest in your house or walking by the way, when you go to sleep and when you get up . . . fixed as a sign on your hand and a mark on your brow . . . lettered on the pillars of your house and over the doors of your towns'.[1]

Thus education—the acquisition of knowledge and its diffusion— takes its place as a vital element in the life of religion. Religion is realized as proceeding from thinking as well as feeling in a unity of theory and practice. It is an amalgam of knowledge and action and love, the knowledge preceding the love and issuing in action.

8. It is a characteristic of the sacred books of the Jews that in them the Jews are not portrayed as perfect. On the contrary, both as a people and as individuals they are shown to stand in especial need of the education in which they saw the essential preparation for religion. Hence the retention in the Hebrew Bible of many survivals of crude and undeveloped ideas. The instances have been industriously collected and are well known. When Jacob deceived his blind father he showed himself (to all appearance) a sneak; when David measured out two-thirds of the Moabites and slaughtered them, he acted as a barbarian. The so-called imprecatory psalms might well have been produced by propagandist hymn-writers of our own day.

All this is obvious and needs no remark. Such were the accepted ways of the time. What is remarkable is that, as against all this, we are offered specific teaching on a different and higher level, and that this higher level is noted and registered as such. If we have got beyond many biblical positions it is at the instance of the Bible itself. For example, Abraham is depicted as teaching a higher morality to God: the innocent should not be punished with the guilty. Again, it is the Bible itself which condemns David as a man of blood; and it is significant that it quietly ascribes to him a psalm of repentance which has become a classic of religion. Nor is it to

---

[1] In this, as in some other passages below, I have taken, with the permission of the publishers, the Basic English version (Cambridge: Cambridge University Press, 1949). Being simple and unfamiliar, it brings the meaning home to the reader more vividly.

the point that, in his last charge to his son Solomon, David seems to have reverted to his earlier courses. For the tradition he remains the accredited author of a different outlook on life altogether: 'Create in me a clean heart, O God, and renew a right spirit within me. The sacrifices of God are a broken spirit: a broken and a contrite heart, O God, thou wilt not despise.'

I stress the phrase 'for the tradition' because it is the tradition that matters. The painful accuracies of historical criticism are valuable in their own sphere, but they have little significance outside it. The psalm is inscribed 'of David, when Nathan the prophet came to him, after he had gone in to Bathsheba'. We are deliberately sent back to a great crime; and although the story is well known it is worth considering it here briefly since its point is closely relevant to our subject.

In order to gain possession of Bathsheba, David had her husband killed. The method, which would presumably not be considered un-usual, is recounted in graphic detail. But at the end we are removed to another sphere. Another kind of note is struck. As if casually there are introduced the words: 'But the thing that David had done displeased the Lord.' With this there begins another story altogether. The prophet appears, and through him God takes a hand.

The point to be remarked on is this. Story no. 1 is conventional. It is the ordinary run of life, whether in the so-called fierce Orient in the distant past or anywhere else in our own day. Its analogue can be found in any history book and in countless poems and novels. Story no. 2 is Hebrew Bible, that is, Jewish thought in its quintessence. To the question what in Jewish thought is significant for humanity it would be a brief and not inadequate answer to say: the story of Nathan and David, and Psalm 51.

We may take another example, not less known. Ahab, the king, prompted by his queen, dispossesses Naboth: again the conventional story of greed backed by power. And again God intervenes, this time through Elijah the Tishbite. But in this case there is no softening of the blow by parable or argument. 'Hast thou killed and also taken possession?' The indictment is direct and sears like fire.

9. These two examples suffice to illumine a fundamental problem. It is often asked whether the way of life ordained in the Hebrew Bible is tribal custom or universal law, that is, whether we have in it, in the full sense of the term, morality. The occasions are of course local, indeed, tribal. Any human occasion is bounded by space and time and is therefore of necessity limited. But in the cases quoted, however local the occasion, the significance is universal; and it is not only universal but it is offered and recognized as such. Not to kill and seize your neighbour's vineyard or your neighbour's wife is not offered as a temporary piece of advice under special circumstances which may never recur. Nathan's parable, like Elijah's sentence, is completely general. Generality, indeed, is the very essence of both. The parable is of any rich man and any poor man, that is, of man as man, while King Ahab is condemned by Elijah on entirely general grounds as a common murderer and thief. When Nathan says to the king: 'Thou art the man', he is giving concrete expression to the idea that there are rules of life with authority over all men, rich and poor, king and subject, without exception. And the case is rated at its full importance. However petty the kinglet in our view, he is yet, to the narrator, king; and the point of the story is that even kings are subject to law.

Nor is this an isolated case, a judgement casually conceived and as casually forgotten. It is of a piece with the whole trend of the biblical narrative in which the idea of one law for all is an ultimate presumption. The very first act of the chosen king, according to the Deuteronomist, is to be the making of a copy of the Law with his own hand '*so that his heart should not be lifted up over his countrymen*'.

10. Thus the religious message of Jewry as seen by Jewry itself comprised, as an essential part, the idea of law as universal and omnipresent. The new life is to be guided by regulation. Men and their passions need direction and control. Even revenge must be regulated: 'an eye for an eye', and no more. (The condemners of the (Roman) *lex talionis* supposed to be exemplified in this phrase would do well to consider the progress involved in turning *talio* into a *lex*. But in its literal sense it was never a *lex* in Hebrew law, since the system of compounding by ransom or punishment by fine was fully recognized and employed. Indeed monetary compensation is specifically mentioned in the very sections in which the phrase is used.) But regulation does not exclude personal feeling. The 'great *commandment*' is to 'love thy neighbour as thyself'. We may consider this injunction in its context (Lev. 19) since we shall find in it a further and significant illustration of the preceding:

Do not be cruel to your neighbour or take what is his; do not keep back a servant's payment from him all night till the morning. Do not put a curse on those who have no hearing, or put a cause of falling in the way of the blind, but keep the fear of your God before you: I am the Lord. Do no wrong in your judging: do not give thought to the position of the poor, or honour to the position of the great; but be a judge to your neighbour in righteousness. Do not go about saying untrue things among people, or take away the life of your neighbour by false witness: I am the Lord. Let there be no hate in your heart for your brother; but you may make a protest to your neighbour, so that he may be stopped from doing evil. Do not make attempts to get equal with one who has done you wrong, or keep hard feelings against the children of your people, but have love for your neighbour as for yourself: I am the Lord.

Now in the last three verses there is, or seems to be, a limitation, as if the rule holds only in connection with one's neighbour or brother or member of one's own people, but whoever is not one's neighbour or brother or member of one's own people may be lied to, hated, and made the object of false witness, with impunity and without reproach. On the face of it this seems unlikely, and the fact is probably the simple one that the rules were laid down in such a way that the plain man could understand them; and it is natural in a small society to say: treat your neighbour and kinsman decently, because your neighbour and kinsman are the only people you meet. But let us read on: 'And if a man from another country is living in your land with you, do not make life hard for him; let him be to you as one of your countrymen and have love for him as for yourself; for you were living in a strange land, in the land of Egypt: I am the Lord your God.'

The notable point about this further passage is both the giving of a reason and the reason given. Through the giving of a reason the action laid down is seen as rational; and the reason given, although historical and personal, is typical and exemplary. *Because* you were foreigners yourselves in Egypt, you can understand a foreigner's feelings, and for that reason you must treat him as one of your own ('love him as yourself'). All men's feelings are much the same, and what holds in one place and for one person holds in another place and for another. Thus both the reason adduced and the action ordained relate to whoever can come to live in your community, i.e. everybody.

As one reads further, this becomes even clearer: 'Do not make false decisions in questions of yardsticks and weights and measures. Have true scales, true weights and measures for all things.' We have here a prosaic, but sound, definition of justice: not only all men, but all yardsticks, should be equal; and they should be equal under all circumstances and every-where—again, a completely general, and hence moral, requirement.

11. The universality of the way of life under which the Jews believed themselves to have been elected to serve is most fitly illustrated by the majestic passage known popularly as the Ten Commandments. I say 'known popularly' for two reasons. First, the Hebrew does not call them the Ten Commandments but the Ten Words; second, a great German biblical scholar found another set of commandments which by careful pruning can be made to look like ten, and which he says are the original set. And so indeed, for all I know, they may be; but they are not the Ten which have impressed themselves upon the imagination, and helped train the conscience, of mankind. Since it is this which interests us we may be forgiven if we turn to them as they are offered in the plain text and as they have been taught throughout the centuries, engraving themselves on the minds of countless millions. Taking them as they are and without attempting a detailed analysis we may note:

(*a*) in their two 'tables' (traditionally related, the first to duty towards God, the second to duty towards man) they comprise both religious and social ethics;

(*b*) they are general, giving universal rules, and uncompromising, allowing no exceptions;

(*c*) they are simple, open to the understanding of all men, and while not demonstrated propositions they are reasonable;

(*d*) they begin with the self-affirmation of the God who intervenes in the concrete events of history and who, although imageless, cares for the conduct of individual men; and end with a condemnation of human enviousness and greed which lead to social disorder and crime.

The Ten Words are thus the very type of absolute law harnessed to the service of humanity, taking account of the 'desire of the eyes' and the 'inclination of the heart' of man, while yet insisting on man's full and final dependence on the immaterial and the unseen.

12. The inclusion of 'thou shalt not covet' among the Ten Words, like the inclusion of 'thou shalt not curse the deaf or put a stumbling-block in the way of the blind' in the 'law of holiness', suggests a wider interpretation of the word 'law' than is current today. The 'law' (Torah) of the Jews was rather 'teaching' than the written words of a legal code; and if it comes from God—and to the Jewish Scriptures there is no doubt on this point—there are many possible media for its communication. It may be brought down from heaven by a voice or on tablets; it may be set up on monuments by the banks of Jordan; it may be transmuted by prophets or transcribed by kings; it may be sought from the lips of priests or wise men. Yet the end is one and the same, that it be engraved on the heart. It is not in heaven or across the sea but 'very nigh unto thee in thy heart', writes the legislator; 'I will put my law in their inward parts, and in their heart will I write it', proclaims the prophet of the destruction; 'A new heart will I give you and a new spirit will I put within you . . . and ye shall keep my judgments, and do them', says the priest–prophet of the exile. The ideal, be it noted, is not that commonly known as 'autonomy', the activity of the will laying down laws for itself. When men see their wills as the sole source and substance of law, the result is chaos and destruction. Law comes from without; but in man's highest development he need not be taught it because it is written within.

Thus the 'way' of which we are now arrived at the culminating expression is as far removed from the orgiastic as it is from the utilitarian; it is neither an intermittent excitement not a *do ut des*, a giving in order to receive. It is an 'enlargement' of the heart, a 'uniting' of the personality; a refreshing, and a refashioning, of the soul. It is life lived, here and now, in the secret place of the most high. It is the irradiation of everyday existence by the eternal. At times it is impatient—'How long, O Lord, how long?'—but its vision is clear, its confidence unshaken. It serves God for naught. It walks in the paths of righteousness for his name's sake. It sees light in his light, in his presence fullness of joy. The way is a 'blessing', the blessing a 'glory'.

13. We see that the account given by the Jews of themselves involves ideas which have become, in one shape or another, part of the heritage of Western man: election and vocation; freedom and equality; the duty of education; the all-importance of the moral element in life; morality as rational and universal; life as community; the coupling of the love of God and of neighbour; the reality and power of the unseen. The survey has been hurried and necessarily incomplete, but it suffices to justify the remark of the translator of Ecclesiasticus (second century BC) that 'many and great things have been delivered unto us by the law and the prophets and by the others that have followed in their steps, for the which things Israel ought to be commended for learning and wisdom'.

In what follows we shall try and examine some of these 'great things'; although we must regretfully remind ourselves, in the words of the same translator, that 'things originally spoken in Hebrew have not the same force in them when they are translated into another tongue'.

III Basic Ideas

1. It has taken many cultures to make our world, and it is tempting to seek one central principle for each. If the contribution of Greece is primarily science and the arts and that of Jewry ethical religion, it may be remarked that both art and science are products of the contemplative spirit while ethical religion is action and creative change.

The Greeks set out from the universe and saw its origin in the generation of world from world or in the imposition of order on pre-existing chaos. For them matter was eternal and the world-process a shaping of matter by form; there never was a fresh beginning, rather, an endless recurrence. Their deity was not a producer or innovator, but—in their highest vision—'thought thinking itself'; and it initiated movement not as an active subject but as the passive object of thought and desire. Their typical achievements, the arts and sciences, represent similarly an acceptance of the existent. As achievements they are free in so far as they proceed from an untrammelled spiritual activity; but the activity, in Aristotle's phrase about God, is an 'activity of immobility'. The pattern of Greek attainment is the autonomy of mathematics discovering abstract relations or of philosophy enquiring into the structure of the real. Its intellectual ideal is the freedom to judge; its moral aim not the doing of what one wills but the willing of what one can.

The Jews set out from God and saw him as essentially creative. He creates the world, creates a way of life for man, and creates a people to bring this way of life into actuality; indeed he is prepared to try again and to create a new man, and a new heaven and a new earth, if those already created prove inadequate to their task and his purpose. The Jewish God is no philosopher and his path is tangled with logical contradictions. So far from being pure thought concentrated on itself he wills a world outside himself and cares for it; and he cares for it all, animate and inanimate alike, and, among the animate, for animals as well as men. He bans all images of himself since nothing physical can express his nature; and although he is a 'devouring fire'—the ideal of the absorption of man in the divine is not Jewish—man is to walk in his ways and cleave to him. Some of the most impressive sections of the Hebrew Bible portray his intense productivity: the first chapter of Genesis with its serene and comprehensive 'in the beginning God created heaven and earth'; the last chapters of Job with their detailed and imposing pictures of the huge beasts which seem to have been created simply from the joy of creation. (Even the staid psalmist realizes that God could have created such a monster as Leviathan only in order to play with it.) The morning stars sing together—doubtless because they have no other purpose or occupation. No wonder the medieval world found such difficulty in reconciling Aristotle and the Bible!

2. But there were 'contemplatives' among the Jews as there were 'activists' among the Greeks and we may well suspect such generalizations and deductions from a supposed ethos of Greek and Jew. Yet it remains true that historically it was the idea of creation which formed the great wall of division between Greek and Jewish thought. We may see this at its most conscious in the decisive criticisms on this score of the Aristotelian world-view which are to be found in the medieval schoolmen both Jewish and Christian; but it appears already in the typical accounts of the first clashes between Greek culture and Jewish. 'Fear not this butcher', the mother of the seven sons is made to say to the youngest (2 Macc. 7), but 'lift thine eyes unto the heaven and the earth and see all things that are therein, and recognize that God made them not of things that were.'

But the point was not conceived abstractly in its philosophical interest, and again we may quote the mother: 'The Creator of the world, who fashioned the first origin of man and devised the first origin of all things, in mercy giveth back to you again both your spirit and your life, as ye now condemn your own selves for his laws' sake.' The doctrine of creation served to comfort these proto-martyrs by giving them a reasoned ground for the hope of immortality.

3. By an illuminating paradox the Jews were greeted in the classical world with the epithet 'atheist'. Neither they nor their God were ever understood. The difficulty felt was put clearly by the Roman historian Tacitus (*Hist.* 5. 5): 'The Egyptians worship animals of many kinds and images made by men's hands.' (Their gods are thus understandable.) 'The Jews acknowledge one God only, and they conceive of him by the mind alone' (*mente sola unumque numen intelligunt*). He then goes on to specify further: 'The Jews condemn as impious all who, with perishable materials wrought into the human shape, form representations of the deity. That Being, they say, is above all and eternal, given neither to change or decay.'

Tacitus' cold reference to the object and nature of Jewish worship ('one God only and conceived by the mind alone') had a political as well as a religious aspect, 'for it was in consequence of this [conception of God's nature]', he continues, 'that they allow no effigies of him in their cities, much less in their temples: their kings are not given this flattery, nor the Caesars this honour'.

As is well known, the refusal of the Jews to accord divine honours to Caesar played a large part in the events which led to their destruction as a political entity. 'They had been taught from their very swaddling clothes', writes the Jewish thinker Philo of Alexandria, in connection with the Roman Emperor Caligula's order to set up a statue of himself in the Temple at Jerusalem,

by their parents and teachers and instructors, and even before that by their holy laws, and also by their unwritten maxims and customs, to believe that there was but one God, their father and the creator of the world.

For all others, all men, all women, all cities, all nations, every country and region of the earth, I had almost said the whole of the inhabited world, although groaning over what was taking place, did nevertheless flatter him [Caligula] . . . and some of them even introduced the barbaric custom into Italy of falling down in adoration before him, adulterating their native feelings of Roman liberty.

But this single nation of the Jews, alone refusing to perform these actions, was suspected by him of wishing to counteract his desires, since it was accustomed to embrace voluntary death as an entrance to immortality, for the sake of not permitting any of their national or hereditary customs to be destroyed, even if it were of the most trivial character. . . . But in this case what was put in motion was not a trifle but a thing of the very greatest importance, namely, erecting the created and perishable nature of man, as far as least as appearance went, into the uncreated and imperishable nature of God, which the nation correctly judged to be the most terrible of all impieties. . . .[2]

(One may add that in this particular case the significance of the general refusal to give a man the status of God was heightened by the man in question being the head of the state, Caesar himself.)

4. A temple whose holy place dared not be occupied by a physical image was a novelty in the Graeco-Roman world, and it aroused the astonishment of the Romans from the time when Pompey first penetrated into the Temple. Philo gives the text of an interesting letter, written to Caligula by King Agrippa of Judaea, in which this point is given reiterated emphasis:

O my lord and master, Caius, this temple has never, from the time of its original foundation till now, admitted any form made by hands, because it has been the abode of God. Now pictures and images are only imitations of those gods who are perceptible to the outward senses; but it was not considered by our ancestors to be consistent with the reverence due to God to make any image or representation of the invisible God. . . .

On which account no one, whether Greek or barbarian, satrap or king, or implacable enemy; no sedition, no war, no capture, no destruction, no occur-

[2] *On the Virtues and Office of Ambassadors* (*Legatio ad Caium*), ch. xvi *et seq.*, in *The Works of Philo Judaeus, the Contemporary of Josephus*, trans. C. D. Yonge, 4 vols. (1854–5).

rence that has ever taken place, has ever threatened this temple with such innovation as to place in it any image, or statue, or any work of any kind made with hands. For though enemies have displayed their hostility to the inhabitants of the country, still either reverence or fear has possessed them sufficiently to prevent them from abrogating any of the laws which were established at the beginning as tending to the honour of the creator and father of the universe . . .

And he continues:

How many deaths then do you not suppose that the people, who have been taught to regard this place with such holy reverence, would willingly endure rather than see a statue introduced into it? I verily believe that they would rather slay all their whole families, with their wives and children, and finally themselves, in the ruins of their houses and families: and Tiberius knew this well. And what did your great-grandfather, the most excellent of all emperors that ever lived upon the earth, he who was the first to have the appellation of Augustus given to him, on account of his virtue and good fortune; he who diffused peace in every direction over earth and sea, to the very furthest extremities of the world? Did not he, when he heard a report of the peculiar characteristics of our temple, and that there is in it no image or representation made by hands, no visible likeness of Him who is invisible, did not he, I say, marvel at and honour it? . . .

This letter, like many another cited in antiquity, may never have been written or sent, but it reflects admirably the spirit of the situation on either side. God for the Jews was not a human being or an animal or stocks and stones or an idol made with hands, and it was this that made him (and them) a wonder to mankind.

5. The Jewish God was not only not made with hands. He was not a natural object at all. He was spirit, not flesh, God, not man. He was not created. He was the creator. The world which we know and in which we have our being is completely dependent on a Being of another kind altogether.

Thus ultimately only God is real. The heavens can be rolled up like a scroll. The mountains flow down like water. Graven images have eyes that see not, ears that hear not. Men's desires and ambitions are vanity. We are strangers on the earth; our days are like a tale that is told. All flesh is grass, and all its goodliness is like the flower of the field. God alone endures for ever.

The phrases are magnificent but are not offered as rhetoric. They are for the biblical outlook sober truth. The creator God is the beginning and the end, the first and the last.

6. If this were all, however, we should be in the grip of a bare deism. The divine clock-maker would be now a retired workman. He would be resting from his labours in interstellar space unmindful of the fate of his creation. But God for Jewish thought is not only creator. He is father. Indeed, he is much more even than mere father. He is a father who understands children and knows how to deal with them. On this point the biblical story of Jonah is peculiarly instructive. When Jonah is peeved at God's forgiving Nineveh, God teaches him a lesson by a practical illustration. He destroys a plant which shaded Jonah from the sun, and then makes the sun come up even hotter; and when Jonah begins to rage at the loss of the shade, enquires amicably whether Jonah thinks he is right in being angry. Jonah is sure he is right, and the moral is pointed at once. Jonah had not worked for the tree and it was of little value anyway; yet he was rightly sorry for its loss. Is not God to have pity on the 120,000 helpless inhabitants of Nineveh and their cattle, all of them the work of his hands? We may be surprised—or delighted—at the homeliness of the dialogue; but could the point be made more plain? God is not just energy working itself out blindly. He is goodness, and his care extends over all things.

Thus the significant thing for humanity was not the affirmation of the existence of God by the Jews but the kind of God whose existence they affirmed. He is 'living'; he is 'righteous'; he makes demands. He has told man what is good and expects him to live up to it. And he is exigent. He rules with a strong hand. He remembers mercy but is not afraid to be angry. And he is angered when men break faith and kill and are cruel to one another and cast off pity, when they take bribes and turn aside the needy in the gate.

7. Scholars disagree about the origin of Jewish monotheism. Some see in it a gradual growth from more primitive conceptions, some a primary and irresistible intuition. It will be conceded however that, once achieved, it was, in idea, complete. Indeed it could not have been otherwise. The God who created all things by the word of his mouth could not be other than universal; and being the creator of all things he could not be, nor could he be imaged by, any one of them. Thus creation becomes a moral idea as much as a physical process. It involves a qualitative difference between God and his world. God is one and there is none like him. 'Thus shall ye say unto them', says Jeremiah, presumably giving a summary creed to the exiles who were being taken to Babylon (the sentence is in Aramaic): 'The gods that have not made the heavens and the earth, these shall perish from the earth, and from under the heavens.'

This repudiation of all other 'principalities and powers' involved, as a practical consequence, the banishment from the Jewish world-view of all magical content and practices, traces of which in the classical Hebrew tradition can only be found by the ingenuity of scholars. True, there has been uncovered a considerable body of pseudepigraphical literature which includes much intimate information about angels and other spirits (both good and evil) and the approved methods of conciliating or outwitting them. But it is clear that this literature was not representative or accepted. If it had been, it would not have remained in obscurity all these years. There is no novelty, and certainly nothing specifically Jewish, about a magical conjuration or invocation. The Jewish novelty is the clear and expressed conviction that God's pleasure is not to be bought by incantations or manipulations of divine names but by clean hands and a pure heart. Only upright conduct and truth and kindness give men the right to dwell in God's holy hill.

It is this which, in spite of all the striking similarities of address, of phraseology, of general rhythm and content, differentiates, for example, the Babylonian 'psalms' from those which make up the biblical book. The Hebrew Bible will have nothing to do with idolatry and its concomitants. It made a clean sweep: 'thou shalt have no other gods but me'. It cleansed the religious world.

8. If there are indeed 'no gods but me' the heavens become depopulated and mythology an empty story. Now the Jews were not alone in destroying the basis of mythology, and it will be instructive to compare them in this respect with the thinking portion of the great myth-making people so often considered their rivals.

When the historian is asked what is the new thing which Greek philosophy brought into the world, his answer is, reasoning as opposed to myth-making. Reasoning means 'giving an account', supporting a particular statement by more general considerations and so turning it from 'opinion' to 'truth'. A myth is a presentation of experience in terms of the senses and the imagination. At its best it is a dramatic expression of primary fact; at its worst, a substitution of fact by fiction. Whatever its function may have been (and may still be) in primitive thinking, its consequences for civilization are clear. It beguiles the mind until it becomes immersed in make-believe and loses all touch with reality. Reasoning is the attempt to face up to reality and to dispense with make-believe.

The highest product of the reasoning faculty is science, and Greek science is closely connected with Greek philosophy. Science is the giving of reasons for everything that occurs. And since reasons are always general, science is always becoming more and more comprehensive; it grasps together ever larger groups of occurrences in ever wider generalizations. It is thus a unifying activity, and its ideal end is the displaying of nature as one. Its striving, and in ever-increasing measure its achievement, is monistic.

So far then it would appear that the Greek philosophers and the fathers of Jewish thought were moving in the same direction, and indeed it would be an error to think that the one set of ideas excludes the other. Yet there are great differences between them, the root of them being a difference in the primary field of interest. For the Greeks this would seem to have been nature; for the Jews, man. For the Jews nature was the theatre in which man plays his part. The first five days of the creation story in Genesis set the scene for the creation of man on the sixth.

Now nature as a field of scientific enquiry is, at least proximately, determined. Without regularity and generality there is no nature to watch and report upon. It is by observation of the repeated that science offers its account of the repeatable. Its interest is in prediction; and although all prediction is of particulars, the predictions of science are framed in the light of general laws. The emphasis is thus on the generality, not on the particularity; on what is common to all, not what is particular to each.

In the moral sphere it is the opposite which holds good. Here it is just the individual action which matters. There may be little difference between man and man, but that little is for morals all-important. Variety, both in the person and in the circumstance, is the very stuff of its existence. For morality implies responsibility and responsibility choice, and choice is possible only between alternatives. If the human being is to be moral, he must be responsible for his actions; and for the actions to be his, he must have chosen them.

That there are alternatives is taught in all sections of the Hebrew Bible. Both good and evil are open to man. The adjuration of the legislator, the exhortation of the prophet, the prayer of the psalmist, is that man should choose the good; to choose evil spells disaster and death. But man can, if he will, choose evil. The freedom is there.

In numerous passages God is represented as pleading with man; in others as threatening him. But the threats, like the pleading, only serve to emphasize the point that the virtuous act is not mechanical. There are difficult cases—the 'hardening' of Pharaoh's heart, for example—which have exercised the ingenuity of theologians for centuries; but the main current of thought is clear. Man has a true self to which appeal can be made, and the appeal has some chance of success. From the side of God there is no delay. He has no pleasure in the death of the evil-doer. He is portrayed indeed as being over-eager to cancel the sentence of doom, much to the disgust of a Jonah who sees in such divine weakness the ruin of his profession as prophet. But in this, and this alone, God is obdurate. He will not destroy if he can re-form. Yet he has not left the re-forming in his own hands. It lies with man who can, if he will, re-form—re-create—himself.

Thus the world of moral action is the meeting-place between the human and divine. Just as repentance makes a new man, so, in every doing of the right, man (in the rabbinic phrase) is partnering God in the work of creation.

9. Jewish thought, as we saw, set out from and rested on the idea of creation. But the creation was not mere engineering, the carrying out of a project and the leaving it. God's creation is continuous. It was not exhausted with the six days. The world of the six days may be 'very good' but, as the biblical account of the first men testifies, it is not perfect. In order that it should be perfect, creation must perforce continue. And indeed it is still at work in any case; for the creative activity of God differs from the engineering faculty of man in that the objects he creates are themselves creative. In its simplest form (though here there is no power of initiation) an analogue of this may be seen in the physical world with its 'plants producing seed' and its 'fruit trees giving fruit in which is their seed', and its fertile animal population and pulsating life of all kinds. But in its full and true sense it is only seen in the world of human action.

For human action is not a natural process. It is not inevitable, determined either physically from without or biologically from within. It is what we *do*, not what happens to us. And what we do is the fruit of moral choice and proceeds from character as it issues in motive and intention. At a moment of decision man creates the way in which he is to go. Through chosen action he is creative continuously; and this creativity, at its best and most complete, is one with the divine creative act itself: it is a choosing of 'life'.

This is the meaning of the constant prayer for a 'new heart' or a 'new spirit', of the 'stretching of the hands' and the 'turning of the soul'. Man prays to be granted the strength to become himself and assume his destiny. When the covenant of God is written in the heart of man the transcendent will become completely immanent. The soul of man is seen as the 'lamp of God, searching out all the recesses of the inward parts';

and the law-giver's great saying to which reference has already been made thus finds its literal fulfilment:

For this commandment which I command thee this day, it is not too hard for thee, neither is it far off. It is not in heaven, that thou shouldest say, Who shall go up for us to heaven, and bring it unto us, and make us hear it, that we may do it? Neither is it beyond the sea, that thou shouldest say, Who shall go over the sea for us, and bring it unto us, and make us to hear it, that we may do it? But the word is very nigh unto thee, in thy mouth, and in thy heart, that thou mayest do it.

10. This last phrase 'that thou mayest do it' is worthy of note. It is the essential completion of what precedes. Goodness is not theory or pious aspiration. It is action, and action prescribed. Thus we are told in the Prophets that to 'know God' *means* to judge the cause of the poor and needy; and even the pedestrian Book of Proverbs sees blasphemy in oppression and the honouring of God in doing a kindness to one's fellow men. Religion is not a science of theology removed from the everyday grind and an excrescence, or commentary, on it. God enters into human life in its most ordinary relations and religion is a way of living, all-comprehensive and complete.

For the 'forms' of religion are not dissociable from their 'matter' but in it form and matter are an indistinguishable unity. In idea there is no mere ceremony. All outward appearance manifests inward truth. And if outward appearance becomes valued for itself and substituted for inward rightness, the prophetic voice is raised forthwith in crushing denunciation. But 'outward' and 'inward' are corporeal metaphors which represent the spiritual only faultily. A holy life is defined in actions and dispositions to action which, laid down in the Law and the Prophets and the Writings, make up the concrete fullness of living.

It is thus one of the more striking characteristics of Jewish thought that it never remains in the sphere of the abstract but becomes substantial in specific acts and definite institutions. In the same way as justice is no subject for analytical disquisition but the instruction not to use false weights or to take bribes or to have respect of persons, so the idea of freedom becomes the eating of unleavened bread on Passover, the idea of dependence, the dwelling in booths on Tabernacles. (These may have been nature festivals once but like the Sabbath itself they have been transformed.) Doctrine is expressed in action, action embodies doctrine; or rather action and doctrine are one. It is significant action which counts. This is the fast that I have chosen, cries one prophet: to free the oppressed and to give bread to the hungry; Tear your hearts and not your garments, urges another; a third: Let us lift up our heart with our hands. As we are told of the Hebrew language by philologists, it is the verb, expressing an action, rather than the noun, expressing a thing or state, which is central. The abstract idea of the new creation of the individual, expressed in the Abrahamic covenant and the later baptism, is given an abiding and recurring mould in the weekly Sabbath and the yearly Day of Atonement; the abstract idea of the new creation of society becomes actual in the physical figure of the restored Davidic ruler and the specific descriptions of the age he is to inaugurate. Before we come to the consideration of these, however, we must revert to the problem of science and the attitude towards it of Jewish thought.

11. It was a late Greek critic who saw the archetype of the sublime in the sentences ' "let there be light!" and there was light; "let the world be", and the world was': the lawgiver of the Jews ('no ordinary man'!), he says, had a proper conception of the power of God and found in these words an adequate vehicle for its expression. Jewish thought started from God as creative power.

Greek interest was in created nature, and Greek reasoning tended to the deductive. Its ideal and highest achievement was geometrical demonstration. The Ionian temperament seems to have had some inclination towards experiment, and Greek medicine rested on observation. But the mathematical trend prevailed; and the aim of science was conceived of as the reduction of the many observed phenomena to the one intellectual principle from which they could be in turn deduced.

It has been pointed out that it was this severe intellectualism which lead to the final sterility of Greek scientific inspiration. Its world was not large enough, its range too restricted. What was required for the revival of science in modern times was the wider vision of ever-fresh possibility. This was given by the Jewish doctrine of creation. For divine creativity is unpredictable and, so far at least as man's knowledge is concerned, it involves contingency in the created. The fountain of being is productive will which creates 'infinite things in infinite ways'. The universe thus becomes 'open', not 'closed'; and an open universe requires, and nourishes, an open mind.

The science of our day begins with humility. It recognizes the universe as mysterious. It has got beyond the arrogance of the nineteenth century and is not ashamed to falter in the presence of the unknown. It sees no final access to the secrets of nature. It may thus be understood as the attempt of the Greek mind to reach out to the world of limitless possibility suggested by Jewish thought.

12. All this is as may be. The point of relevance for our argument is that Jewish thought, although centred around morals, does not deny science. At its worst, it is just not interested. At its best, it offers science that ever-replenished fullness of being without which science is condemned to a treadmill of theory, and it stimulates enquiry by suggesting that our horizons are not final and our explanations not the whole truth. Many shall run to and fro before knowledge be increased.

And we may add a further thought which has been brought into prominence by recent students of the history of scientific ideas. The very conception of Laws of Nature, so important for science, derives in large measure from theology and the 'word' and 'commandments' of God. Jewish thought gave science rational encouragement by suggesting, in the will and wisdom of God, a ground for the existence of discoverable laws.

This holds good not only of later speculation but of the biblical texts themselves. God is not capricious. We may not understand why he does things but he does them in wisdom and measure and order. His word created the world in various departments and appointed for each its plan. His covenant with Noah included the promise of continuity in the physical universe, so that 'while the earth remaineth, seed time and harvest, and cold and heat, and summer and winter, and day and night shall not cease'. So Genesis, the book of the Beginning. Similarly the prophets took as their exemplar of perpetuity the processes of physical nature. God has, they say, a 'covenant' with day and night that they should always come in their season, a covenant which will not be broken. The most cursory glance at biblical similes will show how closely knit life was with the conception of the orderly course of nature. 'As snow in summer, and as rain in harvest, so honour is not seemly for a fool!'

True, we have here no curiosity in the particularities of the workings of nature which in the Ionian Greeks produced the beginnings of the biological sciences; but if curiosity is not there, wonder is, and the Psalms, less spectacularly than the prophetical writings but perhaps more profoundly, breathe a deep sense of the unity behind the variety of nature. The heavens declare the glory of the one God; the light is his robe, the clouds his chariot. The author of the 139th psalm may show little acquaintance with embryological detail; but he knows, no less than the Greek poet, that man is 'curiously and wonderfully made'.

Still, the moral interest is the stronger. If the heavens declare the glory of God, his will for man is declared in rules of living; and it is these, and not the facts of astronomy, which 'give light to the eyes' and are 'sweeter than honey'. But enquiry into nature was not forbidden. The writer of Job would presumably have rejoiced in an addition to his catalogue of natural wonders; and God himself is singled out by the prophet for especial mention because he has knowledge of the names of all the stars.

13. This point will become important since in the medieval period it produced, or at least allowed, among philosophically minded Jews what was practically a worship of scientific knowledge as a propaedeutic to religion. This attitude towards science had, through Spinoza, important results in the development of the European mind; and it is worth remembering this on the credit side since we must animadvert parenthetically to a *mis*use of biblical texts which gave rise to an unfortunate chapter in the history of religion, a chapter which would seem to be not yet closed. I refer to the so-called conflict between science and religion.

We may take the classical instance.

The psalmist says that the foundations of the earth were fixed and could not be moved. By that he meant presumably that the physical world is in reliable hands. He is repeating in his own way the promise of God after the flood and offering the student of nature just that assurance of which he stands in need, the assurance, namely, that the world is a stable affair not subject to sudden and unreasonable change. He is making a general statement that the universe is orderly; and it is interesting to observe that the same phrase about the earth being fixed is used in connection with the final judgment as if to suggest that there is one source for both moral and physical orderliness. But the psalmist is not advancing a theory of physics; and if this saying of his was considered as such and used in order to confute Galileo, that was not the fault of the psalmist. In the same way the first chapter of Genesis has been used to condemn the results of the study of geology and the theory of evolution, and if it was indeed offered as the literal and final truth of the physical and biological constitution of the world, the position of the religionist would be difficult. The question is, was it so offered, and was it meant to bind posterity any more than the nature mysticism of the 104th psalm or the sceptical queries of Agur the son of Jakeh in the Book of Proverbs?

We may leave this problem to the theologians, returning to our main issue, the content of the Jewish outlook. We have seen that it is preeminently moral. We have now to ask what group of ideas clusters round this primary orientation? A first answer will be, History, and all that history implies both for the individual and for the community.

14. We saw that the Greeks, setting out from the world of nature, produced science, and pre-eminently mathematical science. Now science, and especially mathematical science, has always found difficulty with time. Scientific truth is timeless or above time. Time is the measure of change; but scientific truth (ideally speaking) is changeless. The aim of science has been conceived until quite recently as the discovery of eternal truth.

The Jews set out from the world of man. For them time was all-important. The world of man, like the world of God, is a world of will, and will involves process, i.e. time. Again, the world of man, like the world of God, is one of action. Acts have consequences; and the whole point of a consequence is that it is consequent on something that happened before: again, time! Time is required for the working out of plans. It means the chance of improvement, the possibility of failure. Without time there is no purpose or choice.

When one opens one's Bible, one finds a narrative which passes rapidly from Adam to Noah and from Noah to Abraham. Adam, the man created in the likeness of God, is both the physical and moral progenitor of humanity. Noah is its second physical founder. From him and his sons came 'all the nations of the earth'; and the tale of the generations after the flood is peculiarly instructive: it presents a detailed genealogical tree of the whole of mankind.

But this was only a physical rebirth. There was need of a fresh start morally too. For mankind, like its first ancestor, is by original character akin to the divine; and its task is to win back, and to maintain, this first nature. The way was shown by Abraham, and he therefore bore the burden and privilege of vocation. He was called to teach, through his own family, mankind. He was to train his 'children and those of his line after him to keep the ways of the Lord, that is, to do what is good and right'; and the Bible is the following out of this conception and its consequences both for the Jews and for mankind at large.

Thus for Jewish thought history was education. What happened in the world was never, for it, a circular process as in some Greek thinking, an aimless admixture of opposites combining and dissolving and recombining. There was a goal to be striven for and attained, a goal which could be understood and which was set before the conscious mind.

This is history. History is not merely the record of a string of occurrences. It is an attempt to seize occurrences in their pattern. The biblical account offers a pattern from the very beginning and groups occurrences in accordance with their relevance to it. Some are more, some less, relevant; some important, some not. An obvious instance is the narrative of the Book of Kings where powerful monarchs are summarily dismissed with the disdainful comment that they caused Israel to sin; or one may recall the prayer of Nehemiah for whom the creation of the world, the choice of Abraham, and the deliverance from Egypt would seem to form a sufficient key to the interpretation of human life. The point is not whether these 'philosophies of history' are sound but that there was a 'philosophy of history'.

The pattern is not limited to any one people. It comprises 'all the families of the earth'. Not only are they castigated in their own right for moral shortcomings, notably, breaking faith and inhuman conduct in war. They also partake of the blessing—'Egypt my people and Assyria the work of my hands'. All are, with Israel, vassals of the one God, instruments for his activities ('Ho, Assyrian, the rod of mine anger!') in the one world. In a famous passage the Persian Cyrus is called God's 'shepherd' and, even more surprisingly, God's 'anointed', i.e., in the Hebrew, his *mashiah* (messiah), that is to say, his chosen servant appointed to carry out his purpose in the plan of time which is history. The great prophetic dooms embrace the world powers of Babylon and Egypt and Tyre as well as the local neighbours Moab and Ammon and Ashdod, and they fill the biblical stage with a universal chorus in which all nature joins. The very firs and cedars of Lebanon, even stones and timber from the wall, exult at the downfall of tyrants. The whole earth, animate and inanimate, together with sun, moon, and stars, suffer and rejoice as one; and when God comes to 'judge the earth' (the *whole* earth, be it noted), they 'clap their hands' and 'sing for joy together'.

Thus occurrences become events, each with its part in and significance for the whole. They are no aimless flux but a movement with a mover and a moved. The movement, like the choice of the individual, is not mechanical. Much depends upon man, who is both moved and, to a certain degree, mover too. The movement is forward only if men choose to make it so. The scenes with Joshua at Shechem, Samuel at Ramah, Elijah on Carmel, all present vivid pictures of crucial acts of free choice determining the future of the whole nation. We have here a *drama*, a 'doing', not a mere happening; and man is an actor who within limits creates his own part.

In this drama God is ready to help. His hand is always waiting to support the stumbler, to receive the returning penitent. He appoints prophets to attempt to guide the nation; he sends his angels to watch over individuals. True, there are conditions. There must be a desire to walk in the right path, or, in biblical phrase, a 'right spirit'; but given a right spirit, whether in an individual or in a community, the helping hand is there.

15. It is a remark of the English philosopher F. H. Bradley that the object of historical record is the 'world of human individuality'. The Hebrew Bible is certainly a world of individuals, and what a gallery it presents: Abraham, Jacob, Moses, Elijah, Amos and Jeremiah; Jezebel and Jehu and Zimri. Its stories—Joseph and his brethren; Jonah and the whale; Daniel in the lions' den—have become common property; even its fleeting mentions—Melchizedek, Lot's wife, Jephthah's daughter—stick in the mind. It is not only that linguistically biblical style has given a basic idiom to European languages. Its attitude to life in general has impressed a particular type of character upon the European mind. We think in terms of the human family described in the early chapters of Genesis; we judge ourselves and our fellows in terms of the moral personality required by the prophets and psalmists. We are at home with the non-conformist Amos and the protesting Job because it is they who taught us the nature of non-conformity and protest. They talk to us in our own language, and that because we have made their language ours. If the Hebrew Bible has given the world a doctrine of God, it has given it no less a doctrine of man.

16. The special place claimed for the Jews in the wider drama of world history has given rise to many misunderstandings, and much has been made of the arbitrary character of the 'choice' of the Jews as if it had been dictated by mere wilfulness on the part of the chooser or tribal vanity on the part of the chosen (and narrators). As a modern epigrammatist put it:

> How odd
> Of God
> To choose
> The Jews!

But this is to miss the point of the biblical narrative, and the counter-epigram goes to the heart of the matter:

> It's not
> So odd.
> The Jews
> Chose God.

There is here something reciprocal, a mutual selection, a choice exchanged. There is a 'covenant', and a covenant is two-sided; a 'marriage' —and how often from the time of Hosea is this simile used. The whole trend of the story is not that of an arbitrary choosing and of an irresponsible chosen. It is told as if God were anxiously watching the footsteps of humanity and begging it to show itself worthy of itself and its origin. The eventual choice of one people is almost a counsel of despair; for the people itself it is almost an imposed duty.

A kindred view sees God not as husband yearning for an erring wife's return but as master refusing to let his messenger withdraw from his service. His dealings with men had been so void of success that he could not allow his Jews to default and become 'like all the nations'. A rabbinic story is here again much in point. It tells that God offered the Law to all the other peoples before he came to the Jews, but only the Jews were willing to accept the moral obligations it imposed. Even so (the story continues) he had to hold Mount Sinai over them and threaten them with extinction before they finally agreed! The right way of living entails restrictions on the natural man which the natural man was, and is, unwilling to submit to.

And indeed the record of disappointments is striking: first, Adam himself, then his children, then the generation of the flood; even the 'righteous' Noah and his family would seem to be only the best of a bad generation. Abraham was indeed chosen, and later tradition delighted in adducing reasons why; but his own first-born was rejected and then the first-born of his chosen son Isaac and then the first-born of Isaac's chosen son. There is at work a continuous winnowing right through the history of the 'chosen' people from the beginning till the very last when, at the end of days, 'many of them that sleep in the dust of the earth shall awake, some to everlasting life and some to shame and everlasting contempt'. It is a moral selection which is working throughout. The 'chosen people' is held up to mankind more often as a warning to avoid than as an example to follow; and even when the chosen of the chosen are commended, suffering is the badge, martyrdom the crown. The chosen people is not good because it is chosen; it is chosen because it is good. And its continuance of being chosen depends on the continuance of its being good.

17. The fact is that the idea of choice has yielded to the idea of service: service to God for the benefit of humanity, service to humanity in the name of God. The way is hard, and both prophets and psalmist are full of the bitterness of suffering. But the ideal of the servant includes suffering,

and it triumphs over suffering. Indeed, it is through (though not in) suffering that it is brought to realize the nature of its own destiny, just as it is brought to realize God in his full majesty as God of the whole earth not in the hour of victory but in the hour of defeat. The remnant, the 'tenth part', is destroyed again and again. Its call and vocation is to teach, its reward abuse and shame. Yet its duty is beyond the limits of Israel, and is clearly laid down and inescapable: 'It is not enough for one who is my servant to put the tribes of Jacob again in their place, and to set back those of Israel who have been sent away: My purpose is to give you as a light to the nations, so that you may be my salvation to the end of the earth.' The moral life, and the education to the moral life, starting from a particular people (or section of a people) and environment, embraces of necessity all peoples and all environments. The God of the spirits of all flesh requires the obedience of all flesh, just as, in his own good time, he will wipe away tears from off all faces.

18. The logical connection between monotheism and ethics is not difficult to trace. It means the setting up of one standard for all. Many gods mean many standards. What one god disapproves of, another can always be found to approve.

As a logical argument against polytheism this is sound and can be found repeatedly in Plato; but logical arguments have little effect on the emotions. The Jewish contribution is not a theory of morals but its practice, and practice depends on feeling.

Many examples could be given, for instance, the 'disgusting things' spurned by the law of holiness. The things are spurned as disgusting, and with such vigour that no doubt is left on the point. We have only to open our bibles to see the source of this vigour. God says to Cain: Where is your brother? And Cain says: Am I my brother's keeper? In this stark dialogue we have the strength of the Jewish genius; and the source is clearly the confrontation of man with his maker.

This confrontation is only possible under a monotheism. Only under a monotheism is there no opening for evasion, no dodging the issue, no appeal from one divine power to another. Deity is one. *Vis-à-vis* the one God, the individual human being takes his proper place and assumes his proper proportions. He is responsible and must give an account.

This confrontation of man with God comes out most clearly in the prophets when they receive their call: Moses on Horeb ('Who hath made man's mouth . . . ? Now, therefore, go'); the boy Samuel in the Temple ('Speak; for thy servant heareth'); Elijah and the voice ('What doest thou here, Elijah?'); Isaiah ('"Whom shall I send?" . . . Then I said: "Here am I; send me"'); Jeremiah ('To whomsoever I shall send thee thou shalt go, and whatsoever I shall command thee thou shalt speak'). A peculiarly impressive account is that of Ezekiel: '"Son of man, stand upon thy feet, and I will speak with thee". . . . And he said unto me, "Son of man, I send thee to the children of Israel . . . and thou shalt say unto them, Thus saith the Lord God".'

The prophet is not to care what the crowd says. He is responsible to God alone. He may beg for release or cry for mercy; pray to be blotted out of the book of life. But the doom is upon him no less than on the peoples to whom he is sent. He can do no other. He must speak; and he can speak only what God puts into his mouth.

19. This is spectacular and needs no further illustration. More striking is the quieter appeal, not the great wind or the earthquake or the fire, but the 'still small voice'. One meets it strikingly in the Levitical law of holiness where with impressive and almost monotonous regularity we are given the refrain: 'and thou shalt fear thy God'. It is a rabbinic comment that the sentence is added in cases when either public knowledge is absent or no public punishment is attachable:

Do not put a curse on those who have no hearing, or put a cause of falling in the way of the blind, but keep the fear of your God before you: I am the Lord. . . . Get up from your seats before the white-haired, and give honour to the old, and let the fear of your God be before you: I am the Lord. . . . Do no wrong one to another but let the fear of your God be before you; for I am the Lord your God. . . . Take no interest from him, in money or in goods, but have the fear of your God before you, and let your brother make a living among you. Do not take interest on the money which you let him have or on the food which you give him: I am the Lord your God, who took you out of the land of Egypt to give you the land of Canaan, that I might be your God.

All these cases are matters 'given over to the heart' (I use the rabbinic phrase). They appertain not to the *forum externum*, the court of law and outward appearance, but to the *forum internum*, the court of conscience.

In that court too there is a judge, but a judge who looks to the heart. Conscience means responsibility, and responsibility is to a person. To be responsible is to be answerable, that is, liable to be questioned about one's actions and, if questioned, bound to answer. Questions can only be put by persons; and it is because the God of Jewish thought is at least personal (though he is clearly much more than that too) that conscience acquires its profound significance for human life. 'What will I do when

God comes as my judge', asks Job, 'and what answer may I give to *his* questions?'

20. We may conclude this brief account with the remark that most of the ideas which we have mentioned have become in our day trite. We are used to the ideas of God and history and conscience. But the God and history and conscience to which we have become used are the God, history, and conscience of the Jewish tradition, and the fact that we are used to them does not derogate from their importance or their decisive influence on men's minds. Like water and air they are the primary and indispensable basis of living, remembered only when they run short.

It has appeared to many observers that in this age it is moral ideas which are running short. It behoves us therefore to turn our attention to them again.

IV Some Illustrations and Applications

1. In the light of what was remarked previously on the nature of ideas, it would be difficult to affirm in their history an exclusive influence from Jewish, or from any other, sources. Yet there are connections; and if there is little derivation, there is much affiliation. I offer an example of some intrinsic interest and then proceed to wider issues.

The philosopher John Locke, among the many pioneer ideas which he embodied in his *Some Thoughts concerning Education* (1690), was anxious to emphasize the value for human beings of fresh air and cold water. He suggested, for example, the training of children to accustom themselves to what we should now call open sandals, remarking sagely that if men are not afraid to expose their face and hands to the weather, there seems no reason why they should be afraid of exposing their feet. He also advocated the use of cold baths; but against these there seems to have been so strong a prejudice that he was constrained to seek precedents in experience. After citing from classical literature the somewhat shadowy cases of Seneca and Horace, both of whom mention that they took cold baths in winter, he says (para. 7): 'But perhaps Italy will be thought much warmer than England, and the chillness of their waters not to come near ours in winter. But if the rivers of Italy are warmer, those of Germany and Poland are much colder than any in this country; and yet *in these the Jews, both men and women, bathe all over, at all seasons of the year,* without any prejudice to their health.'

The reference is clearly to the ablutions required in Jewish religious observance, which indeed rest in part on considerations of personal and communal hygiene. On various occasions the washing of the whole body, or of the hands, is obligatory; and the provision of facilities for bathing in running water is a part of the routine of Jewish community organization. The idea is already full-fledged in the Pentateuch, for which cleanliness is not only next to Godliness but the very condition for the presence of God. As is remarked in connection with the enactment of an elementary hygienic precaution: 'The Lord thy God walketh in the midst of thy camp; therefore shall thy camp be holy.' (The modern reader, prone to sniff at such lofty considerations, should perhaps be reminded that 'ritual' cleanliness is still cleanliness!)

Now it is not suggested that if it had not been for the ritual washings of the book of Leviticus the modern bathroom would not have come into being, any more than that latrines would not be put up by a modern army if it had not been for the precedent of Deut. 23: 12–14. The point is that the religious ideas of the Hebrew Bible entailed ways of living which we now understand to be required by the human situation. (In fact they gave them a force and a driving power which experience has shown regrettably to be wanting to mere medical advice.)

With this in mind we may turn to the wider problem, and I suggest two lines of approach which may prove fruitful. First we should ask ourselves what the world would have been lacking if Jewish thought had never existed; second, we may try to estimate the significance of those ideas from Jewish thought which were so Hebraic as to be untranslatable and which have been preserved therefore in modern languages in their original Hebrew: for example Sabbath, Jubilee, Messiah.

2. To our first question the obvious answer is that if Jewish thought had never existed the world would have been without Christianity and Islam. By this is not meant that Christianity and Islam are solely Jewish in nature and origin. Far from it. They are surely themselves. To be oneself is to be distinct from others; and so far as they are products at all, they are the products of other factors besides the Jewish. And yet Jewish thought is all-important both for them in particular and in the general history of religion.

We may take the latter point first, illustrating it by a conventional analogy which we have used before.

According to the tradition, explicitly phrased in Proclus, the Greek Pythagoras was the first to treat number by and in itself, i.e. he was the creator of mathematics as a *science*. Mathematics as a craft, or as a business device, or as a pre-requisite to religious rites, was known to the Egyptians and Babylonians. But mathematics in the 'pure' sense is Greek; and it is the vision of Pythagoras which was taken up long after by Kepler and Descartes and the mathematical physicists of our own day. Mathematics may therefore be fairly called Greek, although the thought may have changed in its content and detail and although no one can say whether, if Pythagoras and the Greeks had never existed, there might not have arisen other individuals, or another people, to think the same or similar thoughts.

It is somewhat in the same way that we may call religion Jewish. It is in Jewish thought that what is recognized as religion received basic expression. If we are asked what religion is, we can point to certain ideas, or figures, in Jewish thought, much as, when asked what mathematics is, we point to the Greek tradition and the Greeks.

But we may go further than this. It is not only a matter of 'type' or 'inspiration' or 'vision'. The positive content of Greek mathematics is an integral part of modern mathematics, and whole sections of it are given in modern textbooks as its essential groundwork. It is not a mere survival taught for historical reasons like the theory of phlogiston in chemistry. Its value for humanity lies in itself, in its own demonstrated propositions.

Similarly, Jewish thought as such is embedded in Christianity and Islam. It fills their sacred books; and if it were removed, their essential content would be different. Christianity, indeed, on the lips of its founder, proclaimed itself the fulfilment of Judaism; and the prophet of Islam declared that he was the true successor of Moses and, like Moses, a 'prophet with a book'. Thus we may fairly reaffirm the accepted judgement that Judaism is the 'mother' religion, Christianity and Islam its 'daughters'. Without Abraham, Moses, and the prophets, both Christianity and Islam, if they could have come into being at all, would have been strangely other than they are.

But again this is not all. Children often break with their parents and, whether in sorrow or in anger, go their own independent ways; and yet retain for all that, in the very fibres of their being, their parents' characteristics. Whatever be finally accepted as the detailed connection between the three great monotheistic religions, it is clear that they have, and still preserve, a strong family resemblance. They are all vitally interested in conduct; they all conceive the material universe as dependent on spiritual reality; they all see this one and unique spiritual reality as the source of good and of right conduct. There is between them much more in common than this; but it will be agreed that there is at least this, and that this is all-important.

3. If we accept this minimum and turn to our second line of approach, we shall see that it supports the results of our first. The untranslatable words we have mentioned enshrine ideas similar to those just indicated.

The Sabbath is the visible sign of the insufficiency of the material and the need for its reintegration with the spiritual. It is a standing protest against the doctrine of wage slavery. It is the weekly demonstration that although work is good ('six days shalt thou labour' is also part of the command), work is not an end in itself; that although the satisfaction of the body is good, the body is little without the soul. Even the most severe and gloomy of Sabbaths only underlines, in however unpleasing (and possibly mistaken) a fashion, this fundamental lesson; and the Jewish tradition, with its love of home life and its devotion to study, has shown how the Sabbath can be made not only a day of respite from work but a positive factor in human development and well-being.

The Sabbath offers a recurring opportunity for self-discovery. It invites living at a higher and truer level. It presents freedom as an active principle, the felt need to realize potentialities which on a work-day are submerged and forgotten. It is constant reminder that, although men live by bread, they do not live for bread. The Sabbath is thus more than a rest, more even than a recuperation of energy for return to the familiar task. It is, rather, a fresh direction of energy based on a fuller comprehension of the nature and needs of man.

With the weekly Sabbath there should be joined the yearly Sabbath, the seventh year of every 'week' of years. On this year the land rests: again freedom, this time for the soil. After seven Sabbaths of years there comes the Jubilee, the fiftieth year; 'and let this fiftieth year be kept holy, and say publicly that every one in the land is free from debt: it is the Jubilee, and every man may go back to his heritage and to his family'.

The poor man is thus released from the burden of his poverty. He is given a new chance; he is made free. His shackles are struck off from him. He makes a fresh start. He becomes again, in the full sense, a man.

It is important to observe the root idea of this (to us) startling provision. It is given with engaging simplicity: 'No exchange of land may be for ever, for the land is *mine*; and *you are as my guests, living with me for a time.* Wherever there is property in land, the owner is to have the right of getting it back.' The phraseology is exactly parallel with that of the rejection of the very idea of Jewish slavery: 'For they are *my* servants whom I took out from the land of Egypt; they may not become the property of another.' The Jubilee, like the Sabbath, is a return to what should be the norm. It makes the idea of freedom a part of practical human life; it embodies it in the organization of society; and the idea of freedom for man, whether in life or property, is a direct derivative from the dependence of all things, man included, on God.

Our third untranslatable word, Messiah, is in itself a whole history and a whole theology. It has been the unexhausted subject of whole libraries both of research and of popular teaching. It has been the comfort and the hope of centuries. For that reason it need not detain us here. It is too well known for comment. For our purpose it is enough to quote its dictionary definition as the 'promised deliverer of the Jews; Christ as this; liberator of oppressed people or country (French, Latin and Greek from Hebrew *mashiaḥ* anointed)' (*The Concise Oxford Dictionary*). The Messiah is no abstract figure set up for aesthetic contemplation; he is first and foremost a deliverer. And he is a king, the ideal ruler, the embodiment of truth and justice, restoring the divine order in a disrupted world.

He thus represents the re-entry of the spiritual into human affairs. His coming may involve the creation of a new heaven and a new earth. But the new heaven and earth are not ends in themselves. They are the ideal setting of a normal, although reconstructed, life. To the new heart and the new spirit granted to man there will be added a new language, a 'clean language, so that they may all make prayer to the Lord and be his servants with one mind': and the earth will be full of the knowledge of God as the sea is covered by the waters.

4. We may now turn to the later history of the monotheistic religions and observe that after the first few generations Islam attained its full development and maximum variety of interpretation. The longer history of Christianity is more variegated; and, as often happens, the desire for change took the shape of a return to fundamentals. These fundamentals were often found by the seekers in the Hebrew Scriptures, with the result that time and again reform movements in the Church were of a Hebraizing character.

In this connection one thinks readily of the more extreme Protestants in England, Scotland, and Switzerland, all so profoundly affected, not always perhaps (in modern eyes) for the best, by the Old Testament model. Yet sweeter influences should not be forgotten. The Psalter became the hymn-book of all branches of the Church, and who can tell how widely and deeply it has moved the minds of men? True, it has sometimes encouraged them to violence, although not in an evil cause; but for one who appealed to its inspiration to 'avenge thy slaughtered saints' there are countless others who found in its often placid piety both a stimulus in

well-being and a comfort in adversity and loss. Few books in any literature give in such simple language so close a feeling of the divine presence,
fewer still so dignified a practical morality in such easily intelligible
words.

5. Yet there is room still for the thunder of Sinai. Man needs more than
ever to be reminded of the wrath of God. Sin, judgment, punishment—
these must be, and are, alive in any church. The cry of the angels: sanctus,
sanctus, sanctus, rings out on all solemn occasions, and with it the warn-
ings of the day 'which is dark and not light'. *Dies irae dies illa,* as the medieval hymn-writer quotes from the prophets, and a glance at the hymn
itself will show vividly one part of the Hebraic legacy in the Church. The
scene is all biblical. First the signal, the vast assembling, the subjection of
nature, the opened book, the judge who sits, the sinner who trembles;
and then the appeal to the most high king, the trustful abasement, the
confidence that salvation will come. We have in this hymn the hard side of
religion, a side which seems to be lost to view in the modern period: the
fact and sense of wrong-doing; conscience and remorse; the final account-
ing which none can escape.

6. Conscience is bound up with consciousness and conscientiousness,
and these are all connected, both etymologically and in fact, with knowledge (Latin: *scientia*). We spoke before about the public character of the
Jewish revelation and the consequence that teaching became a central
element in the practice of religion. This fact affected the very forms of
worship both in the synagogue and through the synagogue, the church.
The priest was necessarily a teacher: as a late prophet reminds us, his 'lips
kept knowledge, and men waited for the law from his mouth'. The priesthood as such, with its elaborate ceremonial centralized in Jerusalem,
became otiose with the destruction of the Temple, and indeed centuries
before that destruction the dispersion of the Jews was an accomplished
and permanent fact. Thus the synagogue was organized as a 'place of
meeting' and a centre of public instruction. Scholars have pointed out
the survivals of synagogal practice in the ceremonies both of Christianity
and of Islam; but more important than ceremony is the age-long prophetic message, embodied in the very fact of the existence of the synagogue, that God requires mercy and knowledge, not sacrifice and burnt
offering. The indignation of the prophets found its prosaic translation in
the simple prayers and sermons of the 'place of meeting'. Here study
became recognized as an integral part of the service and worship of God.
Classes were established for the young; regular readings and expositions

of Scripture arranged; homily and parable pressed into the service of popular education. This too was taken over by the Church, around which was centred for hundreds of years the only education available; and one remembers also with gratitude the humble priests of the remote monasteries where the tradition of humane letters, despite the obscurantism of the times, was preserved in Europe.

7. One of the least expected by-products of Jewish thought is in the field of political theory. Yet on reflection it is not really a matter of wonder. A religion which salutes God as 'father of the fatherless and judge of the widowed' has laid the spiritual foundation for the welfare state, and biblical legislation, whether ever put into practice or not, contains the essence of all sound social order. That there is one law for all, both citizen and stranger; that before the law all men are equal; that care should be taken, both by individuals and by the community, for the unfortunate and the incapable and the helpless; that birth is an accident and wealth a trust, and neither of them a ground for privilege; that power should not be exercised arbitrarily; that no prince or leader is as such sacrosanct—these and similar lessons stand out from the biblical page for all to see.

It is thus understandable that whole communities should have organized themselves on biblical lines, calling themselves, in Pauline fashion, the true Israel. In particular, the position that all government rests on the consent of the governed was made to depend on the doctrine of the 'covenant'. It was pointed out that covenants and pacts are not imposed but agreed; and that the 'holy people', from Abraham downwards, were willing partners in the covenant with their God. He was in truth their king, but a king who sought for his people and who was freely accepted by them. Further, the secular monarchy among the Jews was also the result of agreement on both sides—witness, for example, the selection of Saul or the invitation extended to Jephthah.

Of course arguments could be found on the other side, and indeed they were. One recalls the typical plea for absolute monarchy, based on a somewhat bizarre use of the Old Testament, given in the political treatise of Dante. In the great crisis of the monarchy in the modern world this plea was revived. The Aristotelian Robert Filmer, for example, summed up centuries of discussion by the affirmation that just as Adam was lord over all creatures by divine command, so the king was a natural father to his subjects by divine right; the king's responsibility is not therefore to his subjects but to God alone, and God alone can remove him. Which statement (and many others of similar character) gave rise to the laborious and devastating criticism of John Locke in the first of his two *Treatises of Government* (1690). The second he devoted to the thesis that kings hold their posts with the consent of, and at the pleasure of, the citizens, and that in extreme cases, when appeal to the temporal power is of no avail, the citizens have the right to 'appeal to Heaven'. The appeal to Heaven is of course rebellion, a turning from the justice of man to the justice of God; and the idea is a biblical one (see Exod. 22: 23 and 27) for which Locke, at the conclusion of his treatise (para. 241) quotes the precedent of the biblical Jephthah (Judges 11: 27). This appeal to the 'supreme Judge' is the last prerogative of the outraged individual conscience. Locke is here voicing the very essence of Protestantism.

It is one of the commonplaces of the history of political theory that this book of Locke's was the direct inspiration of the American Declaration of Independence; and it is fitting that a story which begins with Abraham who left his country and people to set up a home where he could worship God in his own way should have among its later chapters these sturdy and far-reaching documents. And indeed, literary connections apart, there is an inherent link between the Fathers of these different nations and epochs. There is a unity of conviction which binds them together, a unity fostered by the study of the old texts. Like the psalmist they 'know that the Lord will maintain the cause of the poor', and they are ready to lend a hand themselves:

> Not like the brazen giant of Greek fame
> With conquering limbs astride from land to land,
> Here at our sea-washed, sunset gates shall stand
> A mighty woman with a torch, whose flame
> Is the imprisoned lightning, and her name
> Mother of exiles. From her beacon-hand
> Glows world-wide welcome; her mild eyes command
> The air-bridged harbour that twin cities frame.
> 'Keep, ancient lands, your storied pomp!' cries she
> With silent lips. 'Give me your tired, your poor,
> Your huddled masses yearning to breathe free,
> The wretched refuse of your teeming shore.
> Send these, the homeless, tempest-tost, to me.
> I lift my lamp beside the golden door!'

('THE NEW COLOSSUS', A SONNET OF EMMA LAZARUS
ENGRAVED ON THE STATUE OF LIBERTY)

8. It is thus in the field of human relations that Jewish thought has been especially significant. Its interest is in communities and their organization;

and yet it has always realized that communities are made up of individual persons and that life is lived by individual persons. The basis of community life is the person just as the education of the person is its end.

We may refer yet again to a passage cited already:

'And if a man from another country is living in your land with you, do not make life hard for him; let him be to you as one of your countrymen and have love for him as for yourself; for you were living in a strange land, in the land of Egypt.' Here we are exhorted to be kind to others because we know by experience what it means when others are not kind to us; and this ground for decent conduct is enforced by the historical reference: you were foreigners in Egypt and therefore know what it is to be made to feel foreigners yourselves. The appeal is to the person for the person on grounds of the experience of personality.

We might think that we have here a 'law of holiness' for the guidance of a select class of priests; but the same injunction, with the same ground, is repeated continually elsewhere. Indeed, according to the rabbis the command to be kind to strangers is given in the Pentateuch no less than thirty-six times! The experience of Egyptian slavery, like the idolatry of 'beyond the river', seems to have bitten so hard into the consciousness of the whole people that the very memory became an invocation and stimulus to kindness. Even a hired servant, after six years' service, is to be set free, and he is to be 'furnished liberally' and not sent away empty-handed. And again we have the same reason given; you were slaves in Egypt and so know what service means. The whole stress is on our common humanity: 'For ye know the *heart* of the stranger.'

9. It has been worth returning to this point because in it we have the clear and decisive turn in the attitude of man to man which was summed up long after in the Kantian formula that 'persons' are not 'things' and that human beings are never to be treated as instruments only. For Jewish thought the proper attitude of man to man is personal, and that because man, that is, each individual human being, bears in himself the likeness of God. External considerations are thus ultimately of no account. There shall be 'no respecting the position of the poor' just as there shall be 'no honouring the position of the great'. Power, position, riches or poverty, are irrelevant. It is man as man who matters; character; inner worth; what a man is in himself. Men are thus essentially equal, however diverse their circumstances and gifts. Wise and foolish, high and low, rich and poor, meet together in that the one God made them all.

This primary fact of the equality of men as persons is well expressed in the conventional biblical equivalent for a human being, viz., 'son of man'; a phrase which might be translated as accurately 'son of Adam'. A rabbinic synonym is 'he who is created in the Likeness', a term which emphasizes not only the dignity of manhood but also its responsibility. Like 'son of man' (or 'son of Adam'), it also serves to remind us of the oneness of humanity through its common origin and the consequent duty of mutual help. 'Did not God make him as well as me?', asks Job, and the reference is not to friend or neighbour or relative but to man (and woman) servant, i.e. to the depressed class of antiquity: 'Did not God make him as well as me? Did he not give us life in our mothers' bodies? . . . For I was cared for by God as by a father from my earliest days . . .'. It is because we have a common father who looked after us all that we should look after one another. The biological unity of mankind laid down in the narrative of Genesis finds here its full ethical significance.

10. Where all are equally sons of man and creatures of God the only aristocracy possible is that of the spirit. Better a scholar of unknown parentage, runs a talmudic proverb, than a high priest who is an ignoramus. Knowledge is an inalienable possession. 'If you have knowledge, what do you lack?', asks an old Hebrew saw; 'If you lack knowledge, what do you have?' Thus for the worship of power, whether in the form of riches or of birth or of high place, Jewish thought substituted the worship of wisdom; and wisdom, which we are told repeatedly is better than jewels and gold and silver, is not only open to all men but is also the 'master-workman' of God.

Here is not the place to trace out the connection between the well-known praises of Wisdom in the Book of Proverbs, for example, and Greek doctrine, early or late, with its tremendous implications for later theology, though it is often forgotten that knowledge is a key-word not only in the so-called Wisdom literature but throughout the whole Hebrew Bible, Pentateuch and Prophets and Psalms alike. For us the important point is again that we have in it a meeting-place between divine and human, transcendent and immanent, similar to that which we noted before in the sphere of morals. Indeed wisdom here is a moral conception. It is not only the architectural plan of the physical universe, the 'word' by which 'the heavens were created'. It is the hating of evil, of pride, of a high opinion of oneself, of a false tongue. It is the ground for the authority of kings.

Thus ethics and politics are inextricably interwoven, but the primacy is to ethics. A king's will, as we saw in the case of David and Ahab, does not make an action right. One of the most indignant judgements in the whole of the Prophets is that of Ezekiel (17) on the king of Judah of his time for breaking his plighted word to his conqueror. Oaths are oaths, agreements are agreements, even when made for reasons of state or in one's own despite. To break them is a 'wrong done against Me'.

11. The climax of political theory lies in the relationship between state and state. Here again the principle is the use of wisdom in the service of morals; its motto: 'not by might nor by power but by My spirit'. The nations will go up to the house of God which will be high above all mountains, there to be taught knowledge of his ways; and 'he shall judge between the nations . . . and they shall beat their swords to plow-shares . . . neither shall they learn war any more'. The recognition of one spiritual authority; the submission to its decisions; the consequent turning of the weapons of war to the service of peace—the root of the matter is here. In principle war is no method of settling disputes; and the recognition of that fact is not the least of the achievements of Jewish thought which are of living moment today. Isaiah's well-known description of the 'ensign of the peoples' who is to come from 'the stock of Jesse' voices one of the deepest aspirations of humanity in that it substitutes wisdom for force. One notes again the vision of unbroken unity. The nations form one family and are inter-responsible; and in the final consummation it is not one people or territorial unit but the whole earth which shall be 'full of the knowledge of God'.

12. We have been treating of Jewish thought as if it were confined to the Hebrew Bible. The Bible is not a book but a literature, a literature covering many hundreds of years; and it was continued in the literature called summarily by the name rabbinic of which the abiding monument and epitome is the Talmud. It is yet an unsolved problem how far talmudic law in the technical sense influenced the course of European law; but there is no doubt that as a literature it has a living importance for the student of religion. It is to it that one must turn in order fully to understand the religious atmosphere from which both Christianity and Islam proceeded, and it is in it that we find the deepening of such central ideas as that of the majesty, and the nearness, of God; of study as an act of worship; of the all-importance of conduct and the need for its detailed regulation; of the supreme virtues of piety and modesty and regard for others; of the supreme values of truth and holiness and peace. But even so the creative effort was not exhausted; and literature of a distinctive order has been produced by the Jewish people from that time till today. It comprises all branches, from philosophy and ethics, through law and chronicle, and history to poetry, essay, and romance; and it has been produced both in Hebrew and in the vernaculars of the various diasporas —Greek, Aramaic, Syriac, Arabic, Persian, and medieval Latin—as well as in modern languages. It would be useless to attempt the briefest of catalogues of a varied literature covering 2,000 years. It must suffice to mention the two principal epochs in which it impinged in some measure on later European culture and took some part in shaping it.

These two epochs are those of the scholastic renaissance of the twelfth and thirteenth centuries, and the scientific renaissance of the seventeenth.

The scholastic renaissance, crowned by the great name of Thomas Aquinas, formed a lasting synthesis between religion and science, the two great forces struggling, then as now, for the possession of men's minds. The scientific renaissance, bursting through the scholastic synthesis, demanded a new world-view of its own. In each of these decisive intellectual efforts Jewish thought played a part. As in each instance the channel was largely that provided by the work of Moses Maimonides, a few sentences may be devoted to him.

Moses Maimonides (1138–1204) was the great medieval systematizer of Jewish thought in all its aspects. He expounded the vast collections of rabbinic teaching; he produced a 'digest' of his own; he sought for the whole a philosophical foundation. In this last task he faced squarely the problem of the conflict between religion and the science of his day, and it was through this that he achieved his importance in the two epochs we have distinguished. The synthesis he effected between the Bible and Aristotle blazed the trail for the Christian schoolmen, while the attitude he adopted to the Arab theologians of his own day led to results which profoundly affected Spinoza, and, through Spinoza, the intellectual pattern of the modern world. All this must be looked for in specialist treatises. The surprising thing to observe is how familiar Jewish thinkers seem to have been to the educated public of Europe from the thirteenth to the seventeenth centuries.

13. But here a distinction must be made. In a sense the most important contribution made by Jews in this period was not Jewish at all.

When Maimonides, to be followed by Aquinas, argued powerfully against the prevailing school of thinkers in his day and showed that the accepted arguments against the world's having had an absolute beginning were not logically necessary, he gave a lead to the cause of religion which could fairly be called Jewish. It was because of the 'perplexity' caused by the basic Jewish belief in creation when brought into contact with the Aristotelian doctrine of the eternity of the world that Maimonides was brought to consider the philosophical problem and to propound his solution. Here then is a 'Jewish' contribution in the full sense of the word. It is an attempt by a Jew, steeped in the literature and traditions of his people, to solve a vital intellectual problem, of urgent importance for the thought of the day, in the spirit of that tradition and with its help.

When, however, Jews, through their wide intellectual interests and broad knowledge of languages, took a prominent part in translating into Latin those works of Greek and Arab thinkers which helped to shape the mind of the Middle Ages, it is hard to say that their work was Jewish: it was work of the highest importance, done by Jews. It was a labour not of creation but of transmission; and the books transmitted were the classics of general thought, not only those of Jewish origin or interest. (A similar observation may be made on the participation of Jews in so many fields of endeavour in modern times—philanthropy, journalism, art, music, and the stage, as well as law, economics, medicine, psychology, sociology, and the new developments in mathematical physics. Their contributions are contributions made by Jews but neither in scope or intention are they Jewish contributions; though they may owe much of their inspiration and drive to the love of learning and the general admiration for things of the mind which has characterized the Jewish tradition of life throughout its long and troubled history.)

14. An intermediate and somewhat ambiguous position is occupied by the so-called kabbalah, i.e. Jewish mystical literature. The roots of this literature can be traced back to very early times (although its chief monument, the Zohar or Book of Splendour, was given to the world only in the thirteenth century), and it was treated by its early Christian adepts in the fifteenth century as representing the original Hebrew wisdom. It would seem, however, that its philosophical doctrine is a form of Gnostic and Neoplatonic speculation; and although of importance for the inner history of Judaism it has little original value of its own for the world.

Yet it has attracted many students and has had the most unexpected repercussions, from the religious doctrine of the Swedish and Russian theosophists to the aesthetic theories of the French romantics. It is certainly significant that recent writers on authors so diverse as Milton, Hugo, and Rimbaud are constrained to devote much attention to it. Its masterpiece, the Zohar, is in style exuberant, full of striking images and

extravagant (if not grotesque) similes. In subject-matter it is diverse
and at times confused. It contains many ideas, little system. Always pic-
turesque, it is often exhilarating and occasionally profound. To some it
has appeared a treasure house of divine inspiration, to others a monument of human credulity and self-deceit; it is probably best described as a
puzzling mixture of the two together. Yet it would be a mistake to judge
it from the point of view of pure philosophy. It represents rather a revul-
sion against philosophy, and its interest for a later age is in its turning of
the pentateuchal narrative (on which it is ostensibly a commentary) into
allegories of the inner life and in its insistence on moral intention in the
performance of religious ceremony; though here too it is in the full current of a whole line of thinkers of whom the archetype (and historically
the model for many of the early Church fathers) is the pre-Christian
Alexandrian Jew Philo.

15. We have spoken so far of thought as expressed in literature. But
thought is expressed in life as well; and one must ask what influence living
Jewry has exerted on mankind. 'There is a certain nation living here and
there in small groups among the people in all the divisions of your kingdom; their laws are different from those of any other nation . . .'. So says
Haman in the biblical book of Esther, giving classic expression to the
'dislike of the unlike' which is at the root of so many human ills. Yet
Haman's own attempt to destroy the Jews was unsuccessful; and whether
the narrative is history or not, it has always appeared to be typical. The
Passover festival celebrates annually the many redemptions from the
many Egypts in which the Jewish people escaped destruction. For the
'unlike', remaining unlike, survive as the eternal protestants, leavening
mankind through their very non-conformist existence.

Thus Jewry presents a problem to mankind, theoretical as well as practical. Is it, as (in a sense) is held traditionally by the Church or (in a different
sense) by a modern philosopher, the 'clue to history'? Does it persist in
order to bear witness, now as ever, to a new way of life for mankind?

The form of these questions is as old-fashioned as the old answers. In
an existentialist world 'missions' are out of date. Yet man has become an
urgent problem to himself; and what is true now of all men has been true
for many centuries of the Jew. The mere fact of his survival is disturbing.
He is a perpetual stimulus to the intelligence of mankind, as he is a
constant irritant to its conscience.

Surveys of Jewish history have shown different things to different observers. Some have seen in it the foundation of a true international

community, some an extreme example of the narrowest nationalism. Perhaps the answer is, in Jowett's well-known phrase, 'neither and both'; the disjunction may not be complete. But it will be agreed at least that no ordinary interpretative key will suffice to open this door. The Jew is a living witness to the bankruptcy of most theories of history, and not least of those called by the name of sociological.

V Epilogue

1. Jewish thought is dominated by the idea of God with its immediate and complementary derivatives of freedom and law. The first ancestor, Abraham, was remembered as having been brought out from the bondage of 'beyond the river' just as his descendants were brought out from the bondage of Egypt; and the highest vision of their future was that of a further release from the bondage of the external word through the writing of the law 'in their hearts'. But the freedom is freedom to live under law. Freedom is the basis of all community life; law—justice—is its framework and guarantee; and law, like freedom, is the more firmly established when written in the heart.

Bondage is of many kinds. It may be spiritual as well as material. The ultimate bondage is of the mind.

Mind is bound by being confined to any categories which are less than those of the whole. There are many such—stocks and stones, phrases, myths, wealth, political power. These all cramp and confine, and against them the Jewish mind has always waged war. Its God is jealous and will have none other gods besides himself. He is thus the supreme liberator.

The last and most brutalizing of all the idols created by man is the all-controlling and all-interfering state, and the last freedom comes to men from the recognition of their individual and immediate dependence on the God of the spirits of all flesh. Hence the supreme charter of independence: 'they shall not be slaves because they are *My* slaves'. As the Catholic Péguy wrote of the Jew Lazare: 'Jamais je n'ai vu un homme croire, savoir, à ce point, que les plus grandes puissances temporelles . . . ne sont que par des puissances spirituelles intérieures.'[3]

If there is such a thing as a 'Jewish mind', and if the Jewish mind as such has anything to contribute to mankind's common store, it may be said to consist in this sense of absolutes.

2. We have been tracing out ideas, but the paradox of ideas is that they

---

[3] [I have never seen a man believe, know so firmly, that the greatest temporal powers . . . exist only by spiritual powers within.]

are distinct from fact and yet fact has reality only through its participation in ideas. Few of the ideas we have been expounding are in accord with fact. Yet it might be held that the history of human culture is the history of the attempts to make them fact.

Today they seem farther from fact than ever. With the abominations of the last war—gas chambers, concentration camps, genocide—still vivid in our memory, it is hard to speak convincingly of the goodness of God and of his working in history. Before our very eyes history seems to have collapsed.

3. It is a tragic note on which to end but one true to fact. If ideas can help, it can only be through faith, a faith, however, which is not in contrast with 'works', certainly not divorced from works, but which sustains and invigorates works, the faith by which 'the righteous shall live'. The religious passion is for salvation, whether salvation of the individual alone or of the individual within a community; and salvation is a life to be lived, not a theory to be upheld or a belief to be adhered to.

Such faith does not depend on immediate returns or on any hope of reward or fear of punishment. It is rational but not a calculation of chances. It springs from moral integrity rather than scientific knowledge. It rests on the authority of conscience and it is a choosing, not a blind acquiescence in 'irresistible forces' and 'brute facts'. Its exemplar is the reply of the Jews of Babylon to Nebuchadnezzar the king when he asked what god there was who could rescue them from his hands:

We have no need to answer thee in this matter.

If it be that our God, whom we serve, is able to deliver us from the burning fiery furnace, and from thine hand, O king, he will deliver us.

But if not—be it known unto thee, O king, that we will not serve thy gods, nor worship the golden image which thou hast set up.

'But if not . . .'! One may continue the quotation from Péguy: 'Je n'ai jamais vu un homme croire, à ce point, avoir conscience, à ce point, qu'une conscience d'homme était un absolu, un invincible, un éternel, un libre, qu'elle s'opposait victorieuse, éternellement triomphante, à toutes les grandeurs de la terre.'[4]

'Thou wilt keep him in perfect peace whose mind is stayed on Thee: because he trusteth in Thee.'

---

[4] [I have never seen a man believe so firmly, be so firmly aware, that a human conscience was something absolute, invincible, eternal, free that it opposed victoriously, ever-lastingly triumphant, all the great powers of the earth.]

The Significance of Biblical Prophecy
for Our Time

❧

THE prophets did not talk to scholars. They talked to the ordinary man; and when the old synagogue tradition prescribed weekly readings from the Prophets like those from the Law, it arranged that, just like the lessons from the Law, they should be read both in the original and in a vernacular translation, that is, presumably, for the benefit of the ordinary man.

Of course that was a dangerous practice. Bible reading in the vernacular always was dangerous. It gave people 'ideas'. It sometimes made them disrespectful to the powers that be, and the powers that be did not like it. There is an episode in the history of the *haftarah* (as the weekly lesson from the Prophets read in the synagogue is called) which in this regard I find instructive. A noted rabbi is reported in the Mishnah to have laid it down that the sixteenth chapter of Ezekiel, beginning 'Cause Jerusalem to know her abominations', is not to be used as a prophetic lesson. As the commentators explain (I should have thought superfluously), it is not to the credit of Jerusalem. You see the tendency, and it is the same everywhere and at all times. We must not be told about our misdeeds. It is bad for what is called, somewhat curiously, 'morale'.

I am glad to be able to say that in this particular instance the synagogue did not make that mistake. To its credit, the objection, although from a very famous rabbi, was overruled. The official decision is that the chapter in question may be used as a public lesson, and should be translated and read publicly in the vernacular.

This encourages me in my layman's view that the importance of the prophets, both for their generation and for us, is not that they speak 'comfortable words' (though they do that too at times), but that they dared to say things which are very uncomfortable indeed but which happen to be true. Their interest was not in morale (so-called) but in something very different: morals.

First given as an address to the London Society of Jews and Christians, January 1955, and published as Rabbi Mattuck Memorial Pamphlet 1 (London: LSJC, 1955). Reprinted by permission of the Executive of the London Society of Jews and Christians.

The common conception of a biblical prophet is that of a dancing dervish with a loud voice and an execrable temper; or, alternatively, of a smug preacher ready to call down fire from heaven on anybody who disagrees with him. In sum: a vengeful and self-righteous megalomaniac with an intolerable gift of the gab.

I submit that this picture is false. The typical biblical prophet is the lawgiver, Moses himself, who shows his people the 'paths of life'; and the one quality specifically attributed to Moses by Scripture is the quality of humility. He is the 'man of God', that is, he recognizes God as man's 'dwelling-place'. Pre-eminently he is the teacher, but what he teaches he has himself been taught from on high.

With this in mind, one's first thought in pondering the present significance of biblical prophecy is a simple one. It can be crystallized in a short phrase, the phrase 'spiritual authority'.

Spiritual authority is the opposite of temporal power. The prophet Nathan represented spiritual authority against the temporal power of King David; the prophet Elijah represented spiritual authority against the temporal power of King Ahab; the prophet Amos represented spiritual authority against the temporal power of Amaziah the priest of Bethel. The last instance is important because temporal power is not only the direct power of kings. It is all power (in our day, the power of big business, the power of the press, the power of the trade union, the power of the Church) as well as the power of kings. Wherever and whenever there is organization on a large scale—a corporation, a monopoly, a government—there conscience takes second place and right is endangered.

Biblical prophecy is the resurgence of conscience. It is the affirmation that conscience comes first. 'Thou art the man.' 'Hast thou killed, and also taken possession?' 'Hear ye this, O ye that would swallow up the needy, and cause the poor of the land to fail, saying, When will the new moon be gone that we may sell corn? and the Sabbath, that we may set forth wheat? making the ephah small, and the shekel great, and dealing falsely with balances of deceit; that we may buy the poor for silver and the needy for a pair of shoes, and sell the refuse of the wheat . . . Shall not the land tremble for this?' And, in the prophetic view, it was for this that the land did tremble. Temporal power was struck down for moral sin; and moral sin means cruelty, ill-treatment of the weak, the oppression of the stranger within the gate. When the land was laid waste and its people deported, the prophets saw it as a judgment.

Spiritual authority—temporal power. They still exist, and the opposition between them exists still. Indeed, to judge by our own experience, the opposition between them is fiercer now than ever before. But in our day a new element has been added. With progress, matters have become more complicated. The modern, the all too modern, world has elaborated something new which cuts across the old distinction. There is no longer the bare cleavage between spiritual authority on the one hand and temporal power on the other. We have now in addition a hybrid factor, the factor of spiritual power.

By spiritual power I do not mean what is sometimes meant by the phrase. I am not referring to what is really only the temporal power of so-called spiritual forces—the organized priesthood, the churches and synagogues, the vested interests of episcopacies and rabbinates with their binding and loosing and stoning. Power of that sort is not spiritual. It is only a variant of the treatment of Amos the prophet by Amaziah the priest of Bethel: 'O thou seer, go flee thee away into the land of Judah, and eat bread there and prophesy there.' By the phrase spiritual power I mean, literally, power over the spirit, the 'conditioning' of the spirit, the propaganda, the misuse of love of country and the miscall of patriotism, the devilish misapplication of scientific knowledge and techniques in order to make 'new' men. And do not mistake. It is happening every day and all day and all the world over, not only in time of war and on the 'other side'. It is happening on 'this' side too; and the less it is noticed the more it is happening. Some writers have drawn our attention to it forcefully: the late George Orwell, for example, in his *Animal Farm* and particularly in his *Nineteen Eighty-four* which, in its televized form, has just created such a stir. My only quarrel with that book is its title. It should not have been called *Nineteen Eighty-four*, as if it were the expression of a fear for the future. It should have been called *1954 and 1964 and 1974*. It is a sharpened portrait of our own times. The enemy today, as Orwell saw, is the power (not the authority) of the legend, the power (not the authority) of the lie.

A cursory glance at the biblical prophets will show that they are constantly exhorting us to truth: to know truth, to speak truth, to seek truth, to worship the God of truth. They have the reputation of being narrowly moralistic, but their emphasis on truth suggests they realized that morality falters when it is not steadied by truth. As we might say today: intellectual integrity is a principal element in moral character.

And so to me, the most remarkable point, and the most illuminating point, in the biblical account of prophecy, is the recognition of the existence—the real, the factual, and the terrifying existence—of *false* prophecy and *false* prophets.

The false prophets of the Bible are described as 'hunters of souls'. They 'slay the souls that should not die' and they 'save the souls alive that should not live', and they do this by 'lying to my people that hearken unto lies'. They 'prophesy out of their own heart'; they 'follow their own spirit, but they have seen nothing'. They 'seduce my people, saying Peace; and there is no peace'.

The methods of the old false prophet were the same as those of the new: the manipulation of fact, the histrionic use of language, the endless self-praise, the merciless repetitions: 'The Temple of the Lord, the Temple of the Lord, the Temple of the Lord are these.' Modern science has only refined these old weapons. It conditions and reconditions men to buy goods they do not need and to worship leaders who enslave them.

There was a novel published recently in which the methods of this 're-creating' of personality were described. In this particular case the process failed at the last moment and the man had to be, in the delicious modern idiom, liquidated. But we are all, more or less, becoming 'new men', and science knows no halt in its triumphant onward march. Applied psychology is rapidly perfecting itself. Soon a turn of a knob in a central office will give us not only new opinions but a new mind and a new heart and soul.

You will recall that these phrases—a new heart, a new spirit—are biblical. The call to a new man is the call of the prophets; but their new man is a return to a genuine man, not a plastic toy of the propaganda machine to be manipulated and conditioned at will. The biblical version, even in the mouth of the weary positivist Ecclesiastes, is that 'God made man upright'. It sees man as the son of God, as created in the likeness of God, as the child of God, as the first-born of God, as the witness of God, as little lower than the angels; and however far he may degenerate, he is stamped with the stamp of his origin. 'Ye shall be holy, for I the Lord your God am holy.' 'These are the things that ye shall do; speak ye every man the truth with his neighbour; execute the judgment of truth and peace in your gates: and let none of you imagine evil in your hearts against his neighbour; and love no false oath.' 'Wash you, make you clean; put away the evil of your doings from before mine eyes; cease to do evil; learn to do well; seek judgment, relieve the oppressed, judge the fatherless, plead for the widow.'

I should be hard put to it to define the nature of authority. It is almost as hard to define authority as it is easy to define power. But I think we should all agree that in these and similar utterances of biblical prophets the voice of authority is heard clearly. 'It is not in heaven, that thou shouldest say, Who shall go up for us to heaven, and bring it unto us, and make us to hear it, that we may do it? Neither is it beyond the sea, that thou shouldest say, Who shall go over the sea for us, and bring it unto us, and make us to hear it, that we may do it? But the word is very nigh unto thee, in thy mouth, and in thy heart, that thou mayest do it.'

Bishop Butler, speaking on conscience in a famous sermon, said: 'If it had power as it has authority, it would rule the world.' We have here again the same contrast, the contrast between power and authority.

The reconciliation between power and authority; between force and persuasion—'if only kings were philosophers, or philosophers kings'—is the persistent problem of mankind. In the biblical prophets the promise of reconciliation appears under the image of the Messianic Age, 'In that Day'; the day when the weak shall feel himself strong and nations shall cease to learn war: 'Not by might'—the RV margin reads strikingly, 'not by an army—and not by power but by my spirit.'

A utopia? A mirage? I do not know. But we can at least keep the vision alive, and the vision is that of biblical prophecy. It may well be that it is only by keeping that vision alive that we shall be able to keep ourselves alive.

There is one last point I should like to make. It is not really a fresh point. In principle I have made it already; indeed, I set out from it. But the application is fresh; and I hope I shall not be offending anybody if I make it. In a sense *de me fabula*. The reference is to myself and my own.

Till now I have spoken of this matter as a citizen of the world to citizens of the world. The biblical prophets have their tale to tell. When the prophet wishes to lay down our duty in this life, he says: 'God hath told thee, O *man*, what is good.' He does not say: O Englishman, O Frenchman, even O Jew; but O *man*.

But the prophets had quite a lot to say to us Jews too. They promised us many comfortable things. We do well to remember those promises. But we must remember, too, the condition under which the promises were given. The promises are always limited by an 'if': 'And it shall come to pass *if* ye hearken.'

I sometimes think that we forget that 'if'. We claim the promises. We are very quick to claim the promises. But we forget the condition. We forget that the promises must be earned.

But that *is* the condition, the *sine qua non*. If we 'do *not* hearken', then we have no right to claim the fulfilment of the promises, far less to proclaim to the world that in us of this generation the promises are fulfilled.

So I think the biblical prophets have a special lesson for us Jews over and above the general lesson they have for mankind as such. We seem to have followed the false prophets, always claiming, not always deserving. We seem always to be singing the old refrain: 'The Temple of the Lord, the Temple of the Lord, the Temple of the Lord' are we. *Are we?* Like the patriotic rabbi of the Mishnah, we ban any recital of the abominations of Jerusalem. *Should* we?

We shall have to choose pretty soon. We cannot halt for ever between the two opinions. If it is to be Baal, at least let us have the honesty to say so. But let us rather follow the spirit of the old ruling that that chapter in Ezekiel should both be read in public and translated into the vernacular for the instruction of us plain men.

No doubt the politicians and diplomats will disagree. But politicians, and even diplomats, are sometimes wrong; and that, I believe—that politicians and diplomats are sometimes wrong—is one of the great, and one of the abiding, lessons which the biblical prophets have to teach us all, Jew and non-Jew alike.

Some Reflections on the Interpretation of Scripture

✿

I HAVE first to offer an apology for an unintentional plagiarism in my title. 'The Interpretation of Scripture', as you all know and as I remembered too late, is the name of the contribution to the famous volume of essays and reviews made nearly a hundred years ago by Benjamin Jowett. Jowett was then Regius Professor of Greek at Oxford, but 'owing to his having incurred suspicions of heresy by the liberality of his religious opinions, he was deprived for ten years'—I am quoting the *Dictionary of National Biography*—'of the emoluments of his office'.

Some years later, in 1870, Jowett became Master of Balliol, the college to which in 1879 Claude Montefiore was admitted as an undergraduate; and there is thus some connection, howbeit a distant and tenuous one, between at least the title of my address and the distinguished scholar and religious leader in whose honour it is being delivered.

Having established the connection, however, I shall not dwell on it, since—if I may quote the *DNB* again—'Jowett's essay on the Interpretation of Scripture only served to increase the suspicion of heresy entertained against him.' I can only pray that you will be kinder, or I luckier.

I

In this lecture I propose inviting your attention to a matter which, in one form or another, is always cropping up. It is an old-fashioned problem and does not bother everyone; but it is at the bottom of most disputes on scriptural subjects and indeed on many other subjects too. Someone expresses an opinion and backs it up with a biblical quotation. His friend produces another opinion and another quotation. What are we to do about it? An opinion is an opinion and a quotation is a quotation. Are there any grounds for choosing between them?

Some Reflections on the Interpretation of Scripture, Claude Montefiore Lecture 1955 (London: Liberal Jewish Synagogue, 1956). Reprinted by permission of the Executive of the London Society of Jews and Christians.

As a fact we do choose between them. We follow the one and reject the other. But when it comes to justifying our choice we are almost always at a loss. We cultivate a blind eye. We look the difficulty firmly in the face, and pass on.

But the difficulty remains, and it is not a theoretical one only. We all know, and we have it too on high authority, that 'the devil can cite Scripture for his purpose'; but when we meet such a one—'an evil soul producing holy witness'—how can we hope to set about refuting him? For example, when he brandishes his bow and arrow, or whatever lethal weapon is in fashion at the time, and cries: 'Blot out the remembrance of Amalek!', is there anything we can say to dissuade him?

In this particular case I suppose there is. We can say: the verse is not applicable. Amalek is a historical figure and belongs to the past, and the past has gone. An illuminating instance of this method is provided by a curious talmudic story. An Ammonite, we are told, came and asked to be accepted as a proselyte to Judaism. One authority said No, and quoted the Bible: 'An Ammonite shall not come into the congregation of the Lord.' Said another: 'On the contrary, admit him. Since Nebuchadnezzar [with his policy of transfer of populations] mixed the peoples together, it is impossible to be sure which people is which!'

According to the Talmud it was this second view which prevailed. The Ammonite *did* 'come into the congregation of the Lord'. You will note the grounds. The verse as a verse remained but it was held not to apply.

It is this type of process which I should like to discuss with you this evening. It is not exegesis, the scholarly exposition of the words. There is no attempt to modify, or to change, the accepted meaning of 'an Ammonite' or 'not coming into the congregation of the Lord'. The *exegesis* of the verse remains as it was. It is its application, its use, the sense in which it is to be understood in practice, its *interpretation*, which is called in question.

II

I am venturing, I know, on dangerous ground. Use becomes notoriously ab-use, and the philologist raises his voice. 'Ask *me*', he says, 'and I'll settle the issue; and I'll settle it because I have the facts: I know the words.' Yet, for all its knowledge of the words, philology gives us, and can give us, no final answers; and I should like for a moment to enlarge on this most important, but much neglected, point.

For words, as all agree, have different meanings; and there are meanings which, in a specific context, do not fit. And so the philologist, out of the many meanings which present themselves, has to choose the one he thinks *will* fit. Indeed, at times, as we all know, he has to hie very far afield in order to find any meaning to fit. As one turns over biblical commentaries of all ages one sees, for example, Arabic roots of kindred shape brought in to clear up the obscurities of the Hebrew; and the layman accepts the new rendering with reverent thanks until he finds that, according to other philologists, the Arabic yields yet other roots and other renderings. My point is not the flexibility of philological erudition but its essential subordination to meaning. It would appear that, in the ordinary process of the philological investigation of texts, it is the meaning of the whole which has to be determined first. Then the philologist—*c'est son métier*—will produce the linguistic girder which is deemed adequate to support it.

The most striking case in which we can see this process at work is in the attempted deciphering of inscriptions in unknown alphabets. Guesses, assumptions, hypotheses always come first, and these are all not facts but meanings. We can do nothing unless we assume that the language expressed in the unknown signs is of such and such a type, and that the signs themselves express this, that, or the other type of object—names; numbers; objects for sale; military triumphs or commercial ventures; plaques of honour; temple inventories. The hypothetical meanings are then allowed, as it were, to grope for the words like a skeleton key groping for the wards of a lock. Often one reads, in an interim report of progress, that they have been sustained only in part, and, as for the rest, disappointed: 'It would seem to be a variety of early Greek', one is often told, for example, 'but in that case one would expect . . .'; and then possibly what one would expect has not appeared, and a new approach must be excogitated and tested.

III

My object in these remarks is not to depreciate the work of the philologist (it is indispensable) but to suggest that it has its limits. The word, even with the help of the best of lexicons, is never a fact. It is never self-explanatory. Interpretation is always necessary. Indeed, the better the lexicon and the more varied the philological possibilities put at our disposal, the more need becomes manifest for interpretation. We have all been at times amused by the so-called 'schoolboy howlers' arising from the over-impetuous use of Latin or French dictionaries. The lexicon can be too generous; and if the philologist—rightly—protests 'But one must attend to context and meanings', he confirms my point.

As indeed he does in another field too, when he—again quite rightly —offers us emendations. 'In its present state', he seems to say, 'I cannot understand this verse, and I have tried all the variants of meanings for the words of the verse and still cannot make sense of it. I suggest therefore that in this, that or the other of its words we should read *x* instead of *y*. We shall then have sense.' On which one can only observe again that he starts with the sense and then finds the words to fit it.

This procedure is perfectly right and proper. It is the natural thing to do and follows the natural facts of language. We only find it paradoxical because of the contemporary, and I hope passing, illusion that the arts can progress only by aping the sciences. The sciences aver (whether with justice or not is irrelevant here) that they deal with fact and fact only. For the philologist the fact is apparently the word. He therefore proclaims his duty to concentrate his energies on words, although he knows all the time that what he has really to deal with is not words but meanings. And meanings are expressed not in single words but in collections of words; and not only in collections of words but in question marks, and exclamations, and inflections of voice and gesture. May I remind you of Thomas Hardy's remark about the language of Casterbridge: 'The yeomen, farmers, dairymen, and townsfolk, who came to transact business in these ancient streets, spoke in other ways than by articulation . . . The face, the arms, the hat, the stick, the body throughout spoke equally with the tongue.'[1]

A distinguished philologist[2] has suggested recently an explanation of a well-known difficulty in Ezekiel on the assumption of the existence of an aposiopesis, that is, the omission of words in order to suggest the un-mentionable—the kind of thing expressed in modern languages by a succession of dots. The explanation is certainly plausible but it implies that in any given context the important thing may be not the words *put in* but the words *left out*. A true, and indeed important, consideration, but incompatible with the exclusive and unique preoccupation with the single words as such.

IV

The conception I wish to bring before you this evening is that interpretation is a question of meaning; and meaning, which is *not the product*

---

[1] *The Mayor of Casterbridge*, ch. 9.
[2] G. R. Driver on Ezek. 23: 43, in *Biblica* (1954), 155.

but the controller of words, has canons of its own. I have mentioned one already. It is the canon of context. Context is the whole of which the word, the sentence, the passage, is a part; and meaning has to do with context.

One difficulty with contexts is the determination of their extent. The context is a total occasion; but the total occasion might be held to be the isolated specific occasion, or the specific occasion within its own total history, or the total history of that occasion within the totality of history as such; or rather, since history is not a mere collection of facts but an interpretation of facts, the context might be held to be the general interpretation of the totality of facts as arising from a study of the whole literature. This last is in effect the way which is used by most of us and which causes all the trouble. 'The general tendency of the Scriptures', we each say, 'is such and such; and in the light of this tendency I propose to understand this, that or the other detail.' 'Understand?' cries our opponent; '*Mis*understand, you should say. Your interpretation is a *mis*interpretation. You must come back to the plain sense, however un-palatable. Look at the facts, the words!' But I retort: 'What words? *x* and *y* stand in your way? I shall consult my lexicons; or if you don't like analogies from the Arabic or the Mandaic or the Assyrian or the Ugaritic, I shall offer you an emendation. The *words*? They can always be dealt with!'

Let us take the case of 'blotting out the remembrance of Amalek'. Many of us find the injunction distasteful (I shall revert later to the nature of the distaste and its scriptural justification). What are we to do about it? I have suggested already that we might push it back to its historical occasion. We might say: there was indeed, once upon a time, a tribe of that name, but it has long disappeared; the injunction therefore is no longer applicable. Or we can say: let us widen the scriptural context and take into account the parallel passage in Exodus 17. There, there is no in-junction that *we* should blot out the remembrance of Amalek, only the affirmation that *God* will. We can then point out to our valorous friend who is so anxious to do the blotting out himself that, if vengeance is God's, it is not for or from man.[3] If he remains obdurate, we can call on our philologist and ask him to translate the key word not 'remembrance; but 'remembering', and blandly alter our version from 'Blot out the memory of Amalek' to 'Blot out the *remembering* of Amalek!' We can

---

[3] That is how I understand Sifrei on the passage in Deuteronomy and see no reason for Friedmann's note. [Meir Friedmann's edition of the Sifrei was published in Vienna in 1864.]

then assure our friend that the behest of Scripture is not to remember Amalek any more.

I thought I caught a gasp at that rendering, and it is indeed a little surprising. I certainly gasped when I saw it cited in one of my brother's books, and I share his regret that he was not able to trace its source. As a version I consider it an effort of genius. Its author thought in context; but the context he chose was the context not of tribal wars and border fighting—there is plenty of that everywhere to regret and forget about; it was not for that that the Law was given on Sinai[4]—but the wider context of the Law and the Prophets and the Writings in their moral directiveness. And in *that* context, the blotting out of the remembrance of Amalek must be—somehow—adjusted. We have to choose; and it is better, we may well think (nay, *must* think), to give a shock to our dictionaries than to our moral sense.

V

I shall be asked: 'Does it then amount only to this: take what you like, as you like, when you like?' I answer emphatically, No. For we are not taking what we like. We are taking what we must. We are following scriptural directive. We are interpreting, but not imaginatively or from the air. We are interpreting the words of Scripture through the meanings of Scripture. Our moral sense has been largely framed by Scripture. When therefore we interpret Scripture according to the requirement of what we know as morality, we are interpreting Scripture by Scripture. I shall revert to this point in a moment in connection with a famous historical controversy on these matters. I content myself now with the remark that it is because of this fact that the Scriptures are so precious. They are one whole in that they point to one standard. If they were devoid of this unity they would be like the Loeb classics, a miscellaneous collection of material on different subjects assembled together by the accident of composition in (approximately) one language; and their interest would depend on the professional interest of the reader—an architect would turn to 1 Kings 7 or (to taste) Vitruvius, a staff officer to Joshua 6 or to the Aeneas who wrote (I gather) on tactics. But these are professional matters and of interest to professional men. There is an interest common to all humanity, and that is the interest in man not *qua* architect or staff officer but *qua* man; and the interest in man as man is a *moral* interest, an interest in the ends by which he lives or—it may be the same thing—by which he thinks

[4] See Sifrei on the words 'whom thou hast redeemed' (Deut. 21: 8).

he lives, or hopes to live, or, most important, recognizes with regret that he does not live. And that is why the Scriptures are rightly conceived not as a collection or a library but as one book. It has a unity of subject and a unity of tendency as well as a self-affirmed unity of source. It contains both promise and disappointment, both aspiration and degradation. It has hope, illimitable hope; and with it condemnation, although not utter condemnation. It has created our idea of man as he might and should be by condemning the fact of man as he is; for the 'might be' of the Bible is also a fact, living in our minds and creating, or evoking, conscience. There are many horror stories in the Bible, but they are pointed out to us, and condemned, as such. Some of us find the story of Genesis 34 ghastly, but so does the official summing-up (Genesis 49): 'Simeon and Levi are brethren; weapons of violence are their swords. O my soul, come not thou into their council; unto their assembly, my glory, be not thou united; for in their anger they slew men, and in their self-will they houghed oxen. Cursed be their anger, for it was fierce; and their wrath, for it was cruel.'

VI

May I leave these considerations for a moment and draw your attention to an incident in the history of biblical criticism which is at the same time a turning-point in the history of literary criticism in general. I refer to the polemical chapters in Spinoza's *Tractatus Theologico-politicus* in which he indignantly rejects the principle of biblical interpretation adopted by Maimonides.

If you open the *Guide for the Perplexed* of Maimonides, you will find that its first chapters comprise a kind of biblical dictionary; and as you proceed further you will observe that the argument of the book as a whole largely turns around the possibilities of interpreting Scripture which are suggested in this dictionary. Detail apart, the principle is simple. There is only one truth, and that truth is by its nature everywhere the same. The words of Scripture are to be understood therefore in such a way as not to conflict with it. And this is always possible, although sometimes difficult. For words have many meanings, and it is the interpreter's task to find the meaning which fits. As Maimonides remarks in a phrase which became famous: 'The gates of interpretation are never closed.'

You will observe that what Maimonides is doing—and before Maimonides we have in the Jewish tradition the systematic expositions of Philo of Alexandria as well as the whole aggadic literature—what they are all doing is only an extension of what we have noted already, a treatment of words in terms of context; only for Maimonides—and there's the rub —the context is taken to include the general truths of physics and metaphysics. Hence Scripture is judged by what we now consider to be *extraneous* considerations; and since 'the gates of interpretation are never closed', we are sometimes faced with unexpected situations. It is against this that Spinoza rebels so violently and lays down the contrary canon of *internal* interpretation: Scripture can be interpreted only by Scripture.

Spinoza indeed goes even further. He insists on an even more restrictive canon. He seems indeed to be saying about the Scriptures, in his quaint pietistic way, what the modern 'intensive' critic says of literary criticism in general: 'Away with your presuppositions. Fix your eyes on the narrow context. Take this or that passage and see what it implies or involves; and then, in the light of what you find in this way and in this restricted compass, proceed to a judgement of the whole. Do not start with a judgement of the whole and in its light and with its aid interpret, or interpret away, the detail.'

In this issue modern sympathy is on the side of Spinoza; and if we feel any gratitude at all to Maimonides, it is rather for the stimulus he gave to the opposition than for his own ideas. We now recognize, having grown used to the thought, that the Bible was not meant as a text-book of physics or metaphysics. And so we accept Spinoza's thesis that literature is to be treated as literature, science as science; and we frown on Maimonides' allegorizations. 'Fancy seeing propositions of physics in the narrative of Genesis', we say disdainfully; 'It is surely as foolish as Philo's reading of the lives of the patriarchs as a description of the spirit of man in the search for salvation. Abraham is Abraham and not the individual soul of man, and Jacob is a human, all too human, being.'

For myself I like the simplicities. I prefer the plain scriptural tale of Jacob, and Joseph and his brethren, to the involved verbosities of a recently deceased European novelist.[5] I even like my twenty-second chapter of Genesis plain, without the bubble and squeak of Benjamin Britten. But this is a personal peculiarity. We are dealing here with a point of principle. Interpretation is one of the ways in which the monuments of past inspiration are brought afresh to each age as it comes. In one form or another it is both indispensable and inevitable. It is possible that Maimonides went too far. Spinoza did not go far enough. It is indeed wrong to import physics into the Bible. The Bible's concern is not with physics. But it is not wrong to import morals into the Bible, because we are not

---

[5] [The reference is to Thomas Mann, *Joseph und seine Brüder*.]

importing them into it at all. They are already there. We are only bringing back what we have taken out. We are introducing nothing external or alien or strange, because it is just this which is the differentia, the distinguishing and characteristic mark, of Scripture. It is, as it were, *spécialité de la maison*!

VII

It is for this reason that we are justified in treating Scripture as one whole, that is, not book by book or section by section, or sentence by sentence, or, least of all, word by word. As I have said already, it is false to imagine that the interpretation of *any*thing can remain within the ambit of words. There *are* no words in the sense of atomic facts, bricks solitary and self-explanatory out of which the world of meaning arises. In the beginning was the meaning, and the meaning took on the temporary vestment of words, to manipulate and adapt the words to itself rather than itself to the words; and if this is true of individual words and localized meanings, how much more so is it true of the great meanings of literature where words only limn out thoughts struggling for expression, thoughts which only in the widest contexts and the widest frames of reference become, howbeit fragmentarily, comprehensible. The rabbis, who had a shrewd eye for the things that matter, were wont to say that the voice of God, which according to the psalmist is 'powerful' (Hebrew, 'in strength'), is heard by each in accordance with the 'strength' of his understanding; yet it is one voice. They tell us that the Torah was given in seventy languages, or again, that it was given not to angels but to men and in the language of men; yet it is one Torah. They point out that the vision of Isaiah and the vision of Ezekiel were of one and the same King; but Isaiah, they say, being himself of the seed of kings and used to regal splendour, said simply that he saw the King on his throne, whereas Ezekiel, a country bumpkin, wrote down everything he could, reporting the sights for the folks at home. Throughout we have the suggestion that there is one light, however much it is broken up by the prisms of our understanding. Can we plain readers of Scripture see anything of that light? I think we can; and that because—and here is my central point—Scripture itself indicates the way.

I offer two instances.

1. The 'first Word' from Sinai reads: 'I am the Lord thy God which brought thee out of the land of Egypt, out of the house of bondage.'

This is sometimes understood as a metaphysical affirmation of the existence of God. But prima facie it is not metaphysics but history. Further consideration suggests that, just as it is not metaphysics, so it is not history either. It is not a mere record of fact. It is an exhortation. To use a comprehensive word, it is morals; and I submit to you that this is the *Scripture's own* interpretation of it, an interpretation which emerges clearly from its own words elsewhere.

I quote first from the Law of Holiness in Leviticus: 'Ye shall do no unrighteousness in judgment, in meteyard, in weight, or in measure. Just balances, just weights, a just ephah and a just hin, shall ye have: I am the Lord your God, which brought you out of the land of Egypt.' Evidently, *because* 'I am the Lord your God which brought you out of the land of Egypt', *therefore* you shall have just balances. 'An accidental collocation!' you may say. But is it? Let us hear the Deuteronomist: 'Thou shalt not wrest the judgment of the stranger, nor of the fatherless; nor take the widow's raiment to pledge: but thou shalt remember that thou wast a bondman in Egypt, and the Lord thy God redeemed thee hence; *therefore* (a whole and emphatic phrase in the Hebrew) I command thee to do this thing.' Or we may hear the Exodist: 'And a stranger shalt thou not wrong, neither shalt thou oppress him; for ye were strangers in the land of Egypt.' In this the Exodist is in complete accord with the Leviticist: 'And if a stranger sojourn with thee in your land, ye shall not do him wrong. The stranger that sojourneth with you shall be unto you as the home-born among you, and thou shalt love him as thyself; for ye were strangers in the land of Egypt: I am the Lord your God.' One could go on quoting passages of the same type and to the same effect; there are at least a dozen more of them ready to hand. The 'first word' has thus a specific interpretation, a moral interpretation, which is given by and in Scripture itself.

A critic may rejoin that all these various passages are to be attributed to various authors and various epochs of time. But that of course strengthens my point. Not one author alone but a multitude of authors, going through all the letters of the alphabet, maybe, and (in an extended polychrome edition) all the colours and sub-colours of the rainbow—all of them seem to have understood, and to have used, the first Word in the same determinate and striking way; thereby offering a pointer, I venture to suggest, to us who come after, of the *scriptural interpretation of Scripture*.

2. My second example is the scriptural treatment of King David.

As is well known, the Book of Kings records that the building of the Temple was planned by David but carried out only by his son Solomon; and the Book of Chronicles, which would seem to be a kind of Revised

Version of the Book of Kings, gives the reason why: David was a man of blood. That David *was* a man of blood appears from the plain narrative of the early record: 'And he smote Moab, and measured them with the line, making them to lie down on the ground; and he measured two lines to put to death and one full line to keep alive.' What does not appear in the early record is the *condemnation* of such blood-spilling. Possibly it was not approved of; but nobody says so.

The later record *says* so. It does not attempt to blink the issue. It does not even skirt round the facts as (according to the narrative of Kings) his son Solomon did in his message to the king of Tyre. In that message the reason that prevented David from building is given as that of 'busy-ness': he was occupied with other things, and the fact that these other things were war and blood-letting is mentioned only by the way. David in fact (according to the Book of Kings) just had no time to spare! Contrast this with David's statement to Solomon in Chronicles: 'As for me, it was in my heart to build an house unto the name of the Lord my God. But the word of the Lord came to me, saying, Thou hast shed blood abundantly, and hast made great wars: thou shalt not build an house unto my name, because thou hast shed much blood upon the earth in my sight.' Here we have a moral condemnation, one put indeed into the mouth of the sinner himself; a moral condemnation, we may remind ourselves, of a man who, by the time of Chronicles, represented to the people the very type of ideal of kingship and indeed of humanity. The later narrative in fact is bold enough, honest enough, moral enough, to express disapproval of that sort of national hero.

In this connection, I remind you of the superscription to Psalm 51: 'A Psalm of David: when Nathan the prophet came unto him, after he had gone in to Bathsheba.' The commentators discuss learnedly whether the psalm could have been written by David, and if not, by whom and when. But surely the essential fact which is worthy of all attention is the fact that it was ascribed to David at all. It is as if the tradition was concerned to proclaim the necessity of a fresh type, a new ideal, altogether. 'Men of blood and deceit', as other psalms ascribed to the same David (Pss. 5; 55) say, 'are abhorred by God', 'they shall not live out half their days'. 'But I', this last verse concludes—and surely the author of the superscription 'Maschil of David' must have borne in mind that David of the record was just such a one who dealt in deceit and the spilling of blood—'But I will trust in thee.'

In this case I may be held to be over-stressing a mere two words in a casual title which may be no more than a musical instruction. Possibly.

But I cannot think so in the case of Psalm 51. The superscription is so definite, so precise, and so unexpected, that it is difficult to avoid the impression that it was deliberate. It seems to say: '*This* is the David we would have you remember, and *this* is the memorial of his name.' We have here in fact a corrective interpretation of the whole figure of God's chosen king, much as in Amos and Ezekiel we have a corrective interpretation of the whole history of God's chosen people. Scripture itself goes out of its way—or perhaps, goes *into* its own unique and extraordinary way—to point out how, for our instruction and action, it wants the facts interpreted and understood. It seems to say: 'David measured out the Moabites? Forget it. David slew his ten thousands? Forget it. The devious dealings at Nob and Ziklag? Forget them. The last charge to his son and successor? Forget it. Men of blood and deceit shall not halve their days! No, the *real* David—not the *historically* real: who cares for historical history ('and A lived X years and begat B; and A lived after he begat B, Y years, and begat sons and daughters; and B lived Z years and begat C...')?—No, the real King David, that is, the morally real King David, or rather, since the king melts into the man, the morally real person whom we should hold before our eyes for reliving in our own brief span—the 'man who was raised on high, the anointed of the God of Jacob, the sweet psalmist of Israel'—and in this description too we have surely a 'new song'; a transvaluation, if not a deliberate repudiation, of the man of deceit and blood—the real David has other things to say: 'But I will trust in thee.' 'Though I walk through the valley of the shadow of death, I will fear no evil.' 'He guideth me in the paths of righteousness for his name's sake.' And then the prayer: 'Deliver me from blood-guiltiness, O God.'

'I will fear no evil'; 'Deliver me from blood-guiltiness': the Davidic occasions are recognizably here. But they have been transformed. The chronicle has been given significance. The record has become a mere substrate on which moral form has been impressed. The 'man of blood and deceit' has been transmuted into the 'man after God's own heart'. He fears no evil, not because of the help of his 'mighty men' or of his own 'fingers taught to fight', but because 'Thou art with me'. It is God now who guides him, and his 'paths' are not of stratagem and deceit and diplomacy, but 'of righteousness'; and the guidance is given, and received, not for temporal power or for dynasty-breeding, but for 'his name's sake'. I shall not trouble you with parallels on these themes, which would comprise readings from the whole compass of Law and Prophets and Writings. Their importance is that they constitute a revolutionary appraisal of human ambition. They offer a new and totally different scale of values for the life of man.

VIII

We can now see what interpretation ultimately is and wherein its significance lies. It is—ultimately—the determining of an ideal of life, the establishing of preference among possible ends. It is the ordering of types of action in an ascending and descending scale of better and worse, an ordering which shapes the kind of life we choose to live.

In the case just before us, the life of blood and deceit and the life of pure hands and a clean heart, Scripture leaves no doubt which is the right preference; and it seems to be urging us, not only by precept but by offering individual examples, to abhor the one and to choose the other. In other cases its verdict is not explicit, and we have to judge for ourselves in the light of the moral sense awakened in us by those cases in which Scripture leaves no doubt. For there is choice, and we are bidden in general to choose life. Interpretation thus becomes the gateway to life, and in this wide sense is synonymous with education. We have travelled a long way from the niceties of philology, but our path has been implicit from the outset. For (to repeat) *meaning comes first*; and it is the choice of meaning which guides our understanding of the word.

IX

I notice that it is this year just a quarter of a century since the scholar in whose memory this Lectureship was instituted was awarded by the British Academy, in recognition of his many contributions to biblical learning, its Medal for Biblical Studies, a medal itself instituted to commemorate one of the most exact and stimulating scholars of our age, the late F. C. Burkitt. I tremble to ask whether what I have been saying would have met with the approval of these great biblical exegetes. Yet, as Maimonides said, 'the gates of interpretation are never closed'; and I brazenly take up my text and quote (from a letter of Mr Montefiore to Miss Lucy Cohen of January 1893):

When you say that you read the Bible 'looking for the parts whose sentiment or poetry you admire', this is, after all, in the last resort the most profitable way for the lay individual [There speaks the scholar, putting us in our place; but at least he *does* give us *some* place] to read it. Even if you do put some of yourself and the

19th century into it, where is the harm? If we can still (and I think we can still) use the Bible as a spiritual lever, it is a very good use to which to put it.

'A spiritual lever'—that, I think, is just right. It may not be the *best* use (Mr Montefiore seems to be saying) to put the Bible to. The 'best' use would presumably be—but I refrain from poaching on the preserve of scholars. But even if it is not the best one, we have now authority to say that it is a 'very good one'; and in accepting the concession with gratitude, I should only ask permission to add the small gloss that the 'spiritual lever' for which we now have authority to use the Bible is the lever which, as I have tried to show, is provided by the Bible itself.

Let me read to you a well-known passage of the Talmud (Meg. 31*a*), now a part of the Sabbath evening service, which illustrates this admirably:

Rabbi Johanan said, In every passage where thou findest mentioned the greatness of God, there thou findest also his humility. This is written in the Law, repeated in the Prophets, and a third time stated in the Writings.

It is written in the Law, For the Lord your God, he is God of gods, and Lord of lords, the great, mighty and revered God, who regardeth not persons, nor taketh a bribe. And it is written afterwards, He doth execute the judgment of the fatherless and widow, and loveth the stranger, in giving him food and raiment.

It is repeated in the Prophets, as it is written, For thus saith the high and lofty One that inhabiteth eternity, and whose name is holy, I dwell in the high and holy place; with him also that is of a contrite and humble spirit, to revive the spirit of the humble, and to revive the heart of the contrite ones.

It is a third time stated in the Writings, Sing unto God, sing praises unto his name: extol ye him that rideth upon the heavens by his name Jah, and rejoice before him. And it is written afterwards, A father of the fatherless, and a judge of the widows, is God in his holy habitation.

I'm afraid Rabbi Johanan must have been a 'lay individual'; and I can imagine the scholars wagging their fingers at him and saying: 'Now, Rabbi Johanan, in *every* passage? In *every* passage where the greatness of God is mentioned, do you find also his humility? Where is your concordance, Rabbi Johanan?' But I can see Rabbi Johanan nodding his head and saying: 'Yes, in every passage—that is, every passage I intend to see. The greatness of God is indeed linked in Holy Writ with his humility, that is, with his fathering the fatherless and caring for the foreigner; much as the greatness of man is seen by it not in breaking heads and hearts but in having a broken and compassionate heart oneself. It is therein that the Writ *manifests itself* as Holy.'

And I fancy that Rabbi Johanan might have gone yet further. I fancy he might have said that what he had to say required no citations from him ('written in the Law, repeated in the Prophets, and a third time stated in the Writings') since it is attested by the *self*-citation of Scripture itself. 'Let the *power* of the Lord be *great according as Thou* [God] *hast spoken*', we read elsewhere, '*according as Thou hast spoken, saying*: The Lord is slow to anger and plenteous in mercy, forgiving iniquity and transgression.' Thus the power of God, the strength of God, the greatness of God, lies not in his physical but in his moral force. If the devil can cite Scripture for his purpose, here we have Scripture, for its own 'holy witness', citing itself.

It is all so clear; and yet so hard to see. You will remark that Rabbi Johanan relies on no fancy philology or extravagant allegory. The texts speak for themselves. And they have something to say both to the scholar and to the layman, something which it would be difficult to say more simply. They express the primary Jewish intuition that just as the man dear to God's heart cannot be a man of blood and deceit, so the presence of God himself and our knowledge of him means compassion and fellow-feeling with the outcast. Greatness both for God and for man is in fact (*pace* Jonathan Wilde) just goodness in action. It is all so simple; and yet so hard to see.

X

But if it be indeed simple, what need, it may be asked, for interpretation? My answer is an old one; and with it I conclude. *Although* it is all so simple, so clear, it is yet hard to see. Interpretation is the guiding of the eyes which enables us to see what was waiting to be seen all the time.

Baruch Spinoza
His Religious Importance for the Jew of Today

❧

I

BEFORE I come to my theme it may be well to remind ourselves of a few facts of literary history.

Spinoza was born in Amsterdam some ten months after this great and famous university was inaugurated, on 24 November 1632, and died at the Hague on 21 February 1677. His fame rests principally on two books, the *Tractatus Theologico-politicus* published anonymously in 1670 and the *Ethica* published in 1677 by his friends as a part of his *Opera posthuma*. Of these two books it was the former, the *Tractatus Theologico-politicus*, which in its time created the stir. The *Ethica* waited for notice a full hundred years.

Yet, once noticed, the *Ethica* came into its own; the *Tractatus* passed into history. The *Tractatus* belongs to time, the *Ethica* to eternity; and it is this distinction, the distinction between the things of time and the things of eternity, so strikingly exemplified in the history of Spinoza's own work, which is the main lesson that men of religion today can derive from the study of Spinoza.

II

We are assembled this evening in order to learn for our present need from a thinker of the seventeenth century born and bred in this city of Amsterdam; and the first question we should ask ourselves is why it should be just *this* city, *this* people, *this* country and its institutions, which made his life, and thinking, possible. And not his life alone. Seventeenth-century Holland first set the example followed so nobly by Holland of the twentieth century of offering refuge and peace to the wanderer and

First given as an address to the International Conference of the World Union for Progressive Judaism, Amsterdam, 4 July 1957. Reprinted by permission of the World Union for Progressive Judaism, European Region.

homeless. I read to you a few sentences from a letter of one of them written in May 1631:

I walk every day among the thronging crowds as freely and quietly as you could in your private park . . . What other country could one find in the whole world where one can enjoy such complete liberty, and sleep with such a sense of security; where there are armed forces always on the watch to guard us; where poisonings and treacheries and calumnies are less known?

It is René Descartes who is writing, in this very city of Amsterdam, a year before Spinoza was born; and he praises the industry and prosperity of its inhabitants, its public order and private amenities, its allowing everyone to pursue his own affairs without interference. Spinoza, writing nearly forty years later, sees deeper. He sees that all these qualities and characteristics are interrelated; and he boldly proclaims them to be the direct consequence of Holland's declared policy of freedom:

It is the fruit of this freedom (he writes) which the city of Amsterdam reaps in its own great prosperity and in the admiration of all other peoples. For in this most flourishing state, and most splendid city, men of every nation and religion live together in the greatest harmony . . . Religion and sect is considered of no importance. It has no effect before the judges in gaining or losing a cause; and there is no sect so despised that its followers, provided that they harm no one, give every man his due, and live uprightly, are deprived of the protection of the magisterial authority.

This passage, from the twentieth chapter of the *Tractatus Theologico-politicus*, clinches the argument of the whole book. The Treatise—as I propose to call it for short—is a reasoned plea (possibly the first, certainly one of the most striking, in modern literature) for complete freedom of thought and expression (even John Locke's notable Letters on Toleration admit serious restrictions). The Treatise asserts not that the granting of this complete freedom by governments is possible but that it is essential. Freedom can not only be conceded without harm to the community. The community suffers harm if deprived of it. Freedom is the first condition both of social health and of private well-being. It is the prerequisite of civilized living. Without it society becomes rotten, government becomes corrupt, the citizen a mindless automaton.

This lesson has been rediscovered by our generation in the course of the strains and stresses of our own day. When we read such sentences as these:

The ultimate aim of the state is not to tyrannize, or hold men in by fear and make them dependent, but on the contrary to free every man from fear that he may live in all possible security; that is to say, that he may retain in its fullness the natural right to exist and act without harming himself and others. No, I say, the object of the state is not to change men from rational beings into beasts or puppets but, on the contrary, to help their minds and bodies to perform in safety their proper functions, and they themselves to use their reason freely and not struggle against others in hatred, anger or deceit or be stirred against one another in enmity. In very fact, therefore, the true aim of the state is liberty. (ch. xx)

—when we read sentences such as these, we rub our eyes and ask whether they were not written yesterday. The general conclusion of the Treatise is thus startlingly fresh. What is so puzzling about it is the way it is reached. Open the Treatise, and you may think that, in its first half at least, you have before you a biblical scholar's note book written on the interleavings of a volume of sermons. Now it is just this seemingly irrelevant material which is of importance to our immediate subject.

III

For I am asked to discuss with you what the religious Jew of today can learn from Spinoza. By that I understand, not without relief, that you do not wish to hear a disquisition on Spinoza's metaphysics, or on Spinoza's sources, or on the rightness or wrongness of the ban pronounced on Spinoza by the Jewish authorities in Amsterdam three centuries ago. These matters are all interesting and important, and there yet remains on them much to be said. But 'What the religious Jew of today can learn from Spinoza' is a different theme altogether; and in attempting it, I suggest that we start from—I do *not* say, rest in—the seeming irrelevancies of Spinoza's Treatise, for it is among them that we find an account both of religion in general and of Judaism.

Of course the irrelevancies are not really irrelevant. One of the greatest freedoms, freedom of worship, is not unconnected with freedom of expression, and freedom of expression with freedom of belief; and belief has something to do with religion, and religion (dare I say it?) with Judaism, and a primary source, and stimulus, for the understanding both of religion and of Judaism may not unreasonably be seen in the Bible. So the Treatise, although its object is the demonstration of a principle of politics, spends much time in discussing the Bible.

For Spinoza, and indeed his whole generation, especially in Holland (then, as now, pre-eminent in biblical studies), not only knew the Bible well; they took it seriously, much as right down to our own day men took the Greek and Latin classics seriously. In the same way our Treatise uses the Bible as a storehouse of experience, and as a guide in matters of religion and of moral and social thinking.

Taking the Bible in our hands then, and accepting it, as Spinoza insists, in its own light and at its own valuation, what do we find? Well, Spinoza finds a lot of unexpected things. He finds, for example, that—for the Bible—belief in God does not depend on miracle (rather, belief in miracle on belief in God). He finds that—according to the Bible—prophecy was not unique to the Jews. He finds that the pre-eminence of the Jewish prophets was not intellectual but moral, and that their teaching had nothing to do with philosophical or scientific truths. He finds that religion—for the Bible—lies not in knowledge but in obedience, obedience to simple moral rules. He even finds—remember that he is writing in the seventeenth century—that (for the Bible) opinion on matters of religious belief can not only vary (and be allowed to vary) from one man to another, but also in the mind of one and the same man, without the essentials of religion being affected. All this, we read in the Treatise, is the clear doctrine of the Bible; and therefore—according to the Bible—creeds and catechisms, that is, metaphysical formulations of belief, have no place in state legislation. The state can only require its citizens to act morally. It cannot require them to think logically. It can impose upon them rules of conduct. It cannot impose upon them articles of belief. So far as the Bible is concerned, everybody can think what he likes and say what he thinks, provided that he acts justly and is kind to his fellow men. That is religion, the religion of the Bible, says the Treatise. The rest is metaphysics and a man's private affair.

It is not to my purpose here to discuss the validity of these positions. Paradoxical as some of them may appear to be, I fancy myself that Spinoza is right; right, that is, in affirming that these are in fact the fundamental positions of the Bible. But it is obvious that the Bible voices other attitudes as well, attitudes not of tolerance but of intolerance. Spinoza is constrained therefore to enquire into the nature and source of these too.

If only Spinoza had lived in the nineteenth century, his path would have been easier; but in the seventeenth century the historical school was yet to be. Or again, if only he had read a book then in process of composition at Christ's College, Cambridge, the *De legibus Hebraeorum* of John Spencer, he might have gone back to the chapters of Maimonides' *Guide for the Perplexed* which in principle give the required key and which Spencer developed so fruitfully. But the anthropological approach would in any case have been alien to Spinoza's mathematical mind. He seems too, at the time of his writing the Treatise, to have been still sore at his treatment by the synagogue; and, according to a conjecture of one of the greatest of modern students of Spinoza and a lover both of Holland and of Jewry, the lamented Dr Carl Gebhardt, Spinoza probably put into the Treatise part of the earlier Apology which he is said to have prepared when called upon in 1656 to defend himself before the synagogue authorities. But be that as it may, and rightly or wrongly, Spinoza in the Treatise blamed all the intolerance and cruelty of the Bible on the Jews. Broadly speaking, he assigns all the fine things of the Bible to what he calls Universal Religion, all the unpleasant things to what he calls the Hebrew 'Respublica' (that is, Commonwealth) as it is based on the Mosaic code which is tacitly equated by him with Judaism.

We are thus brought to the consideration of Judaism, or rather, of Spinoza's account of it.

IV

Spinoza's account of Judaism is contained principally in his chapters on the Vocation of the Hebrews (iii), the Ceremonial Law (v), and the Hebrew Theocracy (xvii). There is much besides this in the Treatise of interest for the student of Judaism. I should mention in particular his chapters on Prophecy and the Prophets (i, ii), and his remarks on the Interpretation of Scripture (vii) and its Sacredness (xii) and Simplicity (xiii). These chapters touch the very quick of the problem of authority which is one of the great watersheds of theological theory. But the chapters I have indicated (on the vocation of the Hebrews, the ceremonial law and the Hebrew theocracy) deal with the concrete characteristics of Judaism as a separate entity and should therefore engage our special attention.

Briefly—and I remind you yet again that Spinoza is reporting what he says he finds in the Bible—the 'vocation' (that is, the 'call') of the Hebrews was political only. Its end, he says (and I quote his own words) was the 'formation of a society with fixed laws; the occupation of a strip of territory; and the concentration of all forces as it were into one body, that is, the body of the society'. The excellence of the Hebrews, he says, lay in their political organization alone. Their laws were indeed remarkable; but these laws, including the laws of their religion, were intended only to produce obedience to the social order and to promote its conservation. The Mosaic Code was given to and for the Hebrews alone. Its ceremonies, like the inducements it offers to obedience, were local and temporal only. They looked solely to the preservation of the Hebrew community.

The religion which is Judaism is thus (according to this view) the cement which bound together the Mosaic state; and its value, a value which is derivative and adventitious, not intrinsic, lay in its use for the preservation of that state: it was an instrument to aid its survival. It was, as it were, the cocoon spun by the state out of the juices of its own body for the purpose of its own protection.

Spinoza follows the conventional (and, to my mind, unfortunate and misleading) view that there are to be distinguished in it the two parts, of ceremony and morality. The ceremonial consisted in certain customs and habits of behaviour; and with the political disappearance of the community in which it inhered, its reason for existence disappeared. The moral, summed up in the principles of love and kindness and justice, was also intended to strengthen the society; but owing to the intuition of the prophets it became clear that what was salutary for this one society was salutary for all societies, and thus the ideals of love and justice, because they transcended the bounds of the Hebraic state, survived the destruction of that state and became the foundation of the religion of mankind. This religion is non-political in the sense that it is not confined to any one nation or to any one country. It knows no monopolies, that is, no chosen people and no promised land. It rejects the very idea of credal sectarianism; but since men differ in their opinions (as Spinoza remarks) as much as they do in their faces, the uniformity it requires is not of creed but of moral action.

We are here (on biblical grounds) at the general conclusion of the Treatise as a whole. So far as Spinoza's particular account of Judaism is concerned, it will be noted that in his view Judaism is universalist by accident and never so (apparently) for Jews. In essence it is, in the narrow sense, political and (in Spinoza's view) narrowly and savagely political; and those who love to quote his remark on the possibility of the reemergence of the Hebraic state would do well to ponder the reasons he gives in a later passage for its inadvisability. Judaism for Spinoza is a tribal habit of life, isolationist and misanthropic, a device for group survival.

V

And we survive. But by virtue of what? On Spinoza's principles it would seem we have no right to. The cement of a political community would naturally be expected to disappear with the disappearance of that community. In this case, however, the political community disappeared but the cement remained, itself to create a community of a different kind

altogether. But we may leave this general puzzle and ask whether, on Spinoza's own express ground, the ground of the Bible, we need accept
Spinoza's theory at all.

An enquiry of this nature is the proper task of our theologians and I
hesitate to intrude into their sphere. But certain points leap to the eye.
Does Spinoza, as he deals with the evidence from the Bible, take into
account all of it, or the most significant part of it, or even (quantitatively)
most of it? For example, when he speaks of the 'call' of the Jewish people,
he speaks of it as a bare political fact. He says nothing of its moral end. But
according to the Bible which Spinoza says he is expounding, this moral
end is of the very essence of the call: without it the call is no call at all. The
very first charter of Jewry—according to the Bible—makes Jewry dependent on Judaism, almost a 'function' of Judaism. 'For I have known
him', God is represented as saying to Abraham long before the seed of
Abraham grew into the people in which all the nations of the earth are to
be blessed, 'For I have known him *to the end that* he may command his
children and his household after him, that they may keep the way of God,
to do justice and judgment.' For a student of the Bible this is plain
enough; and I need hardly remind students of later Judaism that this
verse is constantly used in this 'charter' sense by the great systematizer
and shaper of our own Judaism, Moses Maimonides. In the Bible itself
the conception is repeated constantly, and in various forms, on other—
biblically speaking—crucial occasions.

Yet of all this I find nothing in Spinoza. Nor do I find the prophetic
conception of Witness; nor the no less striking and prominent doctrine
of the Remnant; nor the constant biblical emphasis that the fulfilment of
the promises is dependent on the fulfilment of the conditions, the moral
conditions, under which the promises were given; nor the constant
calling of the people back to the primary decencies of moral living.
Biblical Judaism is always ahead of the Jewish people, always in advance
of them, always telling them in no uncertain fashion what they should be
doing and what they should not be doing. 'They may cry, We, Israel,
know thee; but Israel hath cast off what is good.' 'God hath a controversy
with the inhabitants of the land, because there is no truth, nor mercy, nor
knowledge of God in the land; there is naught but swearing and breaking
faith and killing and stealing.' That is the authentic voice of Judaism, yet
it is not saying what on Spinoza's theory one would have expected it to
say. On Spinoza's theory one would have expected the 'comforting
words' of the prophets stigmatized in the Bible as false, what we recognize today as the propagandists bolstering up a political regime or giving

'pep' to the morale of its so-called citizens. Spinoza is impressed, and rightly impressed, with the universality of the prophetic teaching. He ignores the moral obligation and the moral function which that very teaching imposed on the Jewish people. Take that away, and (as Amos said) the Jews are just such another wandering tribe as the Ethiopians and the Philistines.

These great omissions and evasions culminate in Spinoza's treatment of the biblical Covenant. The Covenant is not, for the Bible, a political fact, as Spinoza would seem to hold, but a religious act. This act constituted Jewry as a peculiar people, it created the Jewish people in the biblical sense. Whether the act is one of bare acceptance on our part, or something more, I leave to the determination of the theologians. But we should note that there is here (as in any other covenant) another side, a partner, a co-signatory, who in this covenant is all-important; for—according to the Bible and in the formulation of the prayer-book—he 'chose us out of all the nations and gave us his law', thereby—if I may animadvert to the problem of the survival of Jewry—'planting in our midst everlasting life'.

I suggest then that Spinoza has misread his evidence. According to the Bible, the way of life (which is the way of God) created the nation, not the nation the way of life. Judaism is not the product of any community for the reason that it seeks to produce a community. It was never offered as the cement of the Mosaic Commonwealth because that Commonwealth was planned as its realization. Judaism is the idea behind it, not its fruit. It is its programme rather than its present constitution. It is not a fact but a force. As the rabbis put it in their quaint but arresting way, the Torah—Judaism—was created a thousand generations before the world; and I may perhaps be allowed to add the sobering thought that, according to the Bible, the world was created before the Jews.

VI

But we must press on to the deeper issues. We are met to discuss religion, not politics or sociology; and if Spinoza really joins hands with Durkheim and Ahad Ha'am, so much the worse for him. But does he? Let us enquire a littler further.

In the Treatise, Spinoza is arguing to a thesis. As its title, *Tractatus Theologico-politicus*, clearly indicates, he is not proposing to deal with religion as such or politics as such but with their inter-working and combination. He is treating religion from the point of view of government and legislation; and, from the point of view of government and legislation, feeling and opinion and the varying creeds and the differing philosophies can rightly be considered irrelevant. What men do is what matters to government, and what men do can be made subject to control. Religion then, so far as government is concerned, can be treated as a matter of public morals. As he says in his praise of the city of Amsterdam I have already quoted: 'Religion and sect is considered of no importance. It has no effect before the judges in gaining or losing a cause; and there is no sect so despised that its followers, provided that they harm no one, give every man his due, and live uprightly, are deprived of the protection of the magisterial authority.'

But the magistrate's court is not everything. Indeed, I suppose that most of us have not even been inside one. For government and legislation are not the only, and they are not the determining, factors in life, and public order is not the only consideration. These are only the external framework of life, and even so, only from a limited point of view. The flavour and savour of life as it is lived lies just in the feelings and emotions and opinions and creeds which are irrelevant to public order and which do not come up in the courts at all. This is ignored in the Treatise, and (in view of its special and limited purpose) rightly. But it cannot be ignored in any comprehensive view of life. And Spinoza does offer a comprehensive view of life, not, however, in the Treatise, but in the *Ethics*.

And so we can appeal from Spinoza to Spinoza. Does the religion of the Treatise, the religion of charity and good deeds, tally with the religion of the *Ethics*? It may be held perhaps to correspond to the religion of the fourth book of the *Ethics* which describes the life of the 'Free Man' living in accordance with the rule of right reason. But what of the fifth book with its mysterious and suggestive propositions, so calmly enunciated, so elegantly demonstrated, about the eternity of the mind, and the love of man for God and the love of God for man, propositions which would seem to embrace most of what is meant by religion to the ordinary religious man? Our destiny, our highest hopes, our dependence, our independence, our present beatitude, our final salvation—what are these but the great themes of religion as described, or as felt, by all? In the words of Spinoza himself, 'We feel and experience that we are eternal'; or, more positively, 'Man could not exist or be conceived unless he had the power to grasp the eternal and infinite essence of God.' If this is religion (and so it would seem), then in religion lies the source, and the support, and indeed the very fruition, of that very freedom the fostering of which, according to the Treatise, is the end and aim of the political organization of society.

As we pass then from the one of Spinoza's two great books to the other, we find an expansion and supplementation of values which is almost a reversal. Politics and the political view are not enough. The magistrates' courts are not the whole of life. Man is not only a political animal. The time and place, the community and its organization, of the Treatise are cradled in the eternity of the *Ethics*.

Eternity as expounded by Spinoza is an idea of positive *quality*. It is contrasted specifically with quantitative endlessness. It is the completion of existence', reality in its fullness. It is in no sense a 'never-never land'. It is rather, if I may so phrase it, an 'ever-ever land'—the 'absolute affirmation of existence', the 'infinite enjoyment of being', says Spinoza (*Eth.* I. viii; *Ep.* XII)—a land which is not there but here, not hereafter but now, a land which, ever present, beckons us on, and which our highest striving is to go over to and inhabit. It is the Kingdom of Heaven which is within us; and it is notable that Spinoza, when he comes to speak of its central point, the unity of the love of God for man and the love of man for God, and the 'stillness of mind', the *acquiescentia in se ipso*, which is engendered in those who attain it, can think only of the biblical 'Glory' in order to express and illustrate the salvation, the blessedness, the 'liberty', so attained. The Bible, he seems to agree, contains more than the political life. Religion means more than the state.

It means more than the state and it is stronger than the state; as indeed is suggested by recent experience. Only religion has in our day and before our eyes shown the strength to stand up to the great arrogance of our time, the arrogance of the state. Religion too is arrogant. Like the God of the Bible, jealous and terrible as well as full of mercy and love, it makes its demands, presents its claims, from above. But the arrogance of politics enslaves our humanity. The arrogance of religion creates it and gives it shape. The power of the one crushes and destroys; the authority of the other raises up. It dwells in the high and holy place, but with him also that is of a contrite and humble heart, to give new life to the spirit and to proclaim liberty to the captives and to open the doors of the various prisons invented by the ingenuity of our politicians for our bodies and souls alike.

Thus I suggest to you that the religious Jew of today may well turn to the *Ethics*, and particularly to its fifth book, for one of the great needs of our lives (particularly within Jewry), a religious approach to religion. For the 'Free Man' of the fourth book of the *Ethics*, the highest product of the political life, ideal participant in the ideal republic of the supposedly autonomous rule of right reason—the Free Man cannot become himself unless, as is clearly indicated in the last sentence of the fourth book, he receives the support of the truths underlying, and expounded in, the fifth. Humanism is not enough, for the simple reason that man is more than narrowly human.

VII

The fifth (and last) book of the *Ethics* demonstrates in detail the contention of the famous autobiographical passage which opens the unfinished Treatise on the Emendation of the Intellect. In this passage, as you will remember, Spinoza sets out from the futility of ordinary experience; and he describes how he came to see that it is only by love directed towards the infinite and eternal that we can rid ourselves of subjection to the pursuits of the fleeting and evanescent pseudo-goods of life: money, fame, desire. Ultimately, the way of right living and the way of right feeling and the way of right thinking are one and the same. Its practical side is the familiar one of detachment. But it is detachment of a special kind. It is detachment through attachment, attachment to the eternal and infinite object which can never alter and never disappoint, the one object which can arouse an emotion strong enough to master all other emotions.

For emotional life remains the truth of man: desire cannot be extinguished. But it can be diverted. Its object can be changed. Its 'proper' object can be found.

Spinoza's philosophy may thus be accounted as his discovery and exploration of the infinite and eternal. But he could not have set out on the quest if he had not in some fashion already known its end. 'Thou couldst not find me if thou hadst not known me.'

This pre-figuration, or pre-vision, or pre-adumbration, of the infinite and eternal is the first root of religion. We are men, not stones. We start with a sense of eternity; but a sense of eternity is not the knowledge of eternity, certainly not its full consciousness or its fruit. It is a nisus, a striving, a groping, which exists in us owing to the facts of our human, and of universal, nature. It is only slowly and with difficulty and through the exercise of conscious effort that we attain the clarity of the real. But the beginnings are in us from the start. 'We feel and experience that we are eternal.' 'It is no accident but arises out of the very nature of reason, that man's highest good should be common to all . . . For it appertains to the very essence of the human mind to have an adequate knowledge of the eternal and infinite essence of God.'

VIII

Here too we may learn from Spinoza. Salvation is not cheap nor its attainment easy. At the outset of our enquiry we learned the negative lesson that politics is not enough and that the political approach to religion is inadequate. We then learned that moralism too is not enough. Religion includes morals but it is more than morals. We now learn that experience, the experience of eternity, is only a beginning. It is not the bare experience which counts but its depth, its direction, its end. All men have a glimpse of eternity; or, rather, a glimmering of eternity comes to all men. The human task is to develop that first glimmer.

In the view of Spinoza and those who think like him (notably, many of the master-minds of India), this task is shared by religion and philosophy, philosophy (perhaps) rather scrutinizing the road, religion pressing on impatiently to the goal; or, religion gathering up the conclusions of philosophy, philosophy refining the intuitions of religion, but both of them seeing the one end with however varying intensity, both of them suggesting, or imposing, means. Both speak in terms of knowledge, knowledge which the seeker must acquire. What is peculiar to the type of thought represented by Spinoza is that it sees as the essential groundwork of that knowledge the systematic investigation of the physical world which we now call by the name of science. Religion is only the highest rung in the ascending ladder of mind.

For mind too has its reasons; and the reasons of the mind go deeper than the reasons of the heart. And mind, as we are told by Spinoza, is the better part of us; and the satisfaction of mind is the satisfaction of our highest being.

Yet curiosity is not our only instinct, and knowledge of the physical world is not our only channel of satisfaction. We should not ignore science. It is no enhancement of the glory of God to belittle the achievement of man. But we may legitimately rest assured that there are other spheres of aspiration and other instruments of achievement. Scientism too is not enough, and it does not exhaust the windows of our enlargement.

But enlarge ourselves we must. Creatures of time as we seemingly are, it is only through our grasp of eternity (whether our grasp on eternity or eternity's grasp on us) that we can escape from time. If we remain wholly within time, we are time's slaves, not, as we can and should be, time's masters. To those who master time, another world opens:

> Servants of time are slaves of slaves;
>   God's servant hath his freedom whole.
> When every man his portion craves,
>   'God is my portion', saith my soul.
>
> HALEVI, TRANS. SALAMAN

We may then follow the philosophers, we may follow the saints; more simply perhaps, and for us Jews more naturally, we may follow the Law and the Prophets, the psalmists and the rabbis. But whatever we do and however we strive, one thing is sure: the way is difficult, difficult to find, difficult to pursue.

And yet—it is Spinoza speaking—'it can nevertheless be found. It must indeed be difficult [I continue the words of his last grave warning] since it is so seldom discovered. For if salvation lay ready to hand and could be discovered without great labour, how could it come about that it should be neglected almost by all?

'But every excellent thing is as difficult as it is rare.'

Judaism: The Elements

꧁

I

THERE have been many attempts at a pocket definition of Judaism. There is Hillel's, in reply to a would-be convert's request to be taught Judaism while he stood on one leg: 'What you do not like yourself, do not do to others.' There is the medieval rabbi's (in the words of the psalmist): 'In all thy ways know God.' There is the prophet Jonah's: 'I am a Hebrew and I reverence the God of Heaven who made the sea and the dry land.' A famous one is that of Micah: 'He hath told thee, O man, what is good; and what doth God require of thee but to do justice and to love mercy and to walk humbly with thy God?' What is common to all these summary statements is that they are couched in terms of general moral values. Like Micah's pronouncement, they are concerned with no one person or group of persons but with man.

The content of Judaism would thus seem to be universal, yet its bearers are a particular people, the Jews; and the history of Judaism is the story of the balance (often an uneasy one) between the universality of the doctrine and the particularity of its transmitters. The connection between the two is laid down clearly from the very first. God is represented as having 'known' Abraham (that is, singled him out from all others) in order that he should command his children and his household after him to practise the 'way of God, that is, to do justice and judgment'. Here, too, the terms used are completely general: justice, judgement, the way of God; and the children of Abraham are to be the vehicle through which the way of God (that is, the way of justice and judgement) is to be displayed.

This is the doctrine of the 'chosen people', a doctrine which has been misunderstood by both Jews and non-Jews, and which has done much harm. It is so easy to claim to be the chosen people, and to forget that the choice means duty, not privilege. In itself no one people is any better, as in itself no one people is any worse, than any other. But the Jews were chosen to be a 'holy' nation, that is, a nation set apart in order to exemplify a way of living which is right and good for all.

Reprinted with permission from *JUDAISM: A Quarterly Journal of Jewish Life and Thought*, vol. 7, no. 1 (Winter 1958), 3–13. © 1958 American Jewish Congress.

We are discussing the theory of the matter; and it is no argument to say that the Jews we know (and are) are far from being a pattern people. Perhaps they are and perhaps they are not. The point is that Judaism is not to be considered in terms of the Jews but the Jews in terms of Judaism.

This is shown by a fact of some practical importance. When we say that the Jewish people is in idea the bearer or carrier or transmitter of Judaism, the phrase 'Jewish people' has to be understood very carefully and in the widest sense. In principle, the tie constituting this people is not one of 'race' or 'blood'. Judaism does not seek converts, and indeed since talmudic times has actively discouraged them. But a convert once accepted is a full member of the community of Judaism whatever his 'blood' may be. Some of the greatest Jews of history (e.g. the patriot and scholar–saint Akiva) are reported to have been converts or the descendants of converts. 'Let not thy descent be light in thine eyes', wrote Maimonides to a convert of his day. 'If *our* descent is from Abraham, Isaac and Jacob, thine is from *God himself.*'

Thus, the root loyalty of Judaism is not to a person or to an aggregate or persons but, like the root loyalty of Buddhism, to a teaching. This teaching (in Hebrew, Torah) is the 'Law of Moses' as it has been lived and interpreted, with ever-changing emphasis and modification, during the many long centuries of its history. The length of this history should not pass unremarked. The traditional date of the founding father of Judaism, the patriarch Abraham, is roughly the same number of years *before* the Christian era as we are now (1957) *after* it. The traditional date of Moses is some four centuries later (say, 1500 BC); that of David and Solomon (1000 BC), five centuries later still. The great literary prophets (Amos, Hosea, Isaiah, Jeremiah, Ezekiel) range onwards from the eighth century BC. The books classified as the Apocrypha are from Hellenistic times (third to first centuries BC); and it is to the latter half of this period that most of the contents of the newly discovered Dead Sea Scrolls should apparently be ascribed. The Mishnah, the basic rabbinic collection of traditional law, is of the second and third centuries of the Christian era, the Talmud, in its two recensions, of the fourth to sixth. The standard Codes, based on the further discussions of the schools and the decisions of the courts, belong to the eleventh to sixteenth centuries, and they are contemporary with the work of the systematic theologians, moralists, and philosophers; while the mystical movements, with their puzzled doctrine and their often disastrous practical outbursts and their consequences, are a sporadic accompaniment to the whole.

This is all Torah, all—by conscious fiction—the 'Law of Moses'; and we may consider for a moment the treatment of Moses in Jewish tradition since it offers a key to much which to our generation is unfamiliar.

We are accustomed to think of Moses as the law-giver, and we have been taught to contrast the 'spirit' of prophecy with the 'letter' of law as if legal rigorism had to be swept away by prophetic 'inwardness' before religion could be born. That is not so in the history of Judaism, and that for the reason that in Judaism these actors were never dissociated.

Judaism knows Moses not as a law-giver but as a prophet (which means a spokesman of God, not a soothsayer), indeed, as the greatest of the prophets; and 'his' law is not his at all: it is God's. The Law is the detail of the 'way of God', and Moses is only its announcer and expounder. Moses' own exposition is given traditionally in the Book of Deuteronomy; and it is just in the humane legislation of this book that we find the highest combination of 'inner' and 'outer', spirit and discipline. For the traditional Moses there is no opposition between law and feeling, between love and reverence and command. It is 'Moses the man of God' in whose mouth the Bible puts the noble prayer beginning 'Lord, thou has been our dwelling place in all generations' and ending 'Let the beauty of the Lord our God be upon us'; and it is Moses, the Moses of Deuteronomy, who knows that the Commandment is not something far off and distant from man, but 'very near', in our very 'mouths and hearts'.

Yet in the tradition Moses, as an individual, disappears. He never became, as did the Buddha, the centre of a cult. 'No one knows his burial place to this day.' In common Hebrew parlance he is known as Moses *our Teacher*, while the teaching itself has dropped the teacher's name. It is no longer (as in the Bible) the Torah *of Moses* ('Remember the Law of Moses my servant which I commanded him in Horeb before all Israel'), but, barely, and anonymously, *Torah*.

It is this Torah, in its length and breadth and depth, which is Judaism and which, in the words of the prayer-book, 'planted in our midst everlasting life'; and when Hillel gave the definition with which this essay sets out, what he said was not 'This is the whole of *Judaism*', but 'This is the whole Torah.'

Hillel added at once: 'The rest is commentary; go and learn.' The addition is all-important. Judaism is a life and a history and a civilization rather than a bare system of ethics or theology; and from the far-off days of Abraham it has passed through many vicissitudes and many phases of which the biblical, the rabbinic and the philosophical are only the three most easily named. As Hillel recognized over nineteen centuries ago, there is a great deal of 'commentary' and it has to be learned; for religions (like most other things) live not in their generalities but in their specific particulars.

II

Judaism is what is called by theologians a monotheism, that is, devotion to one God; and God is conceived of by Judaism as the creator and maintainer of everything that exists. He is thus not only a distant first cause. He is an ever-present help and supporter.

The unity of God means unity of control in the created world. The king of Aram in the biblical story, having been beaten by Ahab's troops in the hills, was advised to make a second attack in the valley because (his advisers said) the Jewish God is obviously a God of the hills. But he was wrong. The Jewish God, or rather the God of Judaism, is God of the whole earth.

More characteristically, he is the 'God of Heaven', that is, above all geographical considerations. The whole creation is the manifestation of one will. There is one regular order: law, not chaos. 'While the earth remaineth, seed-time and harvest, cold and heat, summer and winter, day and night, shall not cease.'

The physical order we can see through our eyes; and we are bidden to lift up our eyes to the stars and from the sight of nature, see nature's God. More subtly, one of the psalmists says: 'Shall not the creator of the eye have sight?' If we can see, our creator, too, must be able to see; and see (here the metaphor or analogy or inference is bold indeed) 'unto *our hearts* and understand all our actions'. The Pentateuch strikes an even deeper note. 'Be ye holy', it says, 'as I your God am holy.' The meaning is clearly not that God is holy as we are, but that we should try and be holy as God is. God is not only creator of the physical world, and the physical is not the only order. There is a moral order too, and it too is rooted in God. God 'tells us what is good'. He gives the pattern to which our lives should conform. He is the source of our powers, not only of physical but also of moral perception.

The psalmist's sentence is an argument; and it has often been expanded in modern times and used to the effect that the creator of mind cannot, himself, be less than mind. The sentence from the Pentateuch is an injunction. The recognition of God's holiness involves for man an obligation to behave differently. We cannot 'walk before' him without changing our ways. God has a way for us of his own and it is not the way of untutored man; it is something that has to be learned. And what has to be learned has to be taught; whence the need for teaching, i.e. Torah. Thus Torah and its study became the centre of Jewish life, shaping it and elevating it and transforming it through the civilizing influence of learning and education. Without knowledge we are not yet men.

That God is the one creator of all; that he has told man what is good; that man should walk in the path of the good; that in so walking he finds his real nature—all this is traditionally expressed in the biblical formula that man is created in the likeness of God. Yet Judaism would seem to affirm that the uniqueness of man lies not so much in that as a bare fact, as in the further fact that man knows it. 'Beloved is man', as a rabbinic teacher puts it, 'in that he was created in the likeness of God; but it was by a special act of love that it was *made known to him* that he was so created.' For the knowledge brings with it a new status and a new dignity and a new type of obligation, the obligation to measure himself by a higher standard than himself. That man knows that he is made in God's likeness means that he recognizes and realizes that he is to be judged by God's standard.

III

Unity is thus seen as the universal pattern. The one God created one world. In this one world he created one man, the one progenitor of humankind. Mankind constitutes one family, and the moral consequence is drawn explicitly. Since we are one family, why should we fight one another: 'Have we not one father; hath not one God created us?' The Mishnah puts a similar idea in a similarly simple way. Since we are all descended from the one Adam, it says, no one's 'blood' is 'bluer' than any other's.

The ethical objection to polytheism is that it makes possible a variety of moral standards: an act disapproved of by one divinity may be approved of by another. Monotheism cuts all that away. There is one standard only, one right and wrong. And the one God, being a creator God, cares for his creation. He is thus 'father' as well as 'king'.

Judaism registers this in the names with which it addresses God. In the everyday blessings of the prayer-book he is Our God, King of the Universe; in the grace after meals, the Merciful One; in penitential prayer, Our Father, Our King, or 'Our Father which art in heaven'. A favourite rabbinic mode of address is the All-Merciful; another, the Holy

One, Blessed be He. A very usual circumlocution is the simplest of all: The Name.

For there is a sobriety about the attitude of Judaism to God. It rejects familiarity. It keeps distance. It claims no intimate knowledge of God's nature. Indeed, it frowns on over-curiousness. As the Talmud quotes from the book of Ecclesiasticus in the Apocrypha: 'In what is hidden from thee do not enquire.' It is only in the moral sphere that it ventures to make positive assertions about God at all; and these affect rather the practical requirements made by God of man than the metaphysical questions addressed by man to God. We have already seen the prophet Micah's affirmation about what God requires of man. The rabbis follow suit: 'As God is merciful, be thou merciful; as he heals the sick, heal thou the sick; as he feeds the hungry, feed thou the hungry.' These, they say, are the ways of God, and the duty of man is to 'cleave to' them, that is, imitate them and do likewise.

Thus, the doctrine of God in Judaism, however it may have been arrived at, seems in every case to eventuate in a practical outcome. The unity of God, for example, is not an abstract consideration, to be accepted only as an article of theoretical belief. It means one world, one humanity, one universal order, one norm for logic, one standard for morals; it means that truth and justice are not mere words but a way which man is expected to take and to follow. The idea of God is thus not a bare idea but a living force, thrusting itself into every department of life and claiming us (often vainly) for its own.

A striking illustration of this (and it is the more striking because it is unexpected and not in accordance with modern taste) is provided by the pentateuchal law of sanitation. The law in Deuteronomy prescribes that latrines should be *outside* the camp, and the reason given is 'the Lord thy God walketh in the midst of thy camp, *therefore*, thy camp shall be holy'. The comment I would make is this. That God is holy is a conventional statement to be found in the scriptures of most religions; and 'holy men' (particularly in the East today) are no novelty. But the holiness of God in Judaism has a concrete and practical relevance to the way in which ordinary men should live. The English proverb uses abstract terms and says that cleanliness is next to godliness; but Judaism, and the Hebrew language, is always concrete. It is God, the Most High, the Creator of Heaven and Earth, who refuses to abide with us if we live in dirt: '*therefore* shall thy camp be holy'.

This concreteness of Judaism is so important and pervading a characteristic that it requires further illustration.

IV

The American psychologist William James advised the young, whenever they felt inclined to kindness, not to leave the feeling without an outlet but to work it off in a specific act, for example giving up one's seat in a tram-car to an old person, or visiting a neglected aunt. Unless a feeling is exercised, he said, it will become atrophied and dead. In somewhat the same way, Judaism has always insisted on translating general virtues into particular duties. I offer an example or two.

All religions speak of goodness and justice and love in general. Judaism adds concrete specifications. Justice, for example, means having one set of weights only; not taking bribes; not favouring the rich nor (a striking novelty this) the poor. These may not be the only ways in which justice can be exhibited or maintained, but they are at least practical ones and in our power. And they prevent our enthusiasm for the general idea of justice obliterating our interest in particular just acts! Kindness to animals, unexceptionable as a principle but not always exemplified in practice, assumes in Judaism the definite commands not to plough with an ox and an ass together, and not to muzzle the ox when it is treading out the corn; kindness to human beings is to be manifested in such acts as paying your workman every day and not taking in pledge the instruments of a man's livelihood. You love your neighbour by helping him with his load and returning his strayed animals; you look after the poor by leaving them the gleanings of the harvest and vineyard. Love and charity may be something more than this but it is at least this; and it is in and through the practice of particular acts such as these detailed in the Law that the habit of right action, and ultimately right feeling, is formed.

The same characteristic of concrete particularity may be observed in the later great texts of Judaism: the Mishnah, the Talmud, the Codes. A glance at a chapter of Maimonides' Code, for example, will show that he always starts from particular cases, and only afterwards sums up in a general rule. This may be a weakness from the point of view of legal theory but it is a blessing to the public. Law exists in order to help human beings, not human beings in order to help the law; and it is this principle which forms the basis of much which is peculiar to Judaism, and particularly in the Pentateuch itself. For what is remarkable about pentateuchal legislation is that it is concerned deeply with the individual human being and bases itself squarely on his human feelings.

Thus, in the law of punishment, a wrongdoer is not to be punished beyond his strength so that he should not break down in public and be shamed. We are bidden (on thirty-six separate occasions, according to talmudic reckoning) to show kindness to foreigners. And why? Because 'we know the *heart* of the foreigner'. And how do we know the heart of the foreigner? Because (in the land of Egypt) we have been foreigners ourselves. We are enjoined to rest on the Sabbath day and to allow rest to the other members of the household. The phrase used is: 'That thy manservant and thy maidservant may rest *as well as thou.*' That is to say, master and servant are both men and, as such, have the same need of (and enjoyment in) rest; and it is notable that the Hebrew phrase translated in this verse 'as well as thou' is the same as that used in the 'Great Commandment': 'Thou shalt love thy neighbour *as thyself.*' The appeal is from human feeling to human feeling: 'Thou shalt remember that *thou* wast a bondman . . . *therefore* I command thee to do this thing'. A most delicate instance is that of the 'beautiful woman taken in war': 'Thou shalt not sell her at all for money, thou shalt not deal with her as a chattel, *because thou didst humble her.*'

If consideration for the individual human being is at the root of much of pentateuchal legislation, it is not a matter for surprise that the same characteristic pervades historical Judaism as a whole. Moritz Lazarus in his *Ethics of Judaism* describes the working, in the Berlin Jewish community at the end of the nineteenth century, of a 150-year-old system of communal help to families left in immediate want owing to the death of their head. The system was so devised that both givers and takers remained not only unknown but, indeed, unknowable. This is in the full spirit of talmudic legislation. The rabbis of the Talmud held that to help one's fellow man is the best of all deeds but to bring shame on him is one of the worst: a man should be (like Job) 'eyes to the blind' without being himself seen. Similarly, one should not wrong one's fellow 'even in words'; and the thought is developed with such appreciation of human failings as to lead to a prohibition not only of adulteration of articles of food and drink but also of the very asking of a shopkeeper the price of goods if we have no intention of buying.

All this is made a matter for *legislation*. It is the subject of specific articles in the Codes. Just as the Sabbath is the seventh day and no other, and just as charity should be given to the extent of a tenth of one's income, so even the love of God itself, the highest end set before man, is to be practised in specific ways. Feeling is made manifest, as it is fostered, through actions prescribed by law. Law may not attain the ideal maximum of the elect few but it secures the indispensable minimum from the many.

For the 'way' is not left for improvisation. It is a way according to rule. The rule is expressed in specific commandments which regulate conduct. However vivid the indignation felt at social wrong and religious abuse, it is void and useless unless it can be shaped in definite moulds. Judaism not only tells us in general to do good. It exemplifies for us in the Commandments what good to do.

V

The Commandments are conventionally distinguished into moral and ceremonial. The convention, however, like the distinction, is unsound. Ceremony is the device by which the feeling of the presence of God is brought into everyday life. Thus, whatever its detail may be, its total intent is moral. Similarly, morality does not consist in the mouthing of abstract principles but in acting in a particular way. The duties it imposes are specific, and, therefore, in a sense ceremonial.

For life is an all-day affair. It is lived in definite actions. But if actions have no rhythm or pattern, they are the cause of disorder and discontent. The art of living lies in the imposition of form on the indiscriminate welter of feeling, passion, impulse, emotion and phantasy which are the raw material of our lives; and if this is so of our lives as individuals, it is even more so of our lives as lived with others in the social whole.

A notable example of the inextricable blend of ceremony and morals, alike in the individual and in the social sphere, is offered by the Sabbath. 'By nature', as the Book of Ecclesiasticus remarks, all days are the same. The picking out of any one of them is, therefore, an artificial act. It is 'legalism', the imposition of an arbitrary and rigid rule on the glorious fluidity of life. Could there be anything more unnatural than the cutting up of the days into weeks and the selecting of any one day in the artificially constructed series of days over against all others?

Yet although we have in the Sabbath an apparently clear instance of man-made ceremony, it is by no means a meaningless, 'external', act. For the benefits of the Sabbath are spiritual as well as physical. It is at once a signal example of moral legislation, and a call to the individual to remind himself what it means to be a man.

The Sabbath is a typical instance of the way in which Judaism succeeded in turning what may have been originally a magical practice or a sporadic fulfilment of a natural need into a moral institution; and the practical fact of its visible beginning and end (it is kept not from midnight to midnight but 'from evening unto evening') helped powerfully to make its purpose manifest. In the same way, the three great annual festivals, all presumably once nature feasts, were rededicated to moral ideas. Passover becomes the festival of freedom. Pentecost, originally a harvest festival, becomes the festival of the giving of the Law. Tabernacles remains associated with nature; yet it is nature transformed. It is genuine nature as opposed to the artificial civilization of house and town, and brings man back directly to his primary dependence.

But life is much besides Sabbaths and feasts. Man walks before God every day and all the day. His every act is therefore to be hallowed. Those that bear the vessels of God must be themselves clean. The food which comes into our mouth—the meat we eat—can pollute us. We must see, therefore, that it is fit for consumption.

The religious value of the dietary laws lies in the spirit in which they are performed; and those who smile at a 'kitchen religion' would do well to ponder the remark of the early Greek philosopher on entering a poor cottage: 'Here, too, are gods.' Judaism would seem to hold that the occupation of a housewife is a holy one and that a kitchen too is, or can be made, a place of worship. Holiness is not asceticism, a negation of the world and its fullness, It is rather, in the presence and enjoyment of the world and its fullness, a conscious exercise of self-control. It is a guiding, not an obliteration, of natural desire. All hygienic considerations apart, therefore—and yet these should count very strongly—food regulations, however irksome, are of deep moral significance. Just as the weekly Sabbath reminds a man that he is not a mere wage slave, so abstention from certain foods reminds him that he is not a mere animal, following blindly the first desire of his eyes.

VI

In Judaism, man's approach to God is never through a mediator. 'The soul which sinneth, it shall die.' Man has to make his own peace with God. And he has to make his peace with man first. Atonement must be preceded by restitution. This was so by Temple law. The sacrifice was offered only *after* the restitution. It was a public acknowledgement of wrong done, to be made after the wrong had been repaired: 'He shall restore in full, and shall add the fifth part more thereto; unto him to whom it appertains shall he give it . . . And he shall [then and then only] bring his guilt offering unto the Lord . . . and the priest shall make atonement for him . . . and he shall be forgiven.' The doctrine is essentially the moral one of individual personal responsibility. When Moses asked to be allowed to take upon himself the sin of his people, he received the stern reply: 'Whosoever hath sinned against me, him will I blot out of my book.'

How far in time the responsibility extended is not determined. Although the theory of the transmigration of souls is made much of in the kabbalah (as indeed in all Gnostic speculation), Judaism never held to the Eastern doctrine of reincarnation; that is, it never taught that wrongdoing committed in this life can be expiated in another life (or in a succession of other lives) on this earth; and while it believed in an afterlife in which the good persisted and in which wrongs committed were expiated, it was never dogmatic as to its nature. And its emphasis was always on the good. It never insisted on the all-pervading and all-blackening character of sin, and on an everlasting hell. On the contrary. Just as the Bible dwells on the mercy and love of God whose anger does not last for ever, so the living Judaism expressed in the liturgy of the Day of Atonement is one prolonged call to the wrongdoer to change his heart and his ways. It is rather an appeal to the possibilities of good in the worst of us than a threat based on a total and final condemnation of the bad, an appeal based on the conception of the 'presence of God' which we have seen throughout to be a guiding principle of Judaism. In the solemn words of the Atonement liturgy: 'Thou hast set man apart from the beginning, and recognized him that he should stand before Thee.'

Ultimately, the consideration is of the type known as mystical; but Judaism would, I think, hold suspect at least some part of the present connotation of the word. There is in Judaism no special revelation for the hermit or the contemplative, none even for the 'religious'; there is no secret initiation, no opening of hidden mysteries, no esoteric doctrine. God is the preserve of no one man or class of men. The door to him has no special password. It is open always. All men together are made in the likeness of God, and all men may manifest that likeness within them.

But—and the but is all-important—man is not God and God is not man. Man remains man. He stands 'in the presence of' God; he walks 'in the way of' God; he 'appears before' God. He does not *become* God or *disappear in* God. He is not identifiable, certainly never identical, with God. God is the ideal of holiness to which man strives; he is not the psychic or spiritual whole into which man is, or can be, absorbed. The basic religious feeling of Judaism remains that of the Law and the Prophets and the Writings. The eternal God is its dwelling-place, and in his light it sees light. But no more.

VII

A word must be said about the attitude of Judaism to other faiths. The general tone is set by a very early use (or misuse) of the verse in Exodus (22: 28): 'Thou shalt not revile the judges.' Owing to an ambiguity in the Hebrew word translated 'judges', the words could mean: 'Thou shalt not revile God or "the gods"', and the injunction was made to mean: 'Thou shalt not revile the gods *of other people*.' This may have been a counsel of prudence, but it is also a counsel of wisdom. The mature wisdom of Judaism avoided all religious controversy and recognized value in the beliefs of others. The Talmud itself remarks that the pagan is worshipping 'not the mountain but the spirit of the mountain'; and from the Apocrypha and Philo and Josephus to Gabirol and Maimonides we are told that adherents of other religions are also seekers: 'The yearning of them all is to draw nigh Thee.'

But this does not mean that Judaism abandons its own positions, or that it has no positions to abandon. It has its doctrine of the unity of God with its corollaries of one world, one humanity, one truth, and one good. It has its concrete detail of the right way for man: the Ten Commandments, the law of holiness. It has its guiding vision of the creation of man in God's likeness and, with it, the promise of his *re*creation. It has its institutions, its disciplines, its liturgy, its austerities; its historical sorrows, its annual recall of common joys. It has its great acceptance of the world and its fullness, its condemnation of asceticism, its holding fast to the principle of enjoyment under control. It has its great rejection of polytheism and image-worship, and its abhorrence of all forms of cruelty and injustice. It can agree with Buddhism that there are metaphysical questions the solution of which is irrelevant to the religious life; but it clings to the link between God who is at least personal (though he is, too, much more) and the individual soul, a soul which, within our purview at least, is one and enduring. It is this living dependence of the living soul on the living God ('This God is our God for ever and ever; he will be our guide even unto death'; 'Thou wilt keep him in perfect peace whose mind is stayed on Thee, because he trusteth in Thee') which turns what might have been a bare deism, on the one hand, or a bare moralism on the other, into the most lasting, in human history, of all religions.

Dreams are notoriously an index to character. The dream of Judaism is of the coming of the Messiah; or rather, since the Messiah in Judaism is not so much a person as the inaugurator of a new epoch in history, of the coming of the messianic age. A famous picture of this age is that of

Isaiah 11. It depicts its coming into being as the victory of wisdom over violence, of persuasion over force; and it sees the fruit of the victory as the triumph of justice and the advent of universal peace. But all these, peace, justice and wisdom, are manifestations of the spirit patterned on and required by the unity of God. It is only when and because the earth is filled with the knowledge of God that men will do no more violence or wrong.

This is a vision of the end, but it reflects the call constituting Judaism at the beginning. Abraham's family was singled out to follow the way of God, that is, to do justice and judgment. The function of the 'shoot of the stock of Jesse' upon whom 'the spirit of God' is to 'rest' is to complete the task and bring that knowledge of the way to all.

When Maimonides in the concluding chapter of his *Guide for the Perplexed* came to offer in his turn a pocket definition of Judaism, he did so in the words of Jeremiah: 'Let him that glorieth glory in this, that he understandeth and knoweth me that I am the Lord which exercise loving kindness, judgment, and righteousness, in the earth; for in these things I delight, saith the Lord.' The last words ('for in these things I delight') mean, he says, that what God requires from man is the exercise on this earth of kindness, judgement and righteousness: the knowledge of God is to lead to the imitation of his ways. Thus Maimonides, too, the author of the first and greatest of the standard codes of Judaism, gives clear expression to what we have seen to be its essential teaching from the first.

And he does not shrink from the explicit drawing of the logical consequence of monotheism. In principle, there can be no exclusions. As his last word, he added (tradition says in his own hand) a Hebrew distich to the original manuscript of the *Guide* (the book itself was written in Arabic):

> God is very near to all who call him
> If they call him in truth and turn to him
> He is found by everyone who seeks him,
> If he walks forward and goes not astray.

Salvation is from God, but it has to be sought and striven for; and it is for all who seek and strive.

VIII

There are many strands in Judaism, and it is easy (as indeed might well have been done in this paper) to fasten on any of them to the exclusion of any or every other. The only remedy is to follow Hillel's advice: 'Go and learn', and learn as much and as widely and as freely as possible.

Authority, Religion, and Law

❧

I

THE recent Cambridge production of the *Antigone* has given occasion
to ponder again Antigone's spirited declaration on the Unwritten Laws.
King Creon, on political grounds, has forbidden the burial of Polyneices.
Antigone, on religious grounds, has defied him; and she has justified
herself by distinguishing between the changing regulations of a human
ruler and the eternal laws of heaven. Creon says to her: 'Knewest thou the
edict that forbade this deed?', and the dialogue proceeds:

> ANTIG. I knew it. Why, how else? for it was public.
>
> CREON. And such laws thou couldst dare to overstep:
>
> ANTIG. Yes; for it was not Zeus that published them . . .
> I did not deem your edicts of such force
> That a mere mortal could o'erride the Gods'
> Unwritten, never-failing ordinances.
> For these live not today nor yesterday,
> But always: none knows when they first came forth.
>
> TRANS. R. C. TREVELYAN

That is all we hear, the bare affirmation of the difference in kind between *ad hoc* regulation and law; but the action of the play proceeds to
show that it is the eternal law of heaven, not the fiat of the ruler, which
prevails. The play is called by the name of Antigone but its central figure is
not Antigone. It is the bearer of political power, the king; and the play
demonstrates the breakdown, in the person of Creon, of the political
point of view. Political authority is essentially temporary and relative, a
device to meet the changing circumstance of ever-shifting power. It is
myth, not truth. When it claims to be absolute, it is doomed. It nullifies
itself and engenders its own destruction.

The substance of this essay was given as a talk on the BBC Third Programme on
25 March 1959. It was published in the *Hibbert Journal*, 58/2 (Jan. 1960), 115–20. Reproduced by permission of HarperCollins Publishers.

II

There is a very similar, yet very different, story in the Bible, King David lusted after Bathsheba and contrived to have her husband killed. But the thing David had done, we are told, displeased God, and God sent a prophet to David, and the prophet told the king about a rich man and a poor man, and how the rich man took the poor man's one ewe lamb, and David's anger was greatly kindled against the man and he cried: 'As the Lord liveth, the man that hath done this is worthy to die; and he shall restore the lamb fourfold because he did this thing and because he had no pity'; and Nathan said to David: 'Thou art the man. Thus saith the Lord, the God of Israel: Thou hast smitten Uriah the Hittite with the sword. Now therefore the sword shall never depart from thine house.'

It is a deathless story, and a breathless one. It has none of the calm dignity of the Greek. And it presents a clearer case of bare-faced tyranny. Apart from his sordid passion, David had no excuse for his conduct. Creon certainly had. Polyneices was an enemy and had fought against the state. The state had every apparent right to outlaw him and deny him burial. Uriah the Hittite was a hero. He had fought *for* the state and had fallen in its defence. The only thing one can say for David is that he wasted no time in trying to excuse himself. Creon comes on the stage already primed with a political theory. Life and happiness, he says, depend upon the existence of a stable community; any action performed for the stability of the community is therefore justified. The safety of the community is the highest law, and no one can assess it better than the man in charge, and so power and right are identical. David did not descend to such sophistries. The two cases present the same conflict, the conflict between the will of the ruler on the one side and right and God's law on the other. Creon adopts a myth to cover the conflict up. David withdraws his side of it, the ruler's will, and submits to law.

And there is a further and no less important point. Law is seen as harnessed to particularity. General exhortations to do good are of little use. We need to know *what* good to do; and we need to recognize that it is *we* who have to do it, and have to do it whether we like it or not. Law and its authority are not an abstraction. It is for here and now, for the particular situation in which we ourselves stand and act. We talk too easily about '*the* moral law'. Is there a moral *law*, or are there not, rather, moral *laws*? And moral laws have their meaning only with reference to individuals and concrete and specific acts. It is to bring this home that the prophet was sent. *De te fabula*. '*Thou* art the man.'

III

The prophet was *sent*. He is only a messenger. His authority is that of his master. For philosophy (and particularly political philosophy), authority is a problem. For religion, it is a fact. It is worth while to consider the biblical presentation of that fact and to weigh its implications.

Much current opinion will have it that religion has nothing to do with authority. Religion, it holds, is primarily a matter of feeling. It is 'communion', the coming together of the 'I' and the 'thou'. It is personal, the joining of spirit with spirit.

This account of the nature of religion has had a wide appeal. But if we confront it with the Hebrew Scriptures, we shall see that it is unsatisfactory. The Hebrew Scriptures are full of an 'I'; but the 'I' is not human: it is God. And they are full, too, of a 'thou'. But the 'thou', we men, is far from being on an equality with the 'I' which is God. God for the Hebrew Scriptures is not just spirit communing with, or being communed with by, other spirits. He is spirit's creator. In a remarkable phrase found twice in the Pentateuch, he is 'God of the spirits of all flesh'. He is not man's fellow. He is man's maker.

As man's maker he calls man to account. He asks man questions, breaks into man's life; expects every man to do his duty. The prophetic sentence is clear-cut; God hath *told* thee, O man, what is good; God *requireth* of thee to do justice and to act kindly. Here is no dialogue, no debate, no consultation. God *told* us what is good and we must do it; God *requires* of us to act justly and to love kindness. Cruelty and injustice are not bad form or bad for the liver or bad for society; they are in themselves *wrong*. There is here no communion of spirit with spirit but a claim, a demand, a *com*mand. When God asks Job 'Where wast thou when I laid the foundations of the earth?' the question is not a prelude to a friendly tête-à-tête. It is the setting for a declaration of authority based on the only ground for authority that there is.

Authority (this is not a pun) derives from authorship, and biblical religion affirms that the world has an author. The world did not just grow; it was made. Its maker is wise, since as maker he knows the facts. He is good: he cares for the souls which he made. And he manifests himself in moral directions. He told us, for example, what is good. He expects us—*expects* us—to act justly and to love kindness.

IV

This has always seemed to be remarkable. Other gods—the gods of other religions—never did that. They were always busied with personal matters, or they confined themselves to generalities. Only the God of the Hebrew Bible pronounced the Ten Commandments and promulgated the law of holiness, that is, laid down not only general advice to do good but specified what good we should do: 'Thou shalt not glean thy vineyard, neither shalt thou gather the fallen fruit of thy vineyard; thou shalt leave them for the poor and the stranger: I am the Lord thy God . . . The wages of a hired servant shall not abide with thee all night until the morning. Thou shalt not curse the deaf nor put a stumbling-block before the blind, but thou shalt fear thy God: I am the Lord . . . Thou shalt not take up a false report . . . Thou shalt not follow a multitude to do evil . . . If thou meet thine enemy's ox or his ass going astray, thou shalt surely bring it back to him again . . . Just balances, just weights shall ye have: I am the Lord your God . . .'. The Creator turns out to be not only 'great and terrible'—that is, powerful and awe-inspiring (numinous, as we say today). He is a practical moralist, laying down rules for our conduct.

God dominates the Hebrew Scriptures, and one of his favourite phrases seems to be *Get out*. He projected the whole Judaeo-Christian tradition into human life by saying to Abraham: '*Get thee out* of thy country and thy father's house'; and he continued it by 'getting' Abraham's descendants 'out' of the land of Egypt, 'out' of the house of bondage. He says to Moses: 'Go.' He says to Elijah: 'Go.' He says to Amos and Isaiah: 'Go.' The only variant is the awesome summons to Ezekiel: 'Stand up on thy feet and I will speak with thee.'

There is another passage in the Hebrew Scriptures in which God says this to a man. It introduces the chapters in which God answers Job out of the whirlwind. Job seems to have thought that with his questions he could stump God. God's reply is to show Job that the questions man can ask of God are as nothing compared with the questions God can ask of himself. God has no need to apologize. His purposes are wider than man. Where *was* man when God laid the foundations of the earth? And God proceeds to bring before Job a panorama of the vast creation in which man himself holds so small a place.

The instructive thing is that Job is satisfied. He 'laid his hand upon his mouth': 'I had heard of Thee before but by the hearing of the ear, but now mine eye seeth Thee.' What had been brought before Job were the wonders of the Creation; but what Job saw was the wonder, the unique wonder, of the Creator. He says: 'mine eye seeth *Thee*'. He does not say: 'mine eye seeth Behemoth and Leviathan'. He had an immediate apprehension of the one source of all in which power, authority, goodness and wisdom meet together.

V

The difficulties in the idea of creation are notorious. They arise from our human inability to distinguish creation from manufacture. But creation is certainly not manufacture; and the word is used in our fumbling human language in order to express, in however halting a way, the difference in kind between the self-dependent and the dependent. The self-dependent—God—does not need to be pushed into existence, since he is always and already there; the dependent—the world and man—if not pushed into existence, would not be there at all. This is the ultimate seat and secret of religion, the difference in kind between the I AM and the mere 'is'. It is a secret of which perhaps, in our human experience, only the analogy of the arts can give us a distant glimpse. As Samuel Alexander (and more recently Dorothy Sayers) taught us, some slight inkling of the nature of cosmic creation can be taught in the facts of human creation.

The same is true of the effect of creation upon us. Any genuine creation seems to hit us *from without*. It summons us, demands our attention. And so too even for the artist. What he is creating seems to possess an energy of its own. The spectator or audience feels the compulsion in the work of art. The artist feels the compulsion within himself. But it is compulsion. It is what in religion the prophets recognize as a 'burden'. As the Gentile prophet Balaam says in the Bible: 'Have *I* any power to speak anything? The word that God putteth in my mouth, that do I speak.'

The analogy with the arts does not of course demonstrate the fact of divine creation or the existence of a divine creator. It only guides the mind to sympathy with the affirmation from which the whole Bible stems: 'In the beginning God created.'

VI

The Hebrew Scriptures attest to an experience; but it is the experience of the transcendental, a transcendental which manifests itself in law. Law is the control of feeling. It is not so much, as Aristotle called it, mind *without* passion as mind *in control of* passion.

Passion is the experience of the immanent, and its characteristic manifestation is myth. In its place myth has much to give. It is an enrichment
of life. It provides release to feeling. It is one source of plastic and literary
art. But it must be known for what it is, myth, not taken for what it is not,
truth. When we take it for what it is not, we surrender ourselves to the
fraudulent and the sham; we are in the grip of outward seeming.

In religious language, myth is an idol. Idols are manufactured objects
of worship, and the Bible mocks at the men who bow down to the work
of their own hands. Yet graven images are not the only idols. They are
only the more obvious ones. And they are today not the most dangerous.
The dangerous idols are those we make of words, phrases like 'the state',
'race', 'way of life', 'progress', 'democracy'. We fall down and worship
them, and, like Creon in the Greek play, are in the end broken by them.
'They that make them become like them', empty, hollow, unreal.

VII

It is the mark of our semi-literate civilization that it has strengthened the
power of myth and created a new idolatry. In the business world myth
appears as high-pressure advertising, in the political world as slogans and
propaganda; and as an expert in the new sham name given to these
pseudo-sciences is reported as saying recently: 'A community in which
"public relations" assume increasing importance is itself on the down-
grade.' The more myth is accepted as truth, the lower and more degraded
is the society which accepts it.

But there are hopeful signs of a new sanity too. Our world is full of
strife, but whatever the occasion may be, the root issue is everywhere the
same. It is the issue between Antigone and Creon, between Nathan the
prophet and King David. It is that between law and personal will, between law and the darker passions, between law and the deeper feelings.
Slowly, very slowly, law is winning the day, and men's bodies are being
rescued from the consequences of feeling and passion, whether other
men's or their own.

This is the great public drama of our time; and if we follow out its
implications, whether from the vantage-point of New Delhi, where an
international congress of jurists has been working on the theory of the
rule of law, or from that of the practice of the United States today, where
the Supreme Court has taken its place as the educator (the *paidagogos*)
of the nation, we may perhaps find what we are all equally seeking: 'authentic tidings of invisible things'.

But I submit two thoughts for consideration. The first is that just as the struggle of law to re-create our societies is affected by freeing men's bodies from the bondage to feeling and passion, the fruit of which is oppression and violence, so in the same way the struggle of religion to re-create men's souls is effected through freeing them from the bondage to feeling and passion, the index of which is myth.

My second thought is harder and I offer it in fear and trembling. Perhaps the two struggles are one and the same.

Moralization and Demoralization in Jewish Ethics

❧

I

To explain my title, I offer two illustrations. The first is well known, and I adduce it only because its significance is often overlooked.

The Mishnah in Sanhedrin recounts the way in which the old Jewish court tried to bring home to witnesses in a capital case the uniqueness of human life and the consequent responsibility of their position. The court would have them brought in, we read, and would admonish them as follows:

You are not to speak from guesswork or from gossip or from reliance on a third party however trustworthy in your eyes. You must understand that cases involving the death penalty are not like those which involve only money. In money cases a false witness can atone for the damage he has caused by a money payment. In capital cases there rests on his head the blood of the condemned man and the blood of the descendants [who may have yet to be born to him] to the end of days.

The Mishnah then goes on:

It is for this that man was created one, to instruct us that whoever destroys one life, it is accounted to him by Scripture as if he had destroyed a whole world, and whoever preserves one life, it is accounted to him by Scripture as if he had preserved a whole world.

As it stands thus, this statement is completely general. The original creation was of one man, and from that one man came the life of all human beings. To preserve one life is thus to preserve a whole world of humanity: to destroy one life is to destroy a whole world. This is obviously the sense meant, and this is obviously the proper text; and so we find it—I am quoting the late Professor J. N. Epstein—in all exact

First delivered, in a slightly different form, in London as the Leo Baeck Memorial Lecture for 1961, under the auspices of the London Society for Jewish Study and the Leo Baeck Lodge of the Independent Order of B'nai B'rith. It is reprinted with permission from *JUDAISM: A Quarterly Journal of Jewish Life and Thought*, vol. 11, no. 4 (Fall 1962), 291–302. © 1962 American Jewish Congress.

manuscripts and early references. Our printed texts however insert the word *meyisrael*, and therefore read *not* 'whoever preserves or destroys one *life*', *but* 'whoever preserves or destroys one *Jew*'. The addition of the word *meyisrael* produces a sudden, and ludicrous, deflation.

A similar point may be noted in out text of a verse (21) in the last chapter of Isaiah. According to the Septuagint and most modern translations, and with explicit emphasis in the Targum, the verse says that 'some of the Gentiles also will I take for priests and for levites, saith the Lord'.[1] This could be expressed, however, by *lekohanim*, with a *sheva* under the *lamed*, not, as in the Masoretic Text, *lakohanim*, with a *patah*. Now this *patah*, which belongs of course to the sphere not of text but of exegesis (the independent vowel system in our text of the Hebrew Bible being, as is well known, of late date), allows a different translation altogether, *not* 'for priests' *but* (as in the American Jewish Publication Society version of 1917) 'for *the* priests', that is, for the already existing priests. The persons referred to are not to be priests themselves; they are to be 'for', that is, for the use of, the priests already there. Like the Gibeonites of old,[2] they are to do the menial jobs.

I am not decrying this kind of service: 'They also serve who only stand and wait.' I am only pointing out the nature of the change of meaning which is made possible by the choice of vowel. Instead of what at first sight looks like the widest throwing open, to 'all nations and tongues', of the presumed privilege of being priests on the holy mountain, we have, or we seem to have, only the admission of the non-Jew to the offices of hewers of wood and drawers of water. When the repentant Gentile comes to the restored Temple with the assured expectation of being offered, and performing, honourable office, he runs the risk of being told that he has not read the text accurately. The text has a *patah* and not a *sheva*, and therefore his place is (as it were) not in the drawing-room but the kitchen.

II

These instances of 'deflation', or even 'debasement', in Jewish ethics will suffice to explain and illustrate my title. They also reveal its insufficiency. For it is obvious that what they teach us is not so much that such instances exist in Jewish ethics as that we seem to have no Jewish ethics to tell us

[1] The significant references to understand the peculiar interpretation offered by the Jewish commentators are: Midrash *Shohar tov* on Psalm 87; *Yalkut* 207 end.

[2] So Joseph Kimchi, as quoted by his son.

how we may recognize them. The insertion of the word *meyisrael* in the Mishnah passage, or the reading the verse from Isaiah with a *pataḥ*, represents a change in moral conception, yet I do not notice it remarked on as such by our commentators; and this suggests the reflection that having noticed it, they think it of no significance. This would seem to be a monstrous situation. The fact that the latest editor of the Mishnah can allow the printed text to remain with the word *meyisrael* in, and only in his *second* set of additional Notes and Afterthoughts to remark that its omission would be superior, makes one think that our greatest scholars, so sensitive to the minutest points of history and philology, are singularly *in*sensitive to points of moral concern.

Yet these instances cut very deep. Each pair of readings involves a contrary moral attitude; and it is imperative for us, in the normal workings of our lives, to receive guidance between them. Is the view of Judaism on the subject of the place of the non-Jew in the restored Jerusalem that indicated by the Masorah and the American Jewish version; or can we follow the Septuagint and, most explicitly, the Targum, and read our text with a *sheva* and not a *pataḥ*? Is the view of Judaism on the subject of the sacredness of life that indicated by the printed text of our Mishnah,[3] i.e., apparently, that only Jews count; or can we, with the manuscripts and early authorities and Professor Albeck's second Afterthoughts, omit the word *meyisrael*? These are important issues, and we need to know which of the contrary views we are to account as Judaism.

III

It is the consideration of this sort of problem which is the province of the science of ethics; and in the light of the instances I have given it will not be unfair to say that Jewish ethics, or more properly an ethics of Judaism, does not exist.[4] I am not saying that Jewish *morality* does not exist, or

---

[3] See the note of Maharsha (Rabbi Samuel Edels, 1555–1631) in the Romm (Vilna) edition of the Talmud, *Sanhedrin*, appendix, p. 10*a*, col. 2, 1. 4 ff., mercifully omitted in the excerpts given in the current editions of the *Ein ya'akov*.

[4] I regretfully hold to this opinion in spite of the great and justly honoured names of Hermann Cohen and Moritz Lazarus (of which the managing editor of *Judaism* has reminded me). Both of these were too immersed in Kant, and Kantian modes of thought and expression, to be able to do independent justice to our subject. This does not mean that the study of their writings is unprofitable. Very much to the contrary. They are often richly suggestive, as are, too, the essays of Ahad Ha'am, Klausner, Neumark, Shai Ish Hurwitz, and many another writing in Hebrew; and there is much to be learned from books like the posthumous *Bemalkhut hayahadut* of the late Rabbi Abraham Chen. But

that Judaism has no *morals*. It is Jewish *ethics*, or more properly, as I have said, an ethics of Judaism, which does not exist. Ethics is the *theory* of morals. It is the reflective enquiry into the *nature* of morals. It is the reasoned attempt to see, or (possibly) to introduce, order and principle in moral ideas. An ethics of Judaism would be the theory of the morals of Judaism, the attempt to see, or (possibly) to introduce, order and principle in the moral ideas of Judaism. Thus we need two things: the first, a plain statement of the moral ideas of Judaism; the second, the bringing of them together into one intelligible and coherent view. The order of enquiry is important: the statement first, the theory second. So many attempts at an ethics of Judaism have failed because of the mistaken assumption that ethics is a deductive science and that (ideally at least) moral ideas can be excogitated from the blue.

I say that the creation of an ethics of Judaism is an urgent need, but I do not mean that it can be produced by authority. Even the smaller points of morals cannot be determined in this way. It is of no use convening a rabbinical synod in order to change that *pataḥ* into a *sheva*, or to decide that the next official edition of the Mishnah should print the original and not the falsified text. Moral attitudes cannot be changed by acts of synods. I am pleading for something else. I am begging our wise men to turn their attention towards the erection of a coherent set of ideas about the values of Judaism; and by a coherent set of ideas I mean a reasoned account, not a series of oracular pronouncements. It is *a reasoned account of the values of Judaism* which constitutes what I have called an ethics of Judaism. It may necessitate some hard words and severe wrenches. Not everything printed in Hebrew, not even everything printed in some editions of our prayer-books, is Judaism; and I recall to the reader's attention the fact that Maimonides, giving his reasons, felt compelled to dismiss an early kabbalistic classic as sheer idolatry, to be not wondered at as a sublime mystery but, simply, destroyed.

IV

We are sometimes told that the interest in theory, the seeking after principles, the desire for order and coherence, is a heresy of the Greeks,

no one of these offers the reasoned account of the values of Judaism which our subject calls for. For the same reason the *musar* literature, both medieval and modern, is inadequate. It does not contain a coherent set of ideas knit together by thought-out principles.

and alien to Judaism. I do not find this so. On the contrary, I find traces in the oldest tradition of just that of which we are in search. Indeed, what I am going to suggest is that questions of principle and, in particular, questions concerning the principles of morals, that is, questions of ethics, occupied the minds of the creators and upholders of historical Judaism much as they do ours, and in much the same fashion.

I offer a preliminary and simple example:

There is an elementary distinction, basic to all discussions about morals, between the two uses of the word 'can'. Let me turn to the Greeks. Socrates, after his condemnation at the hands of the court, is told by his friends that he can walk out of prison: arrangements have been made and the gaoler will look the other way. Socrates retorts: 'I can; but *can* I?' *Physically*, of course he can. He can flex the muscles of his legs and walk out. But 'can' he *morally*? *Ought* he? Is it not perhaps his duty as a citizen to obey the law and to stay? Just as in the one sense, the physical sense, he can, so in the other, the moral sense, he can not.

We find this ambiguity of the word 'can' in the Hebrew of the Pentateuch itself. We are told that if we see our neighbour's animal astray in the fields, we *cannot* shut our eyes. But *can* we not? Of course we can—in one sense. A famous cartoon in *Punch* once showed a cross-Channel passenger in the middle of a rough passage taking refuge in a freshly carpeted private cabin. A steward comes up to him and says: 'But, sir, you can't be sick here.' To which he retorts: 'Oh, *can't* I?'—and *is*. Of course we can keep our eyes shut. There is nothing easier—physically. But morally? Ought we? Perhaps, after all, morally, we can *not*.

This distinction was noticed specifically in rabbinic literature. We read in Deuteronomy 12: 7: 'Thou canst not eat in thy gates.' Canst not? Of course we can; we can eat anywhere. But as Rabbi Joshua b. Korchah remarks explicitly: *Yakhol ani aval ein ani rasha'i* (I can, but I am not allowed); and he quotes in support Joshua 15: 63, where the children of Judah 'could not' drive the Jebusites out. Could not? Of course they could—physically; but morally they could not because of their oath, and therefore *yekholim hayu aval einam rasha'im*.

The distinction is simple but fundamental. It is that between the 'is' and the 'ought'. But the important thing to observe is that the distinction was not only recognized in our literature. It had its special terminology assigned to it—in our instance, the physical *yakhol* is distinguished from the moral *rasha'i*; and this suggests that it was discussed, which means that people had developed a sense not only for moral fact but for ethical theory.

V

We are used to the idea of discussion in matters of halakhah; and we are used to the pronouncements of the aggadists, both among themselves and in controversy with non-Jews, on matters of morals and religion. But these latter are as a rule pronouncements, dicta, supported by verses, not by argument. This is the rule, but there are exceptions; and these exceptions would seem to testify to the existence of regular argument, that is, of rational reflection, on these matters. The theological argumentation with the neighbouring idolaters is well known and is certainly based on a reasoned review of the issues discussed, however meagrely the theoretical basis survives in the short reports preserved in the existing literature. But let us consider the implications of the no less well known *internal* confrontation of some of the great first- and second-century rabbis.

I take a famous, but to my mind imperfectly understood, instance both for its intrinsic importance and because it illustrates further my plea that our printers and scholars pay insufficient attention to the moral significance of our classical literature.

I start with the conventional text of the well-known passage of the Sifra on Leviticus 19: 18: 'Rabbi Akiva said: "'And thou shalt love thy neighbour as thyself'—this is a great principle in the Law." Ben Azzai said: "'This is the book of the generations of man'—this is a greater principle than that."'

On the face of it we have here a confrontation not of reasoned arguments but of biblical verses, the verses being arbitrarily chosen and set one against the other. Akiva gives us no reason for his choice of verse; and Ben Azzai gives no reason for his assertion that his verse embodies a greater principle than Akiva's. We are not even told in what sense one principle is 'greater' than the other, or for that matter what a 'principle' (*kelal*) is. So far as this report is concerned we may make any guess we like. The accepted explanation of Ben Azzai's statement that his verse embodies a greater principle than Akiva's is that Akiva's verse speaks only of neighbour, Ben Azzai's of man in general; and if we happen ourselves to think that concern with all men is superior to concern with the man next door (though obviously Akiva did not mean that restriction at all), we approve Ben Azzai and accept his valuation.

But this, as I say, is guesswork. For reasoned argument we need *reasons*, a considered statement in the light of a comprehensive principle; and this fortunately is preserved for us, although in a mutilated form, in the midrash of Ben Azzai's verse *in situ*.

I translate the conventional text:

Ben Azzai said: ' "This is the book of the generations of man"—this is a great principle in the Law.' Rabbi Akiva said: ' "And thou shalt love thy neighbour as thyself"—this is a great principle in the Law. For thou shouldst not say: "Seeing that I have been treated contemptuously, let my fellow be treated contemptuously with me; seeing that I have been cursed, let my fellow be cursed with me." ' Rabbi Tanhumah said: 'If thou actest thus, know who it is thou dost contemn. "In the likeness of God he made him." '

The key to the understanding of this passage as a whole is to be found in an acute remark of the brilliant (and concise) seventeenth-century commentator on the Midrash, the Matnot Kehunah, who saw that an 'etc.' (*vegomer*) had dropped out of our conventional text, and in order to understand Ben Azzai's point we have to see the whole of the verse he quotes, and not its first words only. In its entirety it reads: 'This is the book of the generations of man (or Adam): when God created man (or Adam), it is in the likeness of God that he made him.' If this remark of the Matnot Kehunah is accepted (as it clearly must be; incidentally, the addition of such an 'etc.' to many other difficult passages would help solve many mysteries), all we have to do is to see that the words 'for thou shouldst not say' belong to Ben Azzai and not to Akiva. The whole passage then becomes:

Rabbi Akiva said: ' "And thou shalt love they neighbour as thyself"—this is a great principle in the Law.' Ben Azzai said: 'The verse "This is the book of the generations of man; in the day that God created man, in the likeness of God made he him" is a greater principle. It teaches us that we must not say [as we might if we only loved our neighbour *as* ourselves]: "Since *I* have been contemned, let *my fellow too* be contemned just as I was; since *I* have been cursed, let *my fellow too* be cursed just as I was." '

Rabbi Tanhumah [a later teacher] explained: 'If you do that, know who it is whom you contemn—you contemn God in whose likeness man was made.'

(In order to anticipate any objection that this is a 'subjective' and doubtful reconstruction of my own, I point out in passing that I am quoting the *ipsissima verba* of the Rabad [Rabbi Abraham ben David of Posquières, c.1125–98], not however the philosopher of that appellation but the twelfth-century French talmudist, anti-Maimunist and kabbalist, in his commentary on the Sifra, a commentary first published by I. H. Weiss in 1862, that is, a couple of centuries or so *after* the death of the Matnot Kehunah. See too Theodor's note in his edition of *Bereshit rabbah*.[5])

[5] Cf. also Hermann Cohen, *Religion der Vernunft*, 137 ff. *Ed.* [This note appears in the original essay.]

These textual considerations are trying, but they are important, for they demonstrate again the insensitivity of our scholars to questions of morals: two recent so-called 'critical' editions of the *Midrash rabbah* on Genesis reprint without comment the conventional text! But apart from this regrettable fact, one should note the genuine importance of our results. We have uncovered in our classical literature a regular argument on a point of morals conducted on rational lines. Ben Azzai does not just produce a verse and make an *ex cathedra* statement about it. He gives a sound reason for his assertion that his principle is greater than Akiva's. If Akiva's principle is to be the determining principle in morals, moral action (Ben Azzai argues) would disappear. It would result in passive acquiescence in the face of wrong. A person who had himself suffered would shrug his shoulders at the suffering of others. He would say, and on Akiva's principles say rightly: 'What then? *I* have been treated badly. Why should not others be treated badly too?' It is to this that Ben Azzai objects. He says: 'Each and every man *in himself* has his dignity. He bears within him the likeness of God. And *therefore*, even though we may have been treated badly ourselves, we should strive that others should be treated properly.'

Ben Azzai is thus more than an empty universalist. He is not only extending the boundaries of moral concern from neighbour to man. He is repudiating the view expressed in that most abominable of modern phrases: 'It's one of those things', or 'It's the same everywhere'. For Ben Azzai the moral claim is independent of our personal situation, or the human situation as such, *because* it derives from the *self-transcendent* character of man.

But what of Akiva? I think he accepted Ben Azzai's argument. We know that he was big enough to change his mind on points of halakhah. I suggest that he changed his mind on this point of morals too. Recall the great saying preserved in that book of great sayings, the *Pirkei avot*: 'Beloved is man in that he was created in the likeness, and even greater love was shown him in making him conscious of the fact that he was created in the likeness.' We have no mention here of fellow Jew (this comes in his next sentence) or even neighbour, but *man*, and man (in accordance with Ben Azzai's principle) as 'created in the likeness'. We would seem thus to have unearthed in the literature not only a reasoned argument on morals between our early teachers but that most unusual of all things, an argument in which one of the disputants was convinced by the other and changed his views accordingly.

VI

The value of such a principle as Ben Azzai's, a principle not just asserted but supported by reasoning and tested in discussion, is that it offers a standard. It gives a criterion by which we can determine the comparative quality of our actions. We now know, for example, that to sit passive in the face of wrong, a wrong which we may indeed have suffered ourselves but which is for all that wrong, is to deny morality. We dare not say: 'Oh, it is just one of those things.' Things have nothing to do with persons, and each man is a person, created in the likeness. It is respect for the likeness, not love of neighbour, which is only an instance of it and possibly in some cases a misleading or at least misguided instance of it, which in Ben Azzai's view (and in Akiva's later view) is the spring and criterion of morality. Actions which proceed from it are therefore moral actions and right; actions which deny it or contradict it, immoral and wrong. I have no doubt at all what Ben Azzai would have thought of that *patah* in the verse from Isaiah or the insertion of that word *meyisrael* in the text from the Mishnah with which I started; but my point is that he would have judged, as he would in my view undoubtedly *have* judged, not from whim or emotion but from a clearly articulated first principle, that is, rationally.

A principle, clearly articulated and firmly grasped, enables us not only to judge. It enables us to correct and improve. It enables us, out of the multifarious material accumulated by time, to select. I have pointed out elsewhere[6] that the great service to Judaism performed by Maimonides was to show us how to master the indiscriminate mass of aggadah, the great *dis*service of the kabbalists and their modern followers to attempt to subject us to it again. Basically, the problem is that of the *translation of aggadah into halakhah*; but whereas much attention has been given by our scholars to the rules of hermeneutics by which new guidance was found in (or extracted from) reluctant, or recalcitrant, texts in the sphere of halakhah, little if any, has been paid, apart from in the work of Heinemann, to the similar activity engaged in the sphere of aggadah. Yet I think it can be shown that part of the conscious energy of the talmudic rabbis was devoted to increasing and developing the higher elements in Jewish morality, and depressing or obliterating the lower.

We have here a most inviting field of research for our sociologists, and I welcome with all my heart and all possible encouragement such studies as

---

[6] In my book on Maimonides: *The Guide for the Perplexed: Moses Maimonides* (London: Hutchinson's University Library, 1948).

Professor Jacob Katz's recent *Exclusiveness and Tolerance.*[7] This book opens up almost unlimited fields of enquiry into these important matters and conceptions, and it is particularly valuable in that it treats of them from the point of view of history and of the halakhah. Since we are dealing now with the problem of an *ethics* of Judaism, our concern is with aggadah, in the sense of the preliminary moulding of men's minds to accept ideas which produce finally the concrete practical ruling which is halakhah; and it is sufficient for this purpose to note the existence of the process of what may broadly be called *moralization.*

The meaning of this word will appear from definite examples. Its need is only emphasized by the often violent methods adopted in order to effect it. The rabbis' hands were tied. They were bound to an inviolable text. But they limited, extended, broadened, narrowed, ignored, blandly changed, even in some striking cases perverted, the plain sense, in order to achieve their aim. They knew that philology is a good servant. They knew even better that it is a bad master; and they had grasped the truth that the determining factor in all exegesis is the whole context and not the isolated word or sentence or even paragraph.

By a 'whole context' I mean here something wider than Professor Barr's, in his recent admirable *Semantics of Biblical Language,*[8] or in my own Montefiore Memorial Lecture[9] of some years ago. I mean a general framework of interpretation, consciously adopted and consistently carried through. For example, the prayer-book speaks of God as having given the Jewish people, 'in the light of His countenance', *torat ḥayim ve'ahavat ḥesed utsedakah uverakhah veraḥamim veḥayim veshalom* (a Law of life and a love of kindness, and righteousness and blessing and pity and life and peace). True, the early text of Saadya, which is pretty much that of Maimonides and (with minor variants) of the Spanish and Italian rites in general, reads *torah veḥayim, ahavah vaḥesed* (Law *and* life, love *and* kindness, etc.). But verbal minutiae apart, the collocation of terms— each one of which, and in some cases the pairs of words together, can be documented by countless references both in Holy Writ and in the rabbinic writings—the collocation of words itself expresses succinctly a complete framework of ideas or what I call a 'whole context'.

For traditional Jewry the Torah—that is, please remember, *Judaism*— was essentially and primarily a doctrine of life and love and kindness and fair dealing and pity. It is no use anybody saying anything to the contrary, be he anthropologist or theologian or moral philosopher or mythologist.

---

[7] Oxford: Oxford University Press, 1961.   [8] Oxford: Oxford University Press, 1961.
[9] [See pp. 80–94 above.]

For Jewry the Law, the Torah, is a law of life and kindness and love and decency and pity. This being the guiding principle, what ever appears contrary to it must be explained away.

And it *was* explained away. For example, in the case of a whole city going idolatrous we read (Deuteronomy 13): 'And ye shall gather all its spoil into the midst of its open square, and burn the city and all its spoil with fire.' Its open square? Here is an opportunity for modifying the judgment, and we are told: 'If it has not got a square, you do not do this.' True, the contrary opinion is also expressed that if the city has no square, you should make one and carry the sentence out; but the point is that openings for moralization were sought for. The guiding principle was encouraged to squeeze out the narrower views.

This particular case would be an instance of conscious limitation, and we have the natural consequence in the dictum: 'The case of a condemned city never occurred nor ever will occur.' In the same way the problem of the savage treatment of the 'seven nations' is met by the observation that they have long disappeared and therefore the regulations affecting them are of antiquarian interest only; though even so we are told, on the legal principle that there is no punishment without previous warning, both that, unless proper warning had been issued, the sentence did not hold and that, if the inhabitants changed their ways, no sentence was imposed at all.

The audacity, both philological and historical, by which the process of moralization was effected shows vividly the intense feeling with which a way out was sought. I love that Mishnah which relates how an Ammonite, against the express prohibition of the Pentateuch and the explicit opposition of the official Patriarchate, was admitted into the congregation. The ground was that there were no longer any Ammonites (or indeed any other 'pure' races) in existence because Nebuchadnezzar, with his policy of transferring populations, mixed us all up! But in the same way as the early authorities could on occasion get around the obvious sense of the Pentateuch,[10] so later authorities could on occasion change the clear ruling of the Mishnah. Maimonides, for example, against the explicit ruling of the Mishnah, directed a convert to Judaism to use the full text of the prayer-book blessings and say 'the God of our fathers', and 'Who brought us out of the land of Egypt', etc.; and his ruling is so important in its general attitude, and so helpful for our needs of today,

---

[10] It will be remembered that an Ammonite *woman* was in any case 'admitted into the congregation' on the ground that the prohibiting text says 'Ammonite' in the *masculine*.

that it is worth recalling and pondering. I draw particular attention to its calm conviction and its serene good sense:

Thou hast asked about the blessings and the prayers, and whether thou shouldst say 'Our God and the God of our fathers' and 'Who sanctified us with his commandments' and so on.

Thou shouldst use them all and change nothing but shouldst pray as any born Jew, whether thou prayest in private or whether thou leadest the congregation in prayer.

The root of the matter is that Abraham our father taught the whole people and made them acquainted with the religion of truth and the uniqueness of God, and spurned idolatry and destroyed its worship and brought many under the wings of the Divine Presence. . . . Therefore any stranger who joins us till the end of time, and everyone who recognizes the unity of God as taught in Scripture, is a disciple of Abraham our father; and they are all of them members of his household, and he it is who brought them to the right path.

And therefore thou art to say, 'Our God and the God of our fathers', because Abraham is thy father . . . there is no difference between us and thee in any thing. Thou mayest certainly say in thy prayers 'Who has chosen us', 'Who has given us the Law', and 'Who has caused us to inherit' and 'Who has separated us', because God hath indeed chosen thee and separated thee from the peoples and given thee the Law; for the Law is given alike to us and to the stranger, as it is written: 'One law and one judgment is there for ye and for the stranger who sojourneth with thee.'

Know this: Our fathers who went up from Egypt were, in Egypt, idolaters for the most part; they had mixed with the nations and learned of their ways; until God sent Moses our teacher and brought them under the wings of the Divine Presence, us and the strangers together, and gave us all one statute.

Let not then thy descent be light in thine eyes. If our descent is from Abraham, Isaac and Jacob, thy descent is from God himself.[11]

VII

Maimonides' ruling on the subject of the proselyte is not an instance of limitation but of broadening. The term 'Jew' is widened to include people who would naturally be considered to be excluded; and it has a curious parallel in the United States of today where one can still hear immigrants, and sons of immigrants, sing lustily: 'Land where our fathers died'. The point is that in the case of Maimonides the position taken is a reasoned one and based on the fundamental, and deeply felt, theological position

---

[11] [From Maimonides' reply to Obadiah the Proselyte: *Letters of Maimonides*, trans. Leon D. Stitskin (New York, 1977).]

that Jews are definable as members of the household of Abraham which is the household of God. The proselyte is therefore even nearer to God than the born Jew because he is a member of God's household by original conviction like Abraham himself, not merely by the fact of birth.

I take now a more subtle instance affecting primarily theology, but (as always in Judaism) theology, as we shall see especially later, involves morality.

We pray: 'O God the great, the powerful, and the awesome', and according to the Talmud even these epithets would not have been allowed but for the fact that they are recorded as having been used of God by Moses. But what do they *mean?* As the aggadists themselves asked: 'Where now is his greatness; where now his awesome deeds?' On the face of it, 'greatness' means presumably 'power', *physical* power; but is the greatness of God just that of a super-scientist or super-politician, that of the hundred-times-a-hundred megaton bomb? The rabbis say flatly, No! Deuteronomy 3: 24 reads: 'O Lord God, Thou hast begun to show Thy servant Thy greatness and Thy mighty hand'; and the Sifrei (Pinhas §134) says:

Thy greatness: this means Thy goodness, as in the verse (Num. 14: 17): 'And now I pray Thee let the power of the Lord be great.'
Thy hand: this means the hand which is stretched out [i.e. in mercy and pardon] to all those who come into the world.
Thy might: this refers to the might Thou showest when Thou dost in mercy repress the attribute of justice; as it is written, 'Who is a God like unto Thee, forgiving sin and passing over transgression?'

The point of interest is the complete moralization of the idea of power. Power has been transmuted from the physical to the moral; and that this is not a casual eccentricity but a purposeful and deliberate change is clear from the note of the same Sifrei on the verse of Deuteronomy *in situ* (§27 with Friedmann's note 11, p. 71); 'This is the universal meaning of the word "greatness" when applied to God.'

That the greatness of God lies in his goodness and his power to forgive, that is, in the words of the Sifrei we have referred to, in his control of justice by pity, is one of the commonplaces of traditional Judaism, and it is thrust home in the prayer-book by one of the most striking instances of moralization which any purposeful exegesis could offer. In the list of the 'thirteen attributes' of God repeatedly appealed to in the liturgy of the New Year and Day of Atonement the last is *venakeh*, 'and acquitting', that is, 'and acquitting the guilty'. But this, of course, is the very opposite

of the original text which reads: *venakeh lo yenakeh*, that is, 'and not acquitting the guilty'. It would be difficult to find a more blatant, and more
instructive, instance of conscious moralization.

From the point of view of the science of ethics, as distinguished from,
and as giving strength and confirmation to, the code of morals, the point
of interest is the way in which the supreme principle—let us call it summarily *torat ḥayim ve'ahavat ḥesed*, Judaism as a doctrine of life and love
of kindness— is followed consistently throughout and creates an integral
pattern. Moralization in this specific direction, explicit and conscious,
was going on all the time in the expansion and development of the tradition. Indeed, I should say myself that the moralization *constituted* the
expansion and development of the tradition.

VIII

We can descry, I think, some of the main lines of the emerging pattern:
in the warp, the increasing warmth and confidence of the universalism; in
the woof, the recession of justice before pity (not, of course, that these
are new elements but that they are seen to cohere more with the old and
give them support and consistence). But these are delicate matters, and
concern the future science of ethics. On the practical side, within the
sphere of living morality, it is sufficient to indicate the deliberate attempt
on the part of the talmudic rabbis, under the guise of biblical exegesis, to
promote the emergence of a new type of man. The instance I am to give is
remarkable because of its very absurdity, absurdity, that is, as exegesis. In
intention it is so far from being absurd as to raise vividly the most modern
of all issues.

In 2 Samuel 23 we are given an account of David's 'mighty men' and
their deeds of valour. Benaiah the son of Jehoiadah, the son of a valiant
man of Kabzeel who had done mighty deeds, slew the two 'Ariel of
Moab', and slew a lion in the midst of a pit in time of snow; on which we
have the comment in the Talmud (*Berakhot*):

A valiant man—this means that he increased and assembled workers for the
Law;

He smote the two Ariel of Moab—this means that he left no one like him [i.e. for
scholarship] whether in the First or the Second Temple;

He slew a lion—that is, he learned the Sifra of the school of Rav.

You will agree that the comment is astounding. As exegesis it is nonsense. But for that very reason it merits special attention. After all, the author
of the comment, and its recorders and preservers, were presumably as

intelligent as we are, and they would not have wasted time and space for a foolish remark if indeed it were just foolish. But it is far from that. In its sphere it gives expression to exactly the same idea (and here is this unity of pattern so interesting and important for ethics) as the theological statement to which I referred earlier. God's greatness, we were told then, does not lie in the exercise of physical power. His mighty hand is mighty because it exercises the moral virtue of pity. Here we have the parallel for man. Man's greatness, too, does not lie in physical power. Soldiers are not the ideal man. Generals are not the ideal man. Even athletes are not the ideal man. It is the moral qualities which count and which constitute man's power. It is those who 'although themselves treated with arrogance, do not treat others with arrogance, who bear humiliation but do not humiliate others, who fulfil God's will in love and put up with adversity' whom 'Scripture calls the lovers of God and whom it declares to be like the sun when it goes forth *in its power* [*gevurato!*]' (Sabb. 88*b*, on Judges 5: 31).

It is usually said that the talmudists, or some of them, were so afraid of the civil authorities that they allegorized away all mention of military acts. Indeed, we are often told that the suppression, or apparent suppression, of the military achievements of the Maccabees in our editions of the classical rabbinic literature—as is well known, Chanukah is mentioned only sparingly and in connection with the miracle of the oil—was due to fear of the police, whether the Roman or the Parthian or the Arab, or, later, of the censors of Christian Europe. *I wonder;* and in spite of the modern school of Jewish history represented prominently by the late Gedaliah Allon, I even doubt whether it was true of the historical Pharisees themselves. If, as a principle of universal application, *God's* power is to be equated with his goodness, perhaps, in the rabbinic mind and as a principle of equally universal application, *man's power also* is to be equated with his goodness. Perhaps they thought sincerely, apart altogether from the fear of the policeman and other considerations of the higher diplomacy, that there are virtues superior to the military. They made great use of the doctrine of the Imitation of God and constantly urge us to follow God in his moral attributes: 'As he is merciful, be thou merciful.' I am not aware of any passage in which we are urged to follow God in his *military* capacity.

If this contention is sound, we seem to have one instance of a society where the soldier was not held up to admiration as the highest type of man; as indeed, in rabbinic idea, he was not (the supreme type was the student of the 'Law of life and the love of kindness').

But here indeed the question which I raised earlier becomes insistent: which is the higher type and which is the lower? The studious life of scholarship and learning; the practical life of kindness and pity; the religious pursuit of holiness ever beckoning us on and ever far away; or the life of the soldier with its Roman ideal of *parcere subjectis et debellare superbos* (sparing those who are at your feet and destroying by war those who are not)? A recent speaker on the British Broadcasting Corporation, a schoolmaster, observed that a principal cause of war in our societies is the idealization of the military life and the submission of the Churches to the military ideal. Perhaps the rabbis of the Talmud also noticed something of this kind and tried to turn men's minds away, not from the *fact* of war —that, alas, would be impossible—but from the regarding of war, and of the warrior, as an ideal. As they said of the tanner and the perfumer: 'Both are required, but better be a perfumer.' It may be that soldiers, like tanners, are necessary; but that is no reason for our considering them, *pace* Ruskin, the highest type of human being. 'Forgive Thy people Israel whom Thou hast redeemed', says the Deuteronomist, 'and suffer not innocent blood to remain in the midst of Thy people'; and the Sifrei comments: 'It was for this Thou didst redeem us, that there should not be among us men who spill blood.'

But (again!) which *is* the highest type of human being; which, in the scale of virtues, is the high and which the low? And what constitutes their highness and lowness? Wherein does it lie and how do we recognize it? By reason of what can we say that any one kind of activity is better than another, 'better', that is, not in any utilitarian or pleasurable sense, but morally? Aristotle says somewhere that if there is a better, there is a best. I rather fancy that Judaism would say that, since there is a Best, there is a better. But I am beginning to approach my subject and shall therefore, after the fashion of the learned, stop.

Mysticism, Thick and Thin

✤

I

WE are all mystics nowadays but we need not be contentiously so. As we have been told recently by a Professor of Education (and he surely ought to know): 'The hot breath of the charismatic behind one's back is disconcerting.' Yet we of the milder sort may still keep in heart. For it would be strange, would it not, if the alleged greatest of all experiences should be confined to a few, a very, very few? I know that, on a similar plane, there are very few great painters, great poets, great philosophers, great technologists, great chemists, great mathematicians: we ordinary folk lack the power of great *creation*. But we have at least the power of *appreciation*; and I imagine that appreciation is of the same kind, although not perhaps of the same order, as creation. We do have in us something, however scanty, of the creative artist or thinker: we are not cut off from them completely. As Mr E. M. Forster remarks somewhere: 'We are rapt into a region near to that where the artist worked.' So my query with regard to the mystic vision remains. Is it conceivable that just this, allegedly the greatest prize of all, is denied to the vast majority of mankind?

The first of the suggestions I am going to make is that it is not so denied. We all in our own way, and in our own degree, sense the divine. I know I am using doubtful words and I shall seek a later occasion to clear them up somewhat. But if we take as a preliminary pointer a remark from an early essay of the late Clement Webb: 'A theory of the world may fairly be called Mysticism in which the ultimate truth and reality of things is held to be a unity the consciousness of which is attainable as a feeling inexpressible by thought', are we indeed all strange to such a feeling? Have we not all of us, at different times and in various situations, had this conviction of unity thrust, as it were, upon our consciousness without our being able to give a reasoned account of it? Even in the sphere of everyday action, do we not sometimes ponder and ponder some perplexity, and of a sudden, somehow, our path becomes clear. We see our way

First read as a paper to the annual conference of the World Congress of Faiths, September 1962, and published in *World Faiths*, 55 (Dec. 1962), 1–12. Reprinted by permission of the World Congress of Faiths. *World Faiths* was renamed and relaunched as *World Faiths Encounter* in 1962.

through, as we say. A pattern emerges. We 'know'—although not really *knowing*—that 'all is well'. The worry drops; the tension is released, and we go on our way rejoicing. All students can testify to this spiritual enlargement, an enlargement accompanied often by what might even (but we are modest beings) be called rapture. We work for years on a body of material and it seems a vague fog of muddled heterogeneity; and of a sudden the mist clears and a pattern, often to our astonishment, always to our delight, stands revealed. The same felt experience accompanies lesser triumphs, even so trivial a one as the finding of a word, the insertion of a comma. It is just *that* word and no other which expresses our meaning, just *that* comma which pulls the sentence 'into line', as we say, that is, makes the pattern clear. It was at the back of our minds. It haunted us. It was there; and yet it was not there. We pursue it, often 'through the arches of the years'. We catch it, and glow with satisfaction.

Many will remember the passage in *Joseph Vance*[1] in which an account is given of the working on an afflicted soul of the Waldstein Sonata. Vance is standing in the street by the docks watching a barge in midstream when his ears catch the notes of a piano:

Each single note said all that could be said—all that the most exacting could ask —of love and life and the great interminable universe. Each one, as its chance came round to speak, said it again and again, and each as it spoke said too that the end of it all was Death. There is no life but dies, no love but ceases, no sun but shall some day grow cold and be left an ash in dark space. I stood and watched the dropping red sail of the boat, and my heart pleaded with the music for a respite. But the music only said again, if possible more beautifully, all it had said before, and gave no hope.

Stop! What was that? A sudden voice of triumph crying out through the bewildering vortex of resonances—a sound as though the morning stars sang together and the sons of God shouted for joy. And then again—and then again! I stood and listened, and lived in the music.

And I heard what it said so plainly that its repetition made a sentence in my ears: 'Stop—stop—stop! You're quite mistaken. Stop—stop—stop! I know you're wrong.' And when a day or two later . . . I sought Frau Schmidt's [the pianist's] acquaintance, I was able to make her understand, by repeating that sentence, that it was the Waldstein Sonata I was asking for . . .

De Morgan then goes on:

I was indebted to Frau Schmidt for an introduction to Beethoven and have ever since regarded the latter as being not so much a Composer as a Revelation . . . Frau Schmidt would crack her hands backwards and suddenly let Heaven loose.

[1] [William Frend De Morgan's novel *Joseph Vance* was published in 1916.]

How often I said to myself, after some perfectly convincing phrase of Beethoven, 'Of course, if *that* is so, there can be no occasion to worry.' It could not be translated, naturally, into vulgar Grammar and Syntax; but it left no doubt on the point for all that.

'Let Heaven loose'—that's a striking phrase, and I find something later on which is almost as good:

It's a breath of fresh air from the highest Heaven brought somehow into the stuffy cellar of our existence. It's the flash of light that strikes on the wall of the tunnel our train is passing through, and shows us the burst of sunshine that is coming.

Or again:

'All's to come right in the end, Joe, be sure of that!' And the Doctor's voice struck into my reverie like the phrase in the Waldstein Sonata.... 'It will do so in some sense absolutely inconceivable by us—so inconceivable that the simple words I use to express it may then have ceased to mean anything, or anything worth recording, to our expanded senses...'
And again, as he spoke, I heard the phrase of the Waldstein Sonata.

I ask pardon for the long quotation but it brings out a number of things relevant to our subject: the empty void of seeming meaninglessness; the emergence of rightness or pattern and the accompanying enlargement of the mind; the conceiving of the inconceivable; the sudden joy, the sustained satisfaction—are not these the acknowledged marks of the classical mystical experience and are they not common in some degree to us all? I leave it to you but remember, please, that my concern is not to write mysticism down, but to write the rest *up*.

II

I find the key myself in the conception of 'pattern', not 'experience'. Experience cannot be an ultimate because it is necessarily *of* something. It invites, indeed, demands, the question: 'of *what*?' Pattern is the 'what'. It may be grasped dimly and obscurely so as to appear little more than a vague hint; it may offer itself adventurously as a guiding principle; it may stand out clearly and decisively as a fully sustained theory; but in every case the pattern is the thing. It is pattern, whether in the form of a sensuous figure or of the super-sensuous *non*-figured, which appears, or is sought for, in all human achievement and which constitutes the common ground between the arts and the sciences, the philosophies, the logics, the religions, the systems of morality, of mankind. Again I say, not 'experience'. Experience is the matter; structure, pattern, is the form: and it is everywhere form, structure, pattern, which we are led to seek and which, progressively, we find. (Find, or impose? I leave that to the metaphysicians. For myself, I should say, Find.) We are imperfect creatures, as the old philosophers used to say, and we reach out, by the very nature of our being, to perfection; and perfection is self-completeness and lies in wholes, not in isolated particulars, and wholes are patterns, structures, in which the isolated particulars, no longer isolated and no longer mere particulars, find their place, that is, their meaning.

> Much have I travelled in the realms of gold
>   And many goodly states and kingdoms seen;
>   Round many western islands have I been
> Which bards in fealty to Apollo hold.
> Oft of one wide expanse had I been told
>   That deep-browed Homer ruled as his demesne;
>   Yet did I never breathe its pure serene
> Till I heard Chapman speak out loud and bold.
> Then felt I like some watcher of the skies
>   When a new planet swims into his ken;
> Or like stout Cortez, when with eagle eyes
>   He stared at the Pacific, and all his men
> Looked at each other with a wild surmise—
>   Silent, upon a peak in Darien.[2]

Let us consider this sonnet for a moment, torturing it with our prose. We start with a rough survey of the 'realms of gold' which however, are felt inadequate (Homer is missing!). Our demand for completeness (through the reading of Chapman) is met. In the face of the whole thus revealed we stand silent and satisfied. We had dimly sought for something but it was nothing alien or strange: in a sense it was part of ourselves already. The 'new' planet was one we guessed was there, the 'new' sea one we had anticipated. We had a 'hunch' and now have knowledge, and our knowledge of the fact is a filling-out both of the 'hunch' and of ourselves. Mind (shall we say it?) is self-transcendent and its completed state is coterminous with the ordered totality of things. It is this ordered totality to which it reaches out and it is this which, when found, brings it its own amazed and joyful fulfilment.

---

[2] [Keats, 'On First Looking into Chapman's Homer'.]

III

But I begin to stumble and need support.

Professor G. Wilson Knight, one of our leading students of Shakespeare and of the seventeenth century, has just issued a revised edition of his early *Christian Renaissance*. I find the points I am trying to make admirably set out in his first chapters.

First, as to the nature, and ubiquity, of pattern and the search for pattern. He gives a helpful analogy from the game of chess:

Most moderate chess-players . . . try to analyse at every turn the diverging ramifications of the next few moves . . . The complications become swiftly infinite and the baffled mind makes a move in despair . . . A player of a much higher order . . . when making a decision, sees a whole movement simultaneously outrolled and leading to an ideal mate. He does not think in terms of a process but rather visualises what he names a 'pattern' spread out immediately in space and time, or rather in space–time, and rejects moves that do not fit this pattern . . . The good player tries not so much to play the game right as to prevent its playing itself wrong.

This seems to me to be illuminating. Our ideal figure in the field of literature or science or music has the pattern spread out before him and rejects what does not fit. It is not he who is playing the game right or wrong, it is the game which is playing itself or even playing him; and all he does or can do is to help it to play itself right, or at least to prevent it from playing itself (unrolling itself, revealing itself) wrong. 'Art', Professor Knight goes on to say, after reminding us that 'it is reported that Mozart saw, or heard, a complete work as a single whole before setting it down in the time-sequence of composition', 'Art is largely the rejection of incompatibilities whilst having regard to an ideal recognised first in terms of what it is not and realised after by the expression of what it is.'

It would seem to follow that the pattern is in command, pressing down upon the artificer. It is not for nothing that the biblical prophets spoke of the word that came to them, as a 'burden' or as a 'living fire they could not contain'. It was something given to them, not something they had made up themselves. As Balaam said to Balak: 'Have I now any power at all to speak anything? The word that God putteth in my mouth, that shall I speak.' We read the same in the autobiographical statements of many of the great artists. The creative source, they say, is not within but without. They themselves (they say) are but tools. They *do* more than they *know*.

IV

The student of mysticism will at this prick up his ears. For what is this but the well-known doctrine of 'passivity', advanced both as theory and as practical advice, in the writings of many religious mystics? These tell us that the first thing we must learn to do if we would ascend the mystical ladder is to *empty our minds*. In more violent phrase, we must *annihilate ourselves*. 'Only the silent hear.' Power, whether kept privately in the heart and mind or poured out in speech, is infused from the without into the within. The within must therefore first be rid of everything active and personal. It must become solely and completely receptive.

I shall revert later to this doctrine of the voiding of the self. But if what I have said of literature is sound, my general submission would seem to be substantiated. Mysticism is neither a miracle (that is, an isolated phenomenon) nor a mystery (that is, an unintelligible one). Its characteristic signs, far from being unusual, are manifest in all creative activity. Professor Knight says: 'The truth is that life is greater and more divinely ordered than our lower consciousness allows.' We may have some qualms about accepting this particular formulation but on one point at least we can, I think, all be agreed. Mind, in any and every sphere (and I include the scientific), is always going beyond its data.

This leads me, at long last, to my title. It was not meant to be either annoying or profound. Its origins are of the humblest. Hotel soups are notoriously of two kinds: there is the thick, and there is the thin. The thick is the dense, the inspissate, the glutinous; the thin, the watered, the vapid, the dilute: and all my title (and my paper) means is that we should persuade ourselves, when thinking on these matters, to follow Shakespeare's advice and 'forswear thin potations'.

For as one delves into the literature of the subject, one cannot but be struck by the fact that so much of it is 'thin'. To adapt an old French jest reported by Boswell: it has plenty of spirit but very little body. Great interest was aroused some years ago by a book translated from the Russian by Mr R. M. French which had reached three editions by 1954. It is the *Way of a Pilgrim*, and comprises[3] the 'travel diary' of a simple Russian believer before the liberation of the serfs a hundred years or so ago. It begins, you will remember, with his hearing in church the verse from Thessalonians 'Pray without ceasing', and asking himself how this could be put into practice. He goes with his problem from one spiritual

---

[3] I understand that it is now regarded as unauthentic, but as an illustration it will still serve.

teacher to another until finally he is advised to say the 'prayer of Jesus'—
that is, 'Lord Jesus, have mercy on me'—twelve thousand times a day.
He reaches this figure fairly soon, and the repetition becomes for him
what he calls a constant 'interior' player. 'In the end', he says, 'I felt it going on of its own accord within my mind and in the depths of my heart,
without any urging on my part. Not only when I was awake but even
during sleep, just the same thing went on. Nothing broke into it and it
never stopped even for a single moment, whatever I might be doing. My
soul was always giving thanks to God and my heart melted away with
increasing happiness.'

Now I am far from depreciating, certainly from denigrating, this type
of piety or the method of its induction; and I recall that countless saintly
men, of all creeds and at all times, have in their own fashion followed this
path. In our own day no less a person than Mahatma Gandhi prescribed
the constant repetition of the name of the Hindu god Ram as a specific
against all ills, and it is common experience that the going over in one's
mind, at times of stress, of memorable passages from literature is one of
the great props of life. But, so far as I am concerned, I cannot help apply-
ing to the self-hypnotization of the Russian monk and similar states of
mind (or should we not say, rather, with many of the mystics themselves,
mindlessness) the word 'thin'. Like gazing at a point on the wall or listen-
ing to a tom-tom, it may lead to ecstasy; but it is a question whether
ecstasy as such is of significance. As Mr Bennett writes in his recent remarkable volume of autobiography of a dance of dervishes he was privil-
eged to witness:

The experience itself made a deep impression. But who was changed by it? Tomorrow they would all be as before—dominated by the same passions and weaknesses as all other men . . . Men and women are bathed in tears and the heavens
seem to open . . . Did they not all return unchanged in character to the same life
dominated by the same weaknesses?[4]

V

If the Russian pilgrim represents for me what I have called 'thin' mysticism
—and I take him as a type and say again that I am not denouncing it as
worthless; very much to the contrary—what, you may well ask, is the
'thick'? Here I recall two impressive, and almost contiguous, sentences of
Spinoza: the one, in a scholium, or note (V. xxiii), 'Sentimus experi-

---

[4] [John G. Bennett, *Witness: The Story of a Search* (London: Hodder & Stoughton,
1952).]

murque nos aeternos esse' (we feel and experience that we are eternal), the other, a full proposition (v. xxiv), 'Quo magis res singulares intelligimus, eo magis Deum intelligimus' (the more we understand individual things, the more we understand God). One striking thing in these two sentences is the change of verb: '*we feel and experience* that we are eternal'; 'the more we *understand* individual things'. The suggestion would seem to be, though I do not claim it as exegesis, that we have an immediate experience of eternity, an experience however which, like all experiences, needs to be cleared up and seen in its wider connections. We are such creatures as must needs transmute general feeling into specific understanding.

And we may go further. Spinoza does *not* say: 'The more we understand *general laws*, the more we understand God.' He says: 'The more we understand *individual things*', or rather (and the word used is a striking one) '*singular* things', that is, things in their singularity or uniqueness. It is 'the more we understand individual things' *as unique* that 'the more we understand God'. The self-development of mind towards its perfection is a progress from the original vague acquaintance in which feeling and knowledge are indistinguishable, through the abstract apprehension of principles which is science, to the concrete grasp of individual things in which knowledge and feeling come together again. Science in fact is not yet fully knowledge because *science* deals with general laws while *knowledge*, as the scholastics said and as poets and artists have always known (or known till very recently)—knowledge is of *individuals*; and the knowledge of individuals is more than of individuals and points to its and their ground. As a modern philosophical novelist has said memorably: 'What stuns us into a realisation of our supersensible destiny is not, as Kant imagined, the formlessness of nature, but rather its unutterable particularity.'

VI

But I need not worry you with the philosophers. You will all recall what was said of that great contemporary literary artist and religious mystic, Charles Williams:

He could make *each one* seem important and interesting . . . But even more than that, he could make life important and interesting, not some life removed from us by money, opportunity or gifts, but the *very life we had to lead* and should probably go on leading for years.

There was nothing pernicious in his influence, no false glow or secret dependence on himself, no element whatever of intoxication, although he could and did turn the water of our lives into wine. He did not deal in effects like happiness, power, importance or other semi-magical promises, but in causes, origins and ends; and he made us see our day so *immediately related to the creating cause* and the divine end of love that he *restored the sense of value* in us.[5]

And Miss Hadfield goes on: 'For myself . . . I can say that the effect of Charles Williams's thought was to strengthen the feelings and to *restore direction.* He gave back *the ability to make fundamental judgments,* from which there comes vitality in living and, finally, happiness in life' (italics mine).

Charles Williams was a mystic of the 'thick' variety. One has only to read his novels to see that. He was a literary man and his approach to life was in and through literature. But 'thickness' can be achieved in many another way. Physics is of course not the only science, but how much more deep and far-reaching was the mysticism of Eddington because of his intimate acquaintance with physics. Biology too is not, of course, the only science; but Henri Bergson nourished a whole generation of mystical and religious thinkers from a mind which had itself been nourished primarily by a close study of biology. We are seeing something of the same kind now in the new stimulus being derived from the palaeontologist Pierre de Chardin and his *union différencie*.[6] Like Spinoza, these men—Eddington, Bergson, de Chardin and many others—had their vision of God made actual through the concrete revelations of nature, just as their understanding of nature was made actual by their vision of God. This vision may ultimately have been the same as that of the Russian pilgrim, but it was immeasurably more 'thick'.

VII

It is here that I find myself in conflict, or apparent conflict, with some of the accepted masters. Let us take a passage from the *Cloud of Unknowing*:

Lift up thine heart unto God with a meek stirring of love, and mean himself and none of his goods. And thereto look that thou loathe to think on aught but himself, so that nought work in thy mind nor in thy will but only himself. And do that-in-thee-is to forget all the creatures that ever God made and the works of

[5] A. M. Hadfield, *An Introduction to Charles Williams* (London: Hale, 1959), 70.

[6] 'My present topic is more and more "*L'union différencie*". There is a full metaphysics, ethic and mystic, contained in those three words.' Letter of 1935, quoted by Miss L. Swan ['Memories and Letters', in Neville Braybrooke (ed.), *The Wind and the Rain* (London: Secker & Warburg, 1962), 40–9, at 43].

them, so that thy thought or thy desire be not directed or stretched to any of them, neither in general nor in special.[7]

Our author thus tells us to turn away from created things and concentrate our minds on the Creator. But it is surely admissible to ask what we *can* concentrate on as Creator if we shut our eyes to created things. 'Do that-in-thee-is to forget all the creatures that ever God made'; be loth 'to think on aught but himself'? But can one? Is Being separable from Activity, and activity from its exercise and products? Was not Hegel right when he said that 'pure being' is 'pure nothing'? Aldous Huxley is fond of quoting Tauler's definition of God as 'a being *withdrawn from* creatures, a *free* power, a *pure* working'; but the definition contains the very ideas he is concerned to controvert (creatures, power, working) with the addition of the near-negative terms 'withdrawn', 'free', 'pure'. I am far from asserting that the traditional mystical terminology is empty, only that a fuller mind is likely to lead to a fuller content and should not be denied its right of entry *ab initio*. Some traditional mystics, we are told, were 'content to rest in the quiet contemplation of their own soul'. I sometimes wonder whether the soul is not in as much need of continuous, and external, nourishment as the body. One famous mystic spoke of his aim as 'being as he was before he was'. Perhaps his aim should have been to be a bit better, a bit fuller, a bit more what he (not *was*, but) *could become*.

This consideration should persuade us to examine with more care the doctrine of the emptying of the mind. We should not allow ourselves to be deceived by loose metaphors. If mind is, as I have urged, by nature self-transcendent, always reaching out, by virtue of itself, beyond itself, is it not to be expected that, in the reaching out, it becomes (as all experience suggests; otherwise education has no meaning) enlarged, expanded, stretched? It does not remain 'as it was'; and to aim at being (in this sense, at least, which may not be the original author's) 'as it was before it was' is a fundamental denial of its own nature. If (to use the favourite metaphor) the soul 'ascends', is it credible that it only changes its position, never its quality? Surely it gains; becomes fuller, more itself, more complete. And if so, granted that the soul must humbly await the inrush of the spirit, are there not some souls, and some individual souls in the various stages of their own development, which are at a higher point of being and are therefore *more capable* of receiving? Is *spiritual fixation* (arrested development!) the ideal? 'Receptivity'? Certainly. 'Passivity'? If you like to

[7] Quoted by David Knowles, *The English Mystical Tradition* (London: Burns & Oates, 1961), 77.

call it so. *Qualitative immobility?* No! The fuller, the more 'stretched' the soul, the greater its positive capability, and the greater, too, its watchfulness, its attention, its humility: think of men like Faraday, Darwin, Einstein. Empty the soul, by all means; but first see to it that it is *worth* emptying. I know that the heart has its reasons as well as the head, but the heart's reasons are often very bad.

And so too, very often, are the head's. But the head can at least *weigh* its reasons and try to find sounder ones

VIII

So I ask you, even as mystics, to give the head a chance. Give *knowledge* a chance, knowledge not in the Gnostic sense of hidden mysteries revealed only to the adept but knowledge in the plain and simple sense of the ABC and the table of arithmetic, that is, literature and the sciences. For knowledge is not to be confined to what is commonly called science, what at school we used to call 'stinks'. There is knowledge in the arts, and the knowledge of the painter and the poet, and so too of the carpenter and other craftsmen, is perhaps for our enquiry of even greater value. And let us not overlook the knowledge shown by migrant birds, and the strange certitude granted to the fluke-worm and the bee. Are we not all—flukeworm and bee as well as artificer and philosopher—caught up in one cosmic pattern? 'We feel and experience that we are eternal.'

But yet it is 'the more we understand *individual things*' that 'the more we understand God'. It is in knowledge of individual things, in the detailed elucidation of the adumbrations of feeling, that the pattern, slowly and dimly, emerges, and I am now impelled, howbeit at so late a stage, to revise my title 'Thin' and 'Thick'. Even in soups, I believe, the antithesis is not final. I have pleaded, with Shakespeare, that we should forswear the thin, and suggested in its stead the thick. I now suggest that, even better than the thick, we should ask for the 'clear'. 'Clear soup', I understand, is what emerges, in the hierarchy of soups, from the straining of the thick, when the gross accompanying matter is filtered and purged away and the pure essence alone remains. So the thick may be dismissed together with the thin. Thesis and antithesis are alike transcended. Greater than both is *clarity*.

True, even clarity, as Professor Price observed some years ago, is not enough. But at least let us *begin* with it at home. For myself, I am trying to make clear to myself my own mystical trilogy: Unity, Pattern, Meaning.

IX

But I stand before you a self-confessed heretic. My key-word is inter-relatedness, not isolation, and my central thought not the flight of the alone to the alone but the striving of the lesser towards the greater full-ness. I urge not the uniqueness of personal experience but the all-pervasiveness of pattern and meaning, so that religion is not what man does with his solitariness but what he does (or rather, perhaps, what is done to him) by virtue of his *togetherness*, his togetherness not only with his fellow men but with all other created things. And as I seem to be tres-passing on high matters, may I be allowed to venture further and express my belief that the greater fullness is creative and, in some small measure, manifest in the creative power of every created thing, so that, if we are to understand anything of ourselves, the way is not that of self-emptying and negation but of ever fuller expression and affirmation? I believe in fact that—but you will remember the interchange between Boswell and Colman when Dr Johnson put himself on record, after his tour in the Hebrides, as 'willing to believe the second sight':

BOSWELL   He is only *willing* to believe: I *do* believe. The evidence is enough for me, though not for his great mind. What will not fill a quart bottle will fill a pint bottle. I am filled with belief.

COLMAN   Are you? Then cork it up.

The advice is good.

Back To, Forward From, Ahad Ha'am?

⁂

I

IN the early years of the century there appeared a remarkable book, by the Italian Croce, entitled: *What is Living and What is Dead in the Philosophy of Hegel?* The subject on which I wish you to direct your attention today is: What is living, and what is dead, in Ahad Ha'am?

By 'living', I mean what is living *for us*, by 'dead', what is dead *for us*. In the recently published volume *Tradition and Change* on the development of the Conservative movement in the Jewry of the United States, there is excerpted an address by the present Vice-Chancellor of the Jewish Theological Seminary of America in which the first of the 'four tested standards' of the movement is declared to be 'scientific knowledge of the whole of Judaism'. The aim is ambitious and I hope the Seminary lives up to it. But even after the 'whole of' Judaism has become known *scientifically*, there still remains the task of its evaluation. Evaluation is not the business of science. Science describes; it does not judge. But life means judgement, discrimination, selection. *On doit choisir.* There are subjects and opinions which for us today are more significant than others and it is these which we have to look out for. What then can we find today of significance in Ahad Ha'am, and, having found it, how and where do we go on further?

II

It should be said at once that we are all of us, in some sense and in some degree, disciples of Ahad Ha'am. We all use his ideas, all speak his language. They are current coin, passed from hand to hand, without thought of the mint in which they were struck. And if we turn again to his writings, we can see the secret of his appeal. Here is a man, we say to ourselves, who talks sense; and he talks sense sensibly. He knows where to

This paper was delivered at the 1960 conference of Anglo-Jewish Preachers. It is reprinted from *Conservative Judaism*, 17/1–2 (Fall 1962/Winter 1963), 20–30. © the Rabbinical Assembly 1963. Reprinted by permission of the Rabbinical Assembly.

begin, and when to stop. His prose is prose, not pastiche. He displays a breadth of vision, a width of interest, a substratum of seminal ideas, which we miss in some other modern Hebrew writers. He is worthy of all admiration; but—and here is my first point—let us admire him for what he *is*, not for what he is *not*. You may have observed that the question I set at the head of this paper was not 'What is living and what is dead in the *philosophy* of Ahad Ha'am?' but 'What is living and what is dead in Ahad Ha'am?' Ahad Ha'am, as I shall explain, was no philosopher and had no philosophy of his own. He was rather, much after the English model, a philosophically minded essayist.

It is not an insult to a man to say he is not a philosopher. There have been very few philosophers in this world: of great ones, say a dozen, of lesser, say a score. Add the ordinary labourers in that particular vineyard of the Lord and you might count, all told, a hundred. Giving us Jews our proper percentage—one, two, three, four, five? Surely five per cent is enough even for us!—you will see that we have better candidates than Ahad Ha'am. But it is a question whether he is to be counted even as a candidate. To be able to hold together in his thought—as Plato put it— 'all time and all existence'—that is traditionally what it means to be a philosopher. Such a claim cannot be made for Ahad Ha'am, and Ahad Ha'am himself would never have dreamed of making it. Ahad Ha'am saw himself as a 'publicist', that is an occasional writer on current issues. And so he was in fact. He was a singularly clear-minded and keen-witted man, widely read (particularly in the field of what is now called that of the social sciences), passionately interested in certain aspects of the Jewish problem as manifested in his day, who used ideas derived from his reading—his past and present reading—in order to illumine the questions of the day. His interest was not in '*all* time and *all* existence' but in a *particular* time and *one slice of* existence. He was emphatically and confessedly a child of his age and environment; and ages and environments change.

This became clear even in his own life. He was never a genuine part of the new Yishuv. Even in Hampstead he wrote something. In Tel Aviv, like Bialik, he wrote nothing. Inspiration ceased. He belonged to Odessa, he belonged to Berlin, he belonged to the city. He may have hated them all, but it was with a hatred which served as a stimulus. He may have loved Tel Aviv; but he was only *in* it, not *of* it.

This fact has come out clearly in one of the most revealing episodes in the cultural history of the new state. There is a revolt against Ahad Ha'am. The 'young men', whether 'angry' or placid, will have nothing to do with him. Some of you may have seen the controversy in the literary pages of

Israeli newspapers a few years ago, and in particular the articles of Gideon Katznelson and others of the younger novelists. Their judgement is not due only to the fact that they had been made to read Ahad Ha'am in school: that is a reason for boredom, not rejection. They rejected him root and branch; and even the recent symposium at Hillel House in Jerusalem produced from the professors and lecturers of the university an appreciation which, when not openly condemnatory, was cold. If you wish today to find disciples of Ahad Ha'am, you have to go to America.

But they admire him there *for the wrong things*. They treat him as an original and creative thinker who forged new ideas valid for all time. But Ahad Ha'am was never, and never set himself up as, that. He was, as I have said, a philosophically minded essayist who used current ideas in order to help himself and others to see their way through present fact. If you isolate those ideas and treat them as self-subsistent and eternal verities, you are doing Ahad Ha'am a grave injustice. Ahad Ha'am was a writer and an excellent writer. But few writers, however excellent, particularly a casual and incidental writer as he confessedly was, can stand the process of deification. You might as well expect to extract a perennial metaphysic from the leading articles of *The Times*!

III

Ahad Ha'am was not only a leader-writer and an excellent one at that. He was also a man of singular courage. He tried to live up to his own professions. When he said that Judaism was more important than Jews, he meant it. When certain facts first appeared in the Yishuv—facts then only the size of a man's hand—he spoke up, and vigorously. I am going to read to you the text of a once famous public letter. I say 'once famous' because it is now unnoticed and unremarked. It does not appear, so far as I know, in any of the many translations of his works, nor, so far as I was able to observe, is it mentioned in the recent Simon–Heller *Life*. But it is all-important for Ahad Ha'am's memory. Without it his life is a fraud. For his life, which was his work, meant sincerity of feeling and cool acceptance of fact coupled with complete honesty of judgement and expression.

The occasion for this letter was the report in the early autumn of 1922 that, in retaliation for attacks on Jews, some young Jews had killed an Arab boy. On this, Ahad Ha'am published the following letter in *Ha'aretz*. It was reprinted in *Ha'aretz* itself some time in the late thirties and is to be found on page 462 of the one-volume edition of Ahad Ha'am's collected works published by Dvir in 1946. It reads as follows (I have translated literally, hence the halting language):

From the time when I first heard the story which is the subject of your article and in particular as I see the reaction of the community in the country to the affair, my heart is filled with gloomy thoughts and I feel as if there were tottering within me all the foundations upon which I built my views on Judaism and Zionism from my youth up. And if these go, what is there left to me in my old age of all the labour which I have laboured in my life except an empty heart and a soul in despair.

'Jews and blood—are there two opposites greater than these?' It was with these words that I concluded one of my first essays many, many years ago; and I was confident at that time that this was a first principle of the truth of which no Jew could doubt. For what did we save from the overthrow of the Destruction but the teaching of our prophets, which we took with us on the road of the long exile to illumine for us the darkness of our lives on strange soil? Our blood was shed like water in all the four corners of the earth for thousands of years, but *we* did not shed blood. We remembered always that the great moral teaching which our fathers handed down to us is the doctrine of the future which it is our duty to preserve, and to give up our lives for, until it become the possession of all humankind, and the beast which is in man cease to rule individual and social existence. Thus our people lived generation after generation. It lived in strange countries among nations who lived on their sword, and the shedding of blood was the work of their hands all the days. But *our* people, persecuted everywhere, for all its external degradation, looked with disgust on its neighbours with their hands polluted with blood, and knew in the depths of its heart that it never had, and never would have, any connection with that life of savagery; because it was the depository of the great moral truth which is destined to spread over the whole world and put an end to the savagery, the cruelty, the spilling of blood, all over the world. And then it too would live in security in its own land and would see with its own eyes its great victory, the victory of its moral teaching for which it had been slaughtered for thousands of years . . .

And now, what can we say and how can we speak if there is truth in this report? God, is this the End? Is this the goal for which our forefathers yearned and for which they suffered all those tribulations? Is this the dream of the Return to Zion which our people dreamed for thousands of years: that we should come to Zion and pollute its soil with the spilling of innocent blood?

I concluded another article, also many years ago, with the words: 'The people will give its money as a price for the state, but not its prophets.' I thought that that too was a first principle. And now God hath dealt hardly with me and given to me to live and see with my own eyes that I was mistaken, apparently, in this as well. Money? The people is not giving much money even now for the building of its 'national home', in spite of the Mandate and the rest of the 'political victories'.

But correspondingly there is growing in it a tendency to sacrifice, on the altar of the 'revival', its prophets, that is, the great moral principles for which our people lived and for which it suffered and for which only it thought it worthwhile to labour to become a people again in the land of its fathers. For without these— God in Heaven, what are we, and what is the future of our life in this country, that we should make all those unending sacrifices without which the country will not be built? Is it only in order to add another little Levantine people in one of the corners of the Orient to compete with the Levantines there already in all those corrupt moral habits—the thirst for blood, revenge and strife—which make up the content of their lives?

If this is the Messiah, let him come and me not see him.

'Let him come and me not see him.' The phrase is talmudic and is the recorded comment of some well-known sages on the troubles supposed to prelude the coming of the Messiah. In its context the reference is to material troubles, the so-called 'birth-pangs' of the messianic age. Ahad Ha'am, in his use of the words, refers to another kind of trouble, the spiritual troubles of moral anarchy. Ultimately his protest is against the attitude expressed in the phrase 'the end justifies the means' which I should translate into Hebrew as *mitsvah haba'ah be'aveirah* ('a religious act achieved through a wrong deed'—Jastrow), a phrase used by a modern Jerusalem scholar as a title for an essay describing the premises, and the consequences, of the seventeenth-century messianic movement in Jewry. There is an old warning against losing the reasons for life for the sake of living. There are some prices which are too high to pay; and Ahad Ha'am seems to have felt it, as this letter shows, with every fibre of his being. The times were for him clearly out of joint.

IV

But we may leave Ahad Ha'am the man and turn to some of his pronouncements on the theory of Judaism. We may start with his account of Jewish ethics. You will remember that he identified the ethics of Judaism with the demand for absolute justice, in contrast with the ethics of Christianity as understood by him, the ethics of love; and he saw the contrast as manifested and exemplified in the negative and positive interpretations of 'loving thy neighbour as thyself' expressed in the well-known sayings of Hillel and Jesus.

The essays in which these views are given[1] have become classic, and we have all used them time and time again. The contrast between justice and love is so attractive, the opposition between the golden rules of Hillel and

[1] [*Ten Essays on Zionism and Judaism* (London: Routledge, 1922).]

Jesus so neat. But one day I came across the following in a reputable Jewish author:

It is laid down by the rabbis *as a positive command* to visit the sick and to comfort mourners and to take out the dead and to help a bride and to escort travellers and to occupy ourselves with everything requisite for a burial; and similarly to make the bride and bridegroom rejoice and to help them in all their needs. These are the personal acts of charity [*gemilut ḥasadim*] which have no measure.

But although all these commands are rabbinical, they are included in 'And thou shalt love thy neighbour as thyself': all the things which you wish others to do to you, do you them to your fellow.[2]

This passage seems pretty definite. The love of neighbour (the *love* of neighbour!) is a general principle of *positive* action. So Maimonides, at least, is far from interpreting the biblical principle, with Hillel, negatively. Indeed, in another passage he seems to interpret Hillel's *negative* formulation *positively*:

All the commandments between man and man are included in *gemilut ḥasadim*, and if you give your attention to them, you will find them so; since Hillel, when the gentile said to him, Teach me Judaism on one foot, replied, What is unpleasant to you, do not do to your fellow.[3]

I may be misinterpreting him but Maimonides seems to be putting the whole of morals, so far as our positive actions affecting others are concerned, under the rubric of *gemilut ḥasadim*, and the whole of *gemilut ḥasadim*, *as a positive system of behaviour*, under the rubric of Hillel's so-called *negative* formulation of the golden rule.

Now I am not for one moment saying that Maimonides is right and Ahad Ha'am wrong, or that Ahad Ha'am is right and Maimonides wrong, or that either of them is either right or wrong *because* the other is wrong or right. But I suggest that any general statement on the nature of Jewish ethics which runs *counter to* an equally general, and certainly deliberate, ruling of Maimonides cannot be accepted without further examination, without much further examination. The very existence of Maimonides' opinion should make us pause in swallowing Ahad Ha'am's (as we have all swallowed it) whole.

V

The same seems to me to hold of Ahad Ha'am's no less famous opposition between justice and love. You may remember the appearance of the

---

[2] Maimonides, *Mishneh torah, Avel* xiv. 1.   [3] Maimonides, Commentary, *Peah* i.

essay in which it is expounded.[4] Unless my memory deceives me, it was published in English simultaneously with its appearance in Hebrew, in the *Hebrew Review* of Bentwich and Sacher. It created a sensation. It seemed to be a new revelation, or at least, to solve finally a problem which had beset Jewry for many centuries. The occasion for the essay was important. The community had been uneasy about the views and activities of one of its most gifted members, the late Claude Montefiore; and here, it was thought, was a decisive answer to them. But is it?

I have already pointed out that if the iron curtain is to be set in accordance with Ahad Ha'am's view of the golden rule and the contrast regarding it between Judaism and Christianity, no less a person than Maimonides would be found to be on the wrong side. The same, I fancy, would happen with regard to justice and love; for whoever looks with any attention at the last chapters of the *Guide for the Perplexed* knows that, according to Maimonides, the central virtue of Judaism is not justice unalloyed, if indeed justice at all, but justice *plus* both *ḥesed* and *tsedakah*. Maimonides takes (it will be remembered) the great key pronouncement of Jeremiah (9: 23–4), and proceeds to analyse its terms. *Mishpat* (justice) gets only two lines; *ḥesed* ('steadfast love', as it is translated in the new Revised Standard Version) and *tsedakah* (which he interprets as equity, the mildness and extenuation *correcting* the severities of justice), a full discussion. I shall not weary you with detail but on the mere words themselves (and *a fortiori* on their biblical usage) Ahad Ha'am's distinction is astonishingly shaky. If his basic view were sound, the Torah should not have said, 'righteousness, righteousness, thou shalt pursue' (*tsedek, tsedek tirdof*), but *mishpat, mishpat tirdof*, which it does not. As for the 'absolute' (*muḥlat*) of Ahad Ha'am, it is of course a neologism for the German *Absolut* borrowed from the usage of Nahman Krochmal. I shall have something to say about Ahad Ha'am and Krochmal later, but I must now say a bit more about *tsedek* and *mishpat*.

You will remember that the psalmist (89: 15) says: 'Righteousness and judgment are the foundation of Thy throne; mercy and truth go before Thy face.' The parallelism is clearly that of *tsedek* and *ḥesed* and *mishpat* with *emet*. *Tsedek* is thus next door to love and on the other side of the street to the rigorous pair of justice and truth. In rabbinical phrase, the attribute of sheer law needs the counterbalance of the attribute of mercy. *Tsedek* is generally translated as righteousness. I am not sure myself what

---

[4] ['Judaism and the Gospels'; Ahad Ha'am also wrote an extended review of Montefiore's commentary on the Synoptic Gospels, which appeared in English translation in the *Jewish Review* in 1920.]

the English word means. But whatever righteousness may mean, I think that rabbinic tradition is one with Maimonides in suggesting that the meaning of *tsedek* is 'equitableness' or 'fairness'.

For example:

Our teachers laid it down: 'In righteousness shalt thou judge thy neighbour': one litigant should not be allowed to sit while the other stands, one speak his fill and the other told to cut his words short.

Another lesson: 'In righteousness shalt thou judge thy neighbour': judge your neighbour with an inclination in his favour. R. Joseph taught: 'In righteousness shalt thou judge thy neighbour': do your best to judge him *yafeh*.

I shall not press this last of R. Joseph, though if the reference is to absolute justice, its terms ('do your best to'; *yafeh*) seem inappropriate. But both the first and second glosses call for comment, especially the second. Absolute justice has nothing to do with an inclination in man's favour. Rashi explains it to refer not to court cases where there are two litigants but to instances of private behaviour where different interpretations are possible, and to mean that in suspicious circumstances you should give other people the benefit of the doubt. But giving a person the benefit of the doubt has nothing to do with absolute justice. It is, rather, general decency or, as I said earlier, fairness. It is treating him—positively!—as we would like to be treated ourselves!

The point is that, as the Midrash insists so often, 'pure' justice is impracticable. God, in the famous words, cannot hold 'both sides of the rope at once'. If he wants a world at all, he must rule it with mercy, not justice. Or, speaking of man:

'Truth and judgment of peace judge in your gates': surely wherever there is judgment of truth, there is no peace, and wherever there is peace, there is no judgment of truth. Where can you have judgment and peace together? Only where there is compromise [*betsua*]. Similarly we read: 'And David did justice and righteousness [*tsedakah*] for all his people.' Surely wherever there is justice there is no righteousness, and wherever there is righteousness there is no justice. What justice is there in which there is righteousness? Where there is compromise.[5]

Here again, *tsedek* or *tsedekah* is the mitigating virtue which makes justice possible. Justice alone will not work, *cannot* work. May I remind you of those striking passages in which the destruction of Jerusalem is attributed to its affairs having been conducted strictly on the 'Din' of the Torah. Whatever they may mean (and there have been various attempts

[5] Tosefta, *Sanhedrin* 1.

to explain them), there does seem a clear suggestion that 'Din' by itself needs qualification. Is not the special virtue emphasized for Jewry in rabbinical writings that of action '*within* the boundary fixed by Din'?

VI

One may reach the same result from many other sides. For example, there is the famous remark about the three distinguishing qualities of Jewry: 'There are three signs in this people: they are compassionate; they are modest; they are charitable.'[6] The last quality is supported by the verse about Abraham being called in order that he should command his children and his household after him that they may keep the way of the Lord, 'to do justice and judgment' (Gen. 18: 19), as the English has it for the Hebrew *mishpat utsedakah*. Here the rabbis seem to have missed a wonderful opportunity. If their view had been that of Ahad Ha'am, they would have said that the third distinguishing mark of Jewry, and the original and indispensable one enshrined in its first charter, is its passion for justice; and they would have pointed out that the text ignores all else and concentrates on the synonyms *mishpat* and *tsedakah* in order to emphasize the absoluteness of the justice required. They seem, however, to have done precisely the opposite. They blandly overlook the presence of the word *mishpat* and lay all the stress on *tsedakah*, interpreting *tsedakah* as blandly, not in the possible sense of something of the nature of justice, but on the contrary in the popular sense of charity and good works (cf. too *Ket.* 8*b*). *Tsedakah* clearly interests the rabbis more than *mishpat*. Anyone (they seem to say) can be just. It takes a Jew to be kind. This remark, by the way, is not mine. It is from my usual source which is itself derived from his usual sources. 'The seed of Abraham our father', says Maimonides, 'feel compassion for all. If anyone does not, you may suspect his ancestry.'

Of course, Maimonides was a 'rationalist' (a recent, and regrettable, term of abuse among Jews); so, at the risk of wearying you, I quote the (*ex definitione*) unimpeachable testimony of a 'mystic':

The terms *tsedakah* and *ḥesed* used in the verse (Proverbs 14: 34) are the twins mentioned together everywhere, as for example, 'He pursues *tsedakah* and *ḥesed*' and, 'I am the Lord who doeth *ḥesed, mishpat* and *tsedakah* on the earth.' The plain sense of the verse is in my opinion that *tsedakah* exalteth a nation when it is present. *Ḥesed* is a reproach to any people when it is absent. The meaning is thus that it is in *tsedakah* and *ḥesed* that the exaltation of any nation lies. Their lack is its reproach.[5]

---

6 BT *Yevamot* 79*a*.   7 Nahmanides on Lev. 20: 17.

We may compare the insistence of another 'anti-rationalist,' Samuel David Luzzatto, on pity (*ḥemlah*) as the root virtue of Judaism. Luzzatto indeed goes further. He says that it is the *whole* of Judaism; and so far as the literary sources go, I have no doubt that he was far nearer the truth than Ahad Ha'am.

VII

I made mention at an earlier stage of the name of Nahman Krochmal, and this brings me to a far more important general point.

It has not been sufficiently appreciated—if indeed it has been noticed at all—that Ahad Ha'am, in so far as he is derivable from any previous Jewish thinker, is to be connected with Nahman Krochmal. A good deal is to be said about Nahman Krochmal's book, the first and most important thing being that it is not a book at all, and that, even if it is, it is not Krochmal's. This is not a paradox but a plain statement of fact. The *Moreh nevukhei hazeman* was so named by Leopold Zunz, who created the volume by putting together some of Krochmal's papers which he found after his death. The result is that we do not know whether what was published in Krochmal's name was meant by him to be published at all, much less whether it was meant by him to be published as a part of the book on the religious philosophy of Judaism which he had planned. We certainly do not know, and have now no means of finding out, whether what *was* published was published in the form Krochmal himself would have liked it to be published.

There has been some discussion on the question whether Krochmal was a Hegelian; and there is reason for supposing that he was not a Hegelian in the sense of recognizing the existence of no other modern philosopher but Hegel. I should guess myself that he was equally impressed by Kant. But the *Moreh nevukhei hazeman* contains as a fact an account of some portion of Hegel's technical logic; and although this may well have been no more than an exercise in translation or vulgarization never meant for publication in this form or in this book, it shows at least that Krochmal was strongly interested in Hegel. And of course Krochmal's celebrated analysis of Jewish history into the three stages of rise and equilibrium and decline has always been said to be Hegelian, especially by people who have not noticed that it misses the whole point of Hegelianism in at least two vital particulars. The topic where the thinking of Hegel is *in fact* preponderant is in Krochmal's treatment of spirit (*ruaḥ*) and the spiritual (*ruḥani*). This is only a variant of the Hegelian account of *Geist* with all its unfortunate confusions of the human and the divine. If you refer to chapter 7 of Krochmal's volume, you will see that this is so. *Geist* is everywhere—in the specific character (or god!) of each one of the peoples of the earth and in the specific character, or god(!), of the people of the Jews; the difference being that, whereas for Hegel the 'absolute' *Geist—hebraice, haruḥani ḥamuḥlat*—manifested itself in, and is identical with, the spirit of the German people, for Krochmal it manifested itself in, and is identical with, the spirit of the Jewish people. Or rather— but it is different to be sure. By an imprecise use of terms, Krochmal keeps on the respectable side of the fence and, verbally at least, remains faithful to transcendence.

Ahad Ha'am did not; but readers of the justly admired essay on Moses are so lulled by the essayist's gentle prose that they either omit to notice this or, if they do, omit to notice its significance. And its significance is made even more significant by the fact that it is so fully in accord with the psychological approach in general which Ahad Ha'am learned from his French masters. The psychological approach looks at things from the point of view of the consciousness of the observer. It has no need of, and no use for, the nature of the observed. It has indeed no need of an observed at all. It studies the states of the observer. It is in the observer that whatever takes place, takes place. Anything outside the observer, even the very existence of anything outside the observer, is hypothetical and superfluous. Read the essay on Moses carefully.[8] God is always within. He is the God of the heart, not of Sinai. The heart has its own promptings, and they are its own in every sense. They well up from within, possibly (as we are told so often now) from archetypal sources in the collective, or the racial, or the universal, *un*consciousness. They create their object (that is, their semblance of an object). They are not called out, not created, *by* an object.

I sometimes fancy that all this is incompatible not only with the God of Sinai but also with the God of religion as such, at least as religion is understood in the West. 'In the beginning God created' is, to my mind, *a* significant statement for religion *in general*; it is certainly central for any account of Judaism, and an account which ignores it, or bypasses it, or even neglects it, cannot be accepted without rigid and searching examination.

---

[8] [In *Selected Essays of Ahad Ha'am*, trans. Leon Simon (Jewish Publishing Society, 1912; repr. New York: Meridian, 1962).]

VIII

So, regretfully, we have to strip Ahad Ha'am down. He is not a philosopher; he was not a son of the Yishuv; he was a man of his own, not of our, time; his interpretation of Judaism, and of Jewish ethics, is doubtful. And yet—imitation and assimilation; priest and prophet; Zionism and Jewish culture; a spiritual centre; nationalists and the Diaspora, rival tongues (Hebrew and Yiddish); the transvaluation of values—as I quote the very names of the essays selected for translation by Sir Leon Simon we hear all the slogans of our day. They have lasted a long time; but—and here I am at a loss to proceed since I am convinced that a great deal of the hollowness in our spiritual life today is due to the presence in it of so many of these slogans. I had almost said, the haunting of it by so many of these pale shades. Even assuming that they were valid once (and men like the learned and acute Shai Ish Horovitz were not so sure), we do not seem to have observed that they have passed into history and that history itself has passed on.

And we have not observed something more important still. I called your attention to the fact that Ahad Ha'am used ideas he found ready to his hand in order to enable him to master and systematize the problems of his age and environment. He *used* ideas he *found*. He did not examine them over-minutely first; and he did not worry overmuch if they were —ultimately—not sound and—ultimately—incompatible with one another. And I am under the uncomfortable impression that many of the ideas he used so fruitfully were ultimately unsound and ultimately incompatible with one another. This may not matter in an essay or a newspaper article, read today, forgotten tomorrow. It does matter, it matters very much, it is of central importance, when the sum of such ideas is taken to be a complete and all-embracing and all-inclusive *philosophy*.

IX

Is there then nothing left? Have we only an implicit Hegelianism or an explicit psychologism leading to the equation of Judaism with an immanent nationalism; or teachings on the content of Judaism which are open to grave suspicion and are certainly opposed to views more deeply based in the authentic line of the tradition? Is there anything left to go back to or forward from?

My own reply would be that there are at least two things, one specific and one general.

The specific thing is Ahad Ha'am's insistence on the overriding character of moral action. In Judaism the moral requirement is supreme. The great sin of today is the 'politicization' of our Judaism, the great need, the 'Judaization' of our politics.

The general thing is the necessity for clear thinking on Judaism. Ahad Ha'am tried and (I submit) failed. We must try again.

Jewish philosophy, or rather the philosophy of Judaism, must resume its rightful place in Jewish studies. You remember F. H. Bradley's call for a critical study of first principles in general. I should be glad if from this assembly of teachers of Judaism in this country there should issue a call for a critical study of the first principles of Judaism.

My plea is for more philosophy in Jewish studies. But I must guard myself against a misunderstanding. Even the most thorough acquaintance with, and the most scientific knowledge of (e.g.) the Arabic original of the Khuzari, *will not do*. Philosophy is not philology. It is not history. It is the study of fact in the light of principles, and the study of principles in the light of fact. I think Ahad Ha'am would have agreed with me there.

Maimonides

❧

I
Life and Writings

MAIMONIDES ('SON OF MAIMON'), MOSES; known by the scholastics as Rabbi Moyses or Moyses Judaeus or Moyses Aegyptius, in Hebrew literature as Rambam, also Maimuni. Born Cordova, south (Arabic) Spain, 1138. Left Cordova as a boy of 13 with his family after the seizure of the country by the religiously intolerant Almohades, and after long wanderings finally settled in Egypt where his father, Maimon, died. When his brother David, a pearl merchant and main support of the family, was drowned at sea, he turned to the profession of medicine, becoming in 1170 physician to the viceroy of Egypt. Died 1204.

His works, all composed under the stress of travel or business, included commentaries on some tractates of the Talmud; a complete Commentary (finished *c.*1168), still widely used, on the early (second- and third-century) rabbinic code, the Mishnah; an original Code of his own, the *Mishneh torah* (Repetition of the Law), completed *c.*1178, preceded by a *Book of Precepts* in which the attempt is made to systematize the approach to the content of Judaism as a religious and moral discipline expressed in the commandments of the Pentateuch; some short medical treatises (e.g. on asthma and diet); some polemical writing (e.g. against Galen's view on teleology and against the prevailing blind belief in astrology); and many 'encyclical' letters to Jewish communities, far and near, on points of law and on public issues of importance. These were his basic preoccupations and interests, and his philosophy was only incidental. The only technically philosophical work is his first, the very slight *Logical Terminology*, a brief account of the elements of Aristotelian logic which concludes with a summary conspectus of the main divisions of the Aristotelian system as a whole. The *Guide for the Perplexed* (completed 1190[1]), which was origin-

This previously unpublished paper was originally written for the *Encyclopaedia of Philosophy* in 1962. It is printed here by permission of the estate of Leon Roth.

[1] The history of the translation and publication of the *Guide* is discussed in section VII below. The standard edition of the text is that of Salomon Munk, Arabic text with French translation and commentary (Paris, 1856–66).

ally undertaken to help a favourite pupil whose studies had brought him into collision with religion and which was afterwards expanded to include 'others like him, however few they may be', is not a set philosophical treatise but, professedly, an unsystematic essay on some problems of philosophical theology.

II
Philosophical Character of all his Writings

Although Maimonides is thus not purely a philosopher, all his work is of a philosophical character in that it harks back to first principles. For example, when the Mishnah lets drop the phrase 'the world to come', Maimonides inserted in his Commentary a special chapter (in effect, a separate treatise) on the nature of the afterlife and the proper use to be made of biblical and talmudic texts. To the Ethics of the Fathers, a collection of moral sayings included in the Mishnah, he prefixed an account of psychological and ethical principles (largely Aristotelian) known as the *Eight Chapters*, while he made the first of the fourteen books of his own original Code a comprehensive *Book of Knowledge*. This is divided into 'Foundations' (a summary of Aristotelian metaphysics and physics turned for the purposes of religion and buttressed with biblical texts), 'Ethics' (where the 'middle way' of Aristotle is shown by apt quotation to be good rabbinic doctrine), the 'Study of the Law' (a treatise on Jewish religious education and ideals), 'Idolatry' (in which a biblical philosophy of history is attempted), and 'Repentance' (a dissertation on practical morals much valued, in the Latin translation, by seventeenth- and eighteenth-century divines). The point of importance is that Maimonides thought it essential to preface a practical code of action by a statement of theoretical principles.

III
Sources of his Philosophical Ideas and his Advice on the Study of Philosophy

So far as these principles are philosophical in the technical sense, they derive from the Arabized Aristotle. On this there has been in recent years much new and illuminating research, but broadly speaking the themes and texts of paramount importance are those of the Four Causes (*Metaphysics* A2 and *Physics* 2. 3); the different 'faculties' of the soul (*Analytics* 1 and *Nicaean Ethics* 1. 13); the different kinds of *nous* (*Analytics* 3, 3–8 and in particular the mysterious chapter 5); the 'unmoved mover' (*Physics* 8. 5

and *Metaphysics* Λ7) God as pure intellection (*Metaphysics* Λ7), and the role of the 'spheres' in the resulting theological cosmology (*Metaphysics* Λ8). The texts themselves are understood largely through the Neoplatonic commentators, a point which has been rightly and fruitfully emphasized in many modern accounts of medieval thought in general; and much of Plotinus himself is given in the much-read *De causis* (= Proclus' *Elements of Theology*) then commonly ascribed to Aristotle. Maimonides himself leaves no doubt as to his views on the philosophers to be followed. In a letter to the Provençal translator of his *Guide* from Arabic into Hebrew (see section VII below) he writes:

Take care not to study Aristotle except in the commentaries of Alexander or Themistius or Averroes. Of the books which you mention as being in your possession or available to you: the *Book of the Apple* and the *House of Gold* are idle speculation and foolishness; they are ascribed to Aristotle but are not his. Al-Razi's *Theology* is his but it is valueless because al-Razi was only a physician. Similarly, Isaac Israeli's *Book of Definitions* and *Book of Elements* are idle and foolish because Isaac Israeli too was only a physician. [Is the meaning that of Pascal's remark on the 'geometrician who is only a geometrician'?] As for the *Microcosm* of Joseph ibn Tsadik, I have not seen it ...

In general, let me advise you not to study any book on logic except that of Abu Nasr al-Farabi. Whatever he wrote, and in particular his *Principles of Existing Things*, is the purest sifted meal, and anyone can learn and profit from him because he was of exceptional wisdom. In the same way, Ibn Bajja [Avempace] was a wise and great philosopher, and his doctrine and writings are 'plain to the attentive, and show the right way in the pursuit of truth' (Prov. 8: 9).

But it is the works of Aristotle which are the source and root of all these books on the sciences, and they cannot be understood except through the commentaries named of Alexander or Themistius or Averroes. Everything else, e.g., the books of Empedocles and Pythagoras and Hermes and Porphyry, is early philosophy and not worth spending time on.

The works of Plato, the master of Aristotle, are profound and of hidden meaning, but the student can dispense with them because the books of his pupil Aristotle are a sufficient substitute for everything which appeared before. Aristotle's doctrine is the crown of human wisdom, unless one has received the divine influence and reached the heights of prophecy than which there is nothing higher.

The works of Avicenna, although accurate and acute, are not on the same level as those of Abu Nasr al-Farabi. But they are useful, and he too is a man whose doctrine is worth occupying yourself with and whose writings you should study.

This is admittedly the advice of an older to a younger man and refers to the books which the younger man had said were available to him. But its direction is clear and confirmed in Maimonides' own writings. A reservation should be made on one point only. Although Maimonides highly recommended to his translator the commentaries of Averroes, it appears from another letter that he himself only became acquainted with them late in life when his own work was already done.

IV
Maimonides' Thinking: The 'Harmonizing' of 'Faith' and 'Reason'

The chapters in the Commentary and the Code indicate already the nature of Maimonides' thinking and his place in the history of thought. It is that of a 'harmonizer' between 'faith' and 'reason'. The great talmudist and student of Holy Writ had to reconcile the Bible with the new culture of the day which centred round the Arabized version of Greek thought current in educated circles, and in the process he came to maintain positions which proved of value outside the synagogue and beyond his time. He was not an original thinker in the full sense. He did not begin philosophy afresh, nor did he offer a comprehensive and detailed reorganization of accepted thought. The *Guide* is a comparatively short book. Its problem is the clash between 'religion' and 'science'; but Maimonides was too good a scientist, and too good a theologian, to accept easy solutions. He is rather suggestive than conclusive. The earlier works (the special chapters in the Commentary and the first book of the Code) are directed to the plain man and are therefore put plainly without discussion of difficulties. The *Guide* discusses some of the difficulties. It is heuristic and, in addition, contains some deliberate mystification the full reasons for which have not yet been satisfactorily explained. In some instances it may be due to the author's professed didactic purpose of stimulating further thought.

V
The Argumentation of the *Guide* and its Main Issues

The *Guide* opens in effect negatively. It sweeps away the anthropomorphisms which are a major obstacle to the thinker's acceptance of the Bible by affirming, and attempting to show in some detail, that they are only a veiled way of conveying philosophical ideas. It passes to a consideration (i. 50 ff.) of the attributes of God in which the *via negativa* is strongly maintained. But God is above, rather than lacking, the excellencies we attribute to him, and it is our description of God, not God's nature, which is to be restrained. In God essence and existence are one; and all that we can say of him truly is that he is the self-sufficient source of all being and spring of all activity. As active cause he is termed in the Bible good and just and merciful, but these attributes (the 'attributes of action') are to be understood not as a description of God but as an index of his requirements from man.

From this discussion we turn to the question of God's existence, the order of enquiry being justified by the reflection that we should know first what the God is whose existence (if we are not satisfied with the Bible) we would have demonstrated, before we attempt the demonstration. The demonstration itself (ii, introduction) is that of the philosophers, i.e. the Aristotelians, and consists of varieties of the arguments from motion and from the existence of the contingent and of potentiality; but before it there is inserted a series of chapters (i. 75 ff.) on the school of Muslim theologians known as the Kalam who based their doctrine of God on a theory of reality approximating to what was called later Occasionalism. This Maimonides uncompromisingly rejects; and when later (ii. 29) he comes to consider biblical miracles, he takes the view expressed in the Code that the supporting of faith by miracle is a sign not of faith but of lack of faith, affirming that, if miracles cannot be explained as having occurred in dreams, they are in some way (as some of the talmudists had maintained long before) embedded in the natural order from the very first, the 'miracles' lying in the circumstances, rather than in the fact, of their happening. The first great positive conclusion of the *Guide* thus emerges. God is the source of order, and the right way to find him is, by the use of the intelligence (which is the 'likeness of God') implanted in us, to unravel the traces of that order. 'Science' is thus to be welcomed, its efforts furthered, and its results accepted.

But current scientific theories are not necessarily science. They are only ways of 'saving the phenomena' (ii. 11), and Maimonides pits himself against the greatest of the theories of science, that of the eternity of the universe. This he does not contravert. He only holds (ii. 13 ff.) that it is not demonstrated. If it were in truth demonstrated, he says (ii. 25) to the great subsequent scandal of Spinoza (*Tractatus Theologico-politicus*, 7), he would have accepted it and accommodated the text of Scripture to it. But since it is not demonstrated (and Maimonides maintains (ii. 15), relying possibly on passages of the *De caelo*, that Aristotle himself did not think it was), the religionist may continue to hold the doctrine of creation. What 'reason' does not forbid, 'faith' may, if its own grounds are sufficient, admit. Yet Maimonides takes, as it were, the worse case, and conducts his demonstration of the existence of God on the scientists' hypothesis of the eternity of the world, not, as his predecessors had done, on that of creation. 'Science' itself is thus forced to the admission of the existence of God.

We pass to God's activity in creation. Maimonides is singularly undogmatic on the nature of the creative act or process because he sees that the real issue for religion is not that between 'emanation' and 'creation' but between necessity and freedom. He argues that the world is a product of God's free activity, and it is his free activity which constitutes, after the creative act (the reason and method of which we cannot know), what we call natural law. All argument to the contrary depends upon analogy with human ways of working with materials *already in* existence; but God called the world *into* existence. This 'transcendental fallacy' being established (ii. 17), we can easily accept the position that, although created and therefore *not* in the philosophical sense 'eternal', i.e. necessary, the universe might endure eternally. The general strategy of the argumentation is remarkable. It is directed first against the theologians who reject the scientific universe, then against the scientists who rely on it too much and take current theories to be demonstrated truth. It then proceeds, on the basis of a more thoughtful science, to construct a more measured theology.

Having pointed out a way round the 'over'-belief of the theologians and the 'under'-belief of the scientists, Maimonides is free to turn to religion. Biblical religion centres round Moses and the prophets, and Maimonides conducts (ii. 32 ff.) an acute enquiry into the nature of prophecy. He notes its characteristic working through the exercise of the pictorial imagination, but holds that in its highest stage it is an intuition deriving immediately from, or even identical with, what the Aristotelians recognized as the 'active intellect' (ii. 38). It is thus brought within the sphere of a general theory of knowledge; and although Maimonides affirms the need of a special descent of the divine spirit before a prophet is made, the whole theory of the 'actualization' of the 'passive' intellect rests on an activity from 'above', and prophecy is seen in principle to be a special case of a general fact. (In a sense, of course, the opposite formulation would also be true, and all knowledge could be seen as a special case of 'prophecy'.) The highest stage of all was achieved by the greatest of the prophets (Deut. 34: 10), Moses, whom 'God knew face to face'; and the knowledge he was given is declared expressly (Num. 12: 6–8) to be imageless, not in 'visions and dreams but mouth to mouth, clearly'.

This rationalization of the figure of Moses allowed Maimonides to vindicate the claims of the 'law of Moses' to be the highest truth. Yet, surprisingly for his day, he was aware to the full of the historical element always present in institutional religion, and he anticipated the methods of comparative sociology by insisting that light should be thrown on the precepts of the Law by a study of the customs of the then neighbouring peoples (iii. 26 ff.). The Law is a discipline, weaning men from erroneous ideas of God and implanting true ideas in their place, and its purpose (iii. 50 ff.) is to lead them to the 'knowledge of God' seen by the prophets as the end of religion. But this 'knowledge' is not an abstract one. It is the certitude of God's existence attained through the recognition of the order displayed in nature, the adoration and consequent love of God to which this leads, and the imitation of God's moral attributes through the practice of kindness, justice, and righteousness on this earth (Jer. 9: 22; *Guide*, iii. 54 end). When this has been achieved, and only when this has been achieved, the way is open to the highest good. This is expressed by Maimonides in terms of the (Aristotelian) ideal of the contemplation of the divine through thought, and it is identical for him with what the psalmist already knew as 'seeing the beauty of the Lord' and the talmudists as 'enjoying the glory of the divine presence'.

The *Guide* concludes with a striking note of universalism: 'God is nigh to all those who truly call on him.' Like the Code (last book, last sentence), it looks to the time when the 'whole earth', that is, humanity as such, 'shall be filled with the knowledge of God as the waters cover the sea'. But the final end is beyond this life and is conditioned by the stage in intellectual advance which in this life man achieves. Divine Providence, understood by the Aristotelians to extend only to the species, reaches down in the case of the human race, endowed as it is with reason (to speak philosophically) or (in biblical terms) made in the likeness of God, to the individual. But the resulting 'immortality' is only for the 'actualized' part of the soul, and only for those whose 'passive' intellect has in some degree become 'actualized' (see Code: 'Foundations', iv. 8–9, 'Repentance', viii. 3). To what extent personal differentiation between and within actualized souls is possible (see *Guide*, i, lxxiv, section 7 and Munk's notes pp. 432–5), is not explained clearly, and thus one of the great questions put by 'faith' to 'reason' is not fully resolved. But Maimonides throughout all his writings maintains the reality of personal immortality in the sense of a constant enjoyment, after this life, of the presence of God. Indeed it is a state acquired by some (e.g. Moses and the Patriarchs: *Guide*, iii. 51 end) in this life. It is thus rather a quality of existence independent of the body which is continued after corporeal dissolution than the usual subject of theological contention.

VI
Repercussions

Maimonides had an austere disdain for everything in the life of the mind but the purest thought (in the Commentary he expressly disapproves of music and poetry), and it was this severe intellectualism, particularly in his account of God and of the life of the soul, which even in his own lifetime aroused a storm in the synagogue. This led historically, *par revanche*, to two important results. The one was the re-emergence of the mystical stream in Jewish thought which culminated in the production of the Zohar in the third quarter of the thirteenth century; the other was the exacerbation of the issue between faith and reason in religion which long afterwards, in the thought of Spinoza, helped to produce the *Tractatus Theologico-politicus* with its classical formulation of the distinction between philosophy and religion and of the necessary severance of Church from State. Yet the violence of the opposition aroused by Maimonides' thought among the religionists was fully equalled by the veneration felt for it by its adherents, and it became and remained the centre of the philosophical movement in Judaism, all subsequent thinkers setting out, in agreement or disagreement, from its main positions.

VII
Maimonides in Western Thought

The *Guide*, written in Arabic, was translated into Hebrew during the author's lifetime, and in consultation with him, by the Provençal Samuel ibn Tibbon (*c.*1150–*c.*1230) to whom the letter quoted above (section III) was addressed. This translation remained standard and exercised a preponderant influence on Hebrew philosophical thought and literary style; it was the source of much of the basic background of the Dutch Jewish philosopher Spinoza. But it is so pedantically exact and faithful to the Arabic original that even in its own day it was found difficult, and at the instance of other Provençal scholars a second Hebrew translation was prepared by the Hebrew poet Judah al-Harizi (*c.*1170–*c.*1235). This second translation, which soon fell out of use among Jews (it was not put into print until the nineteenth century,[2] was the text of the *Guide* translated

---

[2] Ed. Schlossberg (London, 1851–79).

by an unidentified scholar into Latin in the thirteenth century; and it was this anonymous Latin version from the Hebrew of al-Harizi, the same apparently as that printed at Paris under the title *Dux neutrorum* in 1520, which was read by the schoolmen and is referred to by William of Auvergne (d. 1249) and Alexander of Hales (d. 1245). Some of its basic ideas were used (with acknowledgements) by Albert the Great and Thomas Aquinas in the construction of their systems of theology, while recently published manuscripts have shown their importance for the 'intellectual mysticism' of Meister Eckhart. The interest the book excited in its day is also attested to by the curious treatise *De erroribus philosophorum*,[3] in which Maimonides' 'errors' are listed, together with those of Aristotle, Avicenna, Averroes, Algazali, and Alkindi.

The first translation into Hebrew, that of ibn Tibbon, was turned into Latin by Buxtorf the younger (1599–1664); and Buxtorf's *Doctor perplexorum*[4] was the source of the knowledge of the *Guide* shown by, for example, Leibniz, who made some penetrating summaries and criticisms of it,[5] and by John Spencer, the author of *De legibus Hebraeorum* (1669), a book which laid the foundations of the science of comparative religion and which avowedly is a fuller working out of the *Guide*, iii. 26–50. The seventeenth century knew Maimonides well, but rather as a moralist and theologian than as a philosopher, and translated many of his smaller Hebrew treatises into Latin. Edward Pococke's still valuable *Porta Mosis*[6] translated the chapters of the Mishnah Commentary noted in section II above into Latin from the original Arabic.

In the eighteenth century the German Jewish philosopher Moses Mendelssohn, who was wont to say in jest that he had acquired his hump by bending in his youth over the pages of the *Guide*, wrote a standard Hebrew commentary on the *Logical Terminology*, while Solomon Maimon, the critic of Kant and forerunner of Fichte, took his name from Maimonides and wrote a Hebrew commentary on the first part of the *Guide* prefaced by a short account of the history of European philosophy.[7] By the nineteenth century the *Guide* had passed into history and was ripe for the standard edition of the erudite Salomon Munk.[8]

---

[3] Ed. Mandonnet, vol. ii of *Siger de Brabant* (Louvain, 1908).

[4] Basle, 1629.

[5] *Leibniz: La Philosophie juive et la Cabale*, ed. Foucher de Careil (Paris, 1861).

[6] Oxford, 1655.

[7] Berlin, 1791; reprinted, *pietatis causa*, by S. H. Bergmann and N. Rotenstreich (Jerusalem, 1952).

[8] See n. 1 above.

Bibliography

General

W. Bacher, M. Brann, and D. Simonsen (eds.), *Moses ben Maimon*, vols. i and ii (Frankfurt, 1908 and 1914), includes important essays by Ph. Bloch, Hermann Cohen, Jacob Guttmann, and Julius Guttmann. The following octocentenary volumes: S. Baron (ed.), *Essays on Maimonides* (Columbia, Oh., 1941), I. Epstein (ed.), *Moses Maimonides* (London, 1935), and Louis Germain Lévy, *Maïmonide* (Paris, 1911). D. Yellin and I. Abrahams, *Maimonides* (London, 1903); S. Zeitlin, *Maimonides* (New York, 1935). The relevant chapters in standard histories of Jewish philosophy by Julius Guttmann (Munich, 1933; revised and enlarged edn. in Hebrew, Jerusalem, 1951), I. Husik (New York, 1918; new edn., with additional bibliography, 1958), and by G. Vajda, *Introduction à la pensée juive du moyen âge* (Paris, 1947). The relevant sections in Friedrich Ueberweg and Max Heinze, *Grundriß der Geschichte der Philosophie*, ii: *Die mittlere oder die patristische und scholastische Zeit*, 10th edn., rev. Matthias Baumgartner (Berlin, 1915), where the thorny problem of the use made of Maimonides by the great scholastics is discussed with more justice than sympathy; and Leon Roth, *The Guide for the Perplexed* (London, 1948), an attempt to assess Maimonides for modern needs.

Works

Logical Terminology

Hebrew: published as *Introduction to Logic*, ed. L. Roth and E. Baneth (Jerusalem, 1935); with Arabic and Hebrew texts and English translation: by I. Efros, published in the *Proceedings of the American Academy for Jewish Research* (New York, 1938); French: by M. Ventura, *Maïmonide: Terminologie logique* (Paris, 1935).

Philosophical Chapters in the Mishnah Commentary

Latin: by E. Pococke, *Porta Mosis* (Oxford, 1655); English: by J. Abelson, *Jewish Quarterly Review* (1906).

The Eight Chapters

Arabic text with German translation and notes by M. Wolff, 2nd, revised, edn. (Leiden, 1903); English version with notes by J. Gorfinkle (Columbia, Oh., 1912).

Mishneh Torah: The Book of Knowledge [*Sefer hamada*]

English: by M. Hyamson (New York, 1937); by H. H. Bernard, *The Main Principles of the Creed and Ethics of the Jews* (Cambridge, 1832).

The Guide of the Perplexed

In addition to the exemplary and indispensable edition by Salomon Munk, Arabic text with French translation and commentary (Paris, 1856–66), there is an

Italian version by D. L. Maroni (Florence, 1871–6); an English one by M. Fried-laender (London, 1881), frequently reprinted but without the notes, now also in paperback; and a German one by A. Weiss (Leipzig, 1923). There is a shortened English version by Chaim Rabin, with an introduction by Julius Guttmann, in the East and West Library (London, 1952), and a volume of excerpts from the whole of Maimonides' writings by A. Cohen, *The Teachings of Maimonides* (London, 1927). The best Hebrew text is that of J. Ibn Shemuel (Kaufmann), with introductory essays only (Jerusalem, 1946), and with full commentary (1935). Munk's Arabic text has been reprinted with textual notes by I. Joel (Jerusalem, 1921).

Background

There is popular presentation in essays in [I. Abrahams], Edwyn R. Bevan, and Charles Singer, *Legacy of Israel* (Oxford, 1927), but for serious study the work of M. Steinschneider, *Hebraeische Uebersetzungen des Mittelalters* (Berlin, 1893) remains indispensable. For the scientific background consult P. M. M. Duhem, *Système du monde*, 10 vols. (Paris, 1913–59); for the philosophical, W. D. Ross's edition of Aristotle's *Metaphysics* (Oxford, 1924), particularly the introductory essay (no. IV) on Aristotle's theology, and of the *De anima* (Oxford, 1961), introduction, pp. 41 ff. The recent work of R. Walzer, *Greek into Arabic* (Oxford, 1962) throws light on many unexpected places. The many special studies of H. A. Wolfson, listed in the 1958 edition of Husik (see under 'General' above) but unfortunately uncollected, and of L. Strauss (especially *Farabi's Plato* and *The Literary Character of the Guide for the Perplexed*) have not yet been absorbed in the literature.

Bibliography of the Writings of Leon Roth

A BIBLIOGRAPHY of Leon Roth's writings was first compiled anonymously by several of his pupils, and included in a memorial brochure published by the Hebrew University Press in 1963; as the compilers acknowledged, this was almost certainly incomplete. It has been possible to add quite a substantial number of items, and my thanks are due to Professor T. E. Jessop, Mr J. M. Shaftesley, and particularly to members of Leon Roth's family for their help in recovering these titles. The arrangement of material here differs from the Jerusalem scheme somewhat, and, since the present list exceeds the other considerably, I have not felt it necessary to indicate where an item also appears on the Jerusalem list. Unfortunately, personal inspection of most of the Hebrew items, and some of the English ones, was not possible for me, and the completeness of detail is therefore not consistent throughout.

R.L.

I. English

Books

1. *Spinoza, Descartes and Maimonides* (Oxford: Clarendon Press, 1924; reissued New York: Russell & Russell, 1963).

2. *Correspondence of Descartes and Constantyn Huygens, 1635–1647*, edited from manuscripts now in the Bibliothèque Nationale (Oxford: Clarendon Press, 1926).

3. *The Science of Morals: An Essay in Method* (London: Benn, 1928).

4. *Spinoza* (London: Benn, 1929).

5. *Descartes' Discourse on Method* (Oxford: Clarendon Press, 1937).

6. *The Theory and Practice of Government.* Excerpts from *Representative Government* by John Stuart Mill and *The English Constitution* by Walter Bagehot (Jerusalem: D. B. Aaronson, 1945).

This bibliography, compiled by Raphael Loewe, was first published in his *Studies in Rationalism, Judaism and Universalism in Memory of Leon Roth* (London: Routledge, 1966); it is published here, in an edited form, by kind permission of Professor Loewe.

7. *The Guide for the Perplexed: Moses Maimonides* (London: Hutchinson, 1948).

8. *God and Man in the Old Testament* (London: George Allen & Unwin, 1955). Translation of II. 27.

9. *Judaism: A Portrait* (London: Faber & Faber, 1960; paperback edn., New York: Viking Press, 1962).

Pamphlets, Articles, Lectures, Reviews, etc.

10. 'David Nieto and the Orthodoxy of Spinozism', *Chronicon Spinozanum*, 1 (1921), 278–82.

11. 'The *Abscondita Sapientiae* of Joseph del Medigo', *Chronicon Spinozanum*, 2 (1922), 54–66.

12. 'Spinoza and Cartesianism', *Mind*, 32 (1923), 12 f., 160 f. [Later published in I. 1.]

13. 'Miscellanies', *Chronicon Spinozanum*, 3 (1923), 347–8.

14. Review of A. Kaminka's *The Thoughts of Marcus Aurelius* (Heb.), *Jewish Guardian*, 16 Mar. 1923.

15. 'The Goodness of God', *Journal of Philosophical Studies*, 2/8 (1926), 503–15.

16. 'Jewish Thought in the Modern World', in Edwyn R. Bevan and Charles Singer (eds.), *The Legacy of Israel* (Oxford: Clarendon Press, 1927), 433–72.

17. 'Spinoza in Recent English Thought', *Mind*, 36 (1927), 205 f.

18. Review of H. Bergmann's *The Philosophy of Immanuel Kant* (Heb.), *Mind*, 36 (1927), 384.

19. 'The Jerusalem University: Some Personal Notes', *Universities Review*, 2/2 (1930), 111–15. [Describes methods employed to produce Hebrew versions of philosophical texts, and the fashioning of Hebrew for university teaching purposes. Cf. I. 26.]

20. 'Jerusalem Letter', *Universities Review*, 4 (1932), 126–31. [Describes the introduction of teaching in biological sciences, financial difficulties, and administrative experiment in the Hebrew University.]

21. 'Note on the Relationship between Locke and Descartes', *Mind*, 44 (1935), 414–16.

22. 'The Discourse on Method, 1637–1937', *Mind*, 46 (1937), 32–43.

23. 'The Descartes–Huygens Correspondence', *Travaux du IXe Congrès international de Philosophie* ('Congrès Descartes') (Paris, 1937), 101–8.

24. 'The First 25 Years of the Hebrew University', *Bulletin* of the English Friends of the Hebrew University (Oct. 1943).

25. *The Hebrew University and its Place in the Modern World*, Lucien Wolf Memorial Lecture 1945, the Jewish Historical Society of England. [Reported also in the *Jewish Chronicle*, 6 Apr. 1945, p. 5.]

26. Review article: 'Philosophical Classics' *Commentary*, 2 (1946), 298–300. [Outlines the origin of this series of Hebrew translations and the methods employed to produce it. Cf. I. 19.]

27. 'A Plea for Universality in Education', *Scopus*, 2/1 (Mar. 1948). [Cf. II. 54.]

28. 'Judah L. Magnes and the Hebrew University', *Jewish Education*, 20 (1949).

29. 'I[srael] A[brahams] and the Hebrew University', *Zionist Independent*, 1/2 (1949), 20 f.

30. 'General Humanities', in Manka Spiegel (ed.), *The Hebrew University of Jerusalem 1925–50* (Jerusalem, 1950), 98–102. [Outlines the history of the establishment of the various schools of humane studies. A Hebrew edition of this book also appeared.]

31. 'Twenty Five Years [of the Hebrew University]', *Scopus*, 4/1 (Feb. 1950).

32. 'Judaism', *Year Book of Education* (1951), ch. 6, pp. 192–212.

33. 'Ambassador' [review editorial of James G. McDonald's *My Mission in Israel*], *Desiderata*, 4/49 (7 Dec. 1951), 1–3. (Signed A.N.O.R. *Desiderata* was edited by Leon Roth's brother David, the bibliophile.)

34. 'Boloney' [review editorial of Charles G. Finney's *The Circus of Dr. Lao*], *Desiderata*, 4/50 (14 Dec. 1951), 1–4. (Signed A.B.F.)

35. 'Judah Leon Magnes: An Appreciation', *Ner*. Jerusalem, 3rd year, 5–6 (Dec. 1951–Jan. 1952), 20 (English portion of a Hebrew–English periodical). [Cf. II. 71.]

36. 'Philosophy at the University [of Jerusalem] and the Jewish Mind', in Norman Bentwich (ed.), *Hebrew University Garland* (1952), 65–72. Also reprinted as a pamphlet (Welwyn Garden City, 1952). [On the indispensability of scepticism, self-criticism, and intellectual cosmopolitanism.]

37. Letter to the *Jewish Chronicle*, 4 Dec. 1953, p. 21, on the morality of Jewish apologia for the Qibya raid. [Reproduced above, pp. xviii–xx.]

38. *Jewish Thought as a Factor in Civilization* (Paris: Unesco, 1954). Yiddish translation by M. Shenderey (Buenos Aires, 1956). [Reproduced above, pp. 29–73.]

39. 'St George for England' [review editorial of George Orwell's *England, Your England and Other Essays*], *Desiderata*, 7/2 (15 Jan. 1954), 1–3. (Signed A.B.F.)

40. Letters to the *Jewish Chronicle*, 16 Apr. 1954, p. 23, and 30 Apr. 1954, p. 15, on Ahad Ha'am; cf. also issue for 9 Apr. 1954, p. 38.

41. 'Cartesian Studies' [review of Norman Kemp Smith's *New Studies in the Philosophy of Descartes*], *Cambridge Journal*, 7 (1954), 466–75.

42. *The Significance of Biblical Prophecy for our Time*, Rabbi Mattuck Memorial Pamphlet 1 (London: London Society of Jews and Christians, 1955), jointly with W. A. L. Elmslie. [Reproduced above, pp. 74–9.]

43. 'Prophets of All Time', *Common Ground* (Council of Christians and Jews), 9/3 (1955), 3–8. [Abbreviated version of I. 42.]

44. Review of J. C. Wordsworth's *Pain and Other Problems, Philosophical Quarterly*, 5 (1955), 382–3.

45. Letter to the *Jewish Chronicle*, 4 Feb. 1955, p. 14, on J. L. Magnes.

46. *Great Jewish Books, Old and New* (London: Jewish Book Council, 1955).

47. 'A Contemporary Moralist: Albert Camus', R. R. Marett Memorial Lecture, *Philosophy*, 30 (1955), 291–303.

48. *Some Reflections on the Interpretation of Scripture*, Claude Montefiore Lecture 1955 (London: Liberal Jewish Synagogue, 1956). [Reproduced above, pp. 80–94.]

49. 'The "Cherem" on Spinoza', *Jewish Chronicle*, 27 July 1956, p. 15.

50. Address given at the West London Synagogue on the occasion of the inauguration of the Jewish Theological College (subsequently renamed the Leo Baeck College), *The Synagogue Review*, 31/3 (1956), 65 f. In part incorporated in I. 9, 74 f.

51. 'Rabbi and Audience', *Jewish Chronicle*, 14 Dec. 1956, p. 17, and 21 Dec. 1956, p. 15.

52. *Baruch Spinoza: His Religious Importance for the Jew of Today* (Amsterdam: International Conference of the World Union for Progressive Judaism, 1957). [Reproduced above, pp. 95–107.]

53. 'Spinoza and the Religious Jew of Today', *Jewish Chronicle*, 13 Sept. 1955, p. 21, and 20 Sept. 1955, p. 21. [Abbreviated version of I. 52.]

54. 'Encounter and Tensions in World Religions', *Forum* (World Congress of Faiths, London), 32 (1957), 7–15.

55. Review of W. R. Valentiner's *Rembrandt and Spinoza, Jewish Chronicle*, 21 June 1957, p. 23.

56. Review of Arnold Toynbee's *An Historian's Approach to Religion, A[nglo-] J[ewish] A[ssociation] Quarterly*, 3 (1957), 34.

57. 'Judaism, the Elements', *Judaism* (New York), 7 (1958), 3–13. [An earlier draft of ch. 1 of I. 9. Reproduced above, pp. 108–20.]

58. 'Maimonides', *Common Ground* (Council of Christians and Jews), 12/1, (1958), 23–6.

59. Review of M. Waxman's *Tradition and Change, Jewish Chronicle*, 15 May 1959, p. 19.

60. 'The Resurgence of Hebrew', *Jewish Journal of Sociology*, 1/2 (1959), 177 f.

61. 'Authority, Religion, and Law', *Hibbert Journal*, 58 (1960), 115–20. [Reproduced above, pp. 121–7.]

62. 'Back To, Forward From, Ahad Ha'am?', in *Addresses* given at the Thirteenth Conference of Anglo-Jewish Preachers (1960), 35–47. [Cf. 1. 63.]

63. 'Back To, Forward From, Ahad Ha'am?', *Conservative Judaism* (New York), 17/1–2 (1962–3), 20–30. [Cf. 1. 62. Reproduced above, pp. 156–68.]

64. Review of Louis Jacobs's *Jewish Values*, *Jewish Chronicle*, 3 June 1960, p. 20.

65. 'Religion and Piety in Spinoza', in *A Seminar of Saints*, papers presented at the second seminar of the Union for the Study of Great Religions (Madras: Ganesh, 1960).

66. 'Hebraists and Non-Hebraists of the Seventeenth Century', *Journal of Semitic Studies*, 6 (1961), 204–21.

67. Review of Malcolm L. Diamond's *Martin Buber: Jewish Existentialist*, *Journal of Semitic Studies*, 6 (1961), 114.

68. Review of Cyrus H. Gordon's *New Horizons in Old Testament Literature*, *Journal of Semitic Studies*, 6 (1961), 293–4.

69. Review of Samuel Belkin's *In His Image: The Jewish Philosophy of Man as Expressed in Rabbinic Tradition*, *Jewish Chronicle*, 17 Mar. 1961, p. 29.

70. Review of Yeḥezkel Kaufmann's *The Religion of Israel* (English translation), *Jewish Chronicle*, 2 June 1961, p. 24.

71. 'A Secularist Faith', *World Faiths* (formerly *Forum*), 51 (1961).

72. 'Religion and Literature', *Hibbert Journal*, 60 (1961–2), 24–34.

73. 'Religion and Literature' (no. 1. 72), reprinted in *Religion in the Modern World* (London: World Congress of Faiths, n.d.), 24–34.

74. *Foundations*, St Paul's Lecture 1961 (London: London Diocesan Council for Christian Jewish Understanding, 1962).

75. 'Is there a Jewish Philosophy?', in Raymond Goldwater (ed.), *Jewish Philosophy and Philosophers* (London: The Hillel Foundation, 1962), 1–19. [Reproduced above, pp. 1–14.]

76. 'Moralization and Demoralization in Jewish Ethics', *Judaism* (New York), 11/4 (1962), 291–302. [Reproduced above, pp. 128–43.]

77. 'Mysticism: Thick and Thin', *World Faiths* (formerly *Forum*), 55 (1962), 1–12. [Reproduced above, pp. 144–55.]

78. Review of A. C. Bouquet's *Sacred Books of the World*, *Jewish Chronicle*, 7 Dec. 1962, p. 26.

79. Review of Jacob Katz's *Exclusiveness and Tolerance: Studies in Jewish–Gentile Relations in Medieval and Modern Times*, *Journal of Semitic Studies*, 8 (1963), 137 f.

80. Review of S. G. F. Brandon's *Man and His Destiny in the Great Religions*, *Journal of Semitic Studies*, 8 (1963), 217 f.

81. 'Some Observations on Recent Reported Undergraduate Conversions to Christianity', paper read to the Inter-University Jewish Federation [of England] Summer School, Aug. 1954, pp. 22 f. [This item was not technically published but reproduced in cyclostyled form for private circulation only.]

II. Hebrew

The titles of the works Leon Roth wrote in Hebrew are given here in English to enable readers who do not have Hebrew to form an idea of the scope of his writings.

Books

An asterisk indicates books published by the Magnes Press, the Hebrew University, Jerusalem

1. *In Memoriam Ahad Ha'am*. Annual Ahad Ha'am Memorial Lectures, 1929–1937 (also published annually from 1931). Individual titles are:
   (a) 'Philosophy and Ahad Ha'am' (inaugural lecture, 1929).
   (b) '*Imitatio Dei* and the Idea of Holiness' (1931) [English translation above, pp. 15–28.]
   (c) 'Intellect and Will as Religious Factors' (1932).
   (d) '*De erroribus philosophorum*' (1933).
   (e) 'Paganism' (1934).
   (f) 'Middle Axioms in Jewish Ethics' (1935).
   (g) 'The Reasons for the Precepts' (1936).
   (h) 'Development, Definition, and Judaism' (1937).

2. *Guide to Greek Philosophy* (Jerusalem: Mass, 1939; 2nd edn. 1946; 3rd edn. 1952; 4th edn. 1954).

3. *Guide to Modern Philosophy* (Jerusalem: Mass, 1941; 2nd edn. 1950).

4. *Advanced Studies and Contemporary Education* (Tel Aviv: Yavneh, 1944).

5. *Seven Chapters on England and English Democracy* (Tel Aviv: Yavneh, 1945).

6. *Guide to Political Thought* (Jerusalem: Mass, 1947; 2nd edn. 1952; 3rd edn. 1958).

7. *Education and Human Values: Chapters on the Involvement of Humanism in Education* (Tel Aviv: Devir, 1949; 2nd edn. 1961).

8. *Government of the People by the People: Fundamentals of Democracy* (Tel Aviv: Yavneh, 1949).

Translations from the Greek

9. Aristotle, *Metaphysics*, Book I (1934; 2nd edn. 1949).*

10. Aristotle, *Metaphysics*, Book XI (1934).*

11. Aristotle, *Politics*, Books I–II (1936; rev. edn. 1950).*

12. Aristotle, *Ethics*, Books I–II (1943; photographic reproduction 1962).*

Edited Volumes

Leon Roth was connected with the following volumes either as general editor, or through being responsible for annotating or selecting their contents.

13. Leibniz, *The Nova Methodus and Other Writings on Monadology*, Translated by Y. Or (1931; rev. edn. 1951).*

14. Descartes, *Meditationes de prima philosophia*. Translated by Y. Or (1932; rev. edn. 1950).*

15. Rousseau, *Contrat social*. Translated by Y. Or (1932; 2nd edn. 1947; rev. edn. 1956).*

16. J. S. Mill, *Utilitarianism*. Translated by Y. Or (1934; rev. edn. 1951).*

17. Plato, *Theaetetus*. Translated by Aryeh Simon (1934; rev. edn. 1951).*

18. Hume, *Inquiry concerning the Principles of Morals*. Translated by Y. Or (1934).*

19. Locke, *Essay concerning Human Understanding*. Abridged translation by Y. Or, 3 vols. (1935).*

20. Maimonides, *Treatise on the Terminology of Logic*. Moses ibn Tibbon's Hebrew translation from the Arabic, edited with commentary by L. Roth (1935).*

21. Descartes, *Discours de la méthode*. Translated by Y. Or (1936; rev. edn. 1942).*

22. J. H. Muirhead, *Elements of Ethics*. Translated by Y. Or (1937).*

23. Bertrand Russell, *The Problems of Philosophy*. Translated by M. Sternberg (1938).

24. *Illustrations of Post-Biblical Jewish Ethical and Religious Thought*. Selected and edited by L. Roth (Jerusalem: Mass, 1938; 2nd edn. 1946).

25. Berkeley, *Principles of Human Knowledge*. Translated by Y. Or (1939).*

26. *The A. Biram Presentation Volume (Topics of Hebrew Secondary Education in Eretz Israel)*. Includes articles by Roth on 'Problems' relative to the main title of the book, on 'The Teaching of Languages', and on 'Sport'.

27. '*Out of the Mouth of the Most High.*' An anthology chosen from the Hebrew Bible, by L. Roth (1954); also published in English translation: see I. 8.

28. Plato, *The Republic*. Abridged and edited by L. Roth from Z. Diesendruck's translation (Tel Aviv: Schocken, 1945; later edns. also published).

29. A collected volume of essays, *Educating the Citizen*, includes one by Roth entitled 'The Practical Import of the Sovereignty of the People' (1950).*

30. B. Bosanquet, *Logic: or the Morphology of Knowledge.* Translated by Y. Qeshet (Jacob Kopelowitz) (1952).*

Articles, Lectures, Introductions

Several of the articles listed below, although they are printed, include no indication of the publisher: they will presumably have been issued by the Hebrew University of Jerusalem. The same doubtless applies to some of the cyclostyled items (e.g. no. 60) which, in the light of the conditions prevailing in Palestine at the time, are to be regarded as having been virtually published in the same way as is no. 66, a periodical publication issued in cyclostyled form. There may, in some cases, be room for doubt as to whether such items were technically published: but since Leon Roth preserved them together with the file copies of his articles published in conventional form, they are included here.

31. 'The Tercentenary of Spinoza', *Ha'aretz*, 25 Nov. 1932.

32. 'Judaism and the Thought of Spinoza', *Moznayim*, 4/26 (16 Kislev 5693 [1933]).

33. 'The Authority of the Intelligence?' On Maimonides, *Moznayim*, 3 (1935), 370–80.

34. 'Plato in Hebrew', in *J. Klausner Presentation Volume* (Tel Aviv, 1937), 324–9.

35. 'Samuel Alexander"', *Moznayim*, 8 (1939), 383–91.

36. 'What have Greek Education and the Classics to Teach Us?', *Ḥinukh*, 13/2 (Jerusalem, 1940).

37. 'England and the English'. Introductory lecture to a course with the same title given in the Hebrew University, 1939–40, *Moznayim*, 11 (1940–1), 57–66. [Cf. II. 5.]

38. 'Towards the Basis of Democracy', *Moznayim*, 10 (1940), 449–58. [Cf. II. 78.]

39. 'Henri Bergson, *In Memoriam*', *Moznayim*, 12 (1941), 206–8.

40. Rector's opening address, for the academic year 1941/2, the Hebrew University (Jerusalem: Defus Aḥvah, 1941); 8 pp.

41. 'What has the [Hebrew] University Achieved for Hebrew?', *Ha'olam*, 27/8 (1941), 420–2.

42. 'The Place of Religion in the Upbuilding of the Land of Israel'. Synagogue address, *Gilyonot*, 13 (1942), 74–9.

43. 'How our University Goes About It', *Ha'olam*, 7 (1942), 52–3.

44. 'Ahad Ha'am and the Unification of the [Jewish] People', *Moznayim*, 14 (1942), 73–8.

45. The Hebrew Scout movement. Correspondence with Aryeh Kroch (1942).

46. 'The Study of Literature in Secondary Schools'. Opening address at a symposium, in *Miba'ayot ḥinukhenu* (symposium volume) (1942), 30–5.

47. 'Plato and Mendele Mokher Sforim', in *Miba'ayot ḥinukhenu* (symposium volume) (1942), 63.

48. 'Language and Culture', in *Am vasefer* (Tel Aviv: Haberit Ha'ivrit Ha'olamit, 1942), 6–15.

49. Rector's address, the Hebrew University, 24 November 1942; 4 pp.

50. 'Judaism in the Present Age'. Cyclostyled lecture delivered to Ḥug Hadati, 6 Feb. 1943; 3 pp.

51. 'The University and Contemporary Education', *Ha'aretz*, 12 Apr. 1943.

52. 'The Appropriate Orientation for English Studies'. An address to teachers, *Moznayim*, 16 (1943), 144–9.

53. 'National Service'. A broadcast talk to school-leavers, Jerusalem Radio, 2 July 1943; 4 pp.

54. 'Widening the University's Horizons'. Broadcast, Jerusalem Radio, 2 July 1943; 2 pp. [Cf. 1. 27].

55. 'The Diffusion of Culture', *Hagalgal*, 1/1, 22 July 1943.

56. Address to the Palestine section of the Friends of the Hebrew University, 25 July 1943; typescript, 4 pp.

57. 'Adult Education', *Hagalgal*, 1/7, 13 Oct. 1943, p. 14.

58. 'Faith for Living'. Review of E. H. Carr's *Conditions of Peace*, *Hagalgal*, 1/8, 28 Oct. 1943.

59. Rector's valedictory address, commencement of the academic year 1943/4, the Hebrew University, 14 Nov. 1943 (Jerusalem: Defus Aḥvah); 6 pp.

60. Rector's address at degree-giving ceremony (undated: between Autumn 1940 and Summer 1943); cyclostyled, 2 pp.

61. Opening address at a symposium on popular enlightenment in Erets Yisra'el and Hebrew education in the Diaspora, in *Haskalat ha'am ba'arets vehaḥinukh ha'ivri batefutsot* (Jerusalem, 1944), 1–11.

62. 'Education and Religion', *Moznayim*, 17 (1944), 344–8.

63. 'Ahad Ha'am in Retrospect: Fifteen Years', *Ha'olam*, 45 (1944), 308–9.

64. 'National Discipline and Individual Freedom', *Moznayim*, 18 (1944), 84–7.

65. 'Religion, State, and Spinoza's *Tractatus Theologico-politicus*', *Moznayim*, 19 (1945), 170–4, 227–32.

66. 'Religion without Socialism'. Fly-sheet of *Ha'agudah hadatit*, 2/1–2, 22 Dec. 1945, pp. 14–25 (cyclostyled).

67. 'Joseph Hermann Hertz, Chief Rabbi: *In Memoriam*', 14 Jan. 1946.

68. 'The Report of the British Government's Royal Commission on Education in Palestine', *Amudim*, 35, 7–8 July 1946(?).

69. 'The Beginnings of Philosophy' (Tel Aviv: Hotsa'at Aleh, 1947).

70. Address to a teacher's course, *Yediyot lamorim shel beit sefer hareali*, 12/2, 5 Oct. 1947, pp. 5–6 (cyclostyled).

71. '*Homo politicus* (Politics as a Branch of Ethics): *In Memoriam* J. L. Magnes', *Ba'ayot hazeman*, 7 Dec. 1948, pp. 7–8. [Cf. I. 28, I. 35.]

72. 'The Law of the Land: Education for Citizenship in the State of Israel' (Jerusalem: Histadrut Hamorim Ha'ivrim, 1948).

73. 'Wordsworth, Literary Values, and Education', *Mahbarot lesafrut*, 4/3–4 (1949), 47–55.

74. 'The Rights of Man'. Opening address to the Israel Society of Political Science, 5 Nov. 1950; 3 pp. (cyclostyled).

75. 'Religion and Ethics', *Yediyot lamorim shel beit sefer hareali*, 15/3, 1 Dec. 1950, pp. 15–22.

76. 'Why is an Association for Civil Rights Necessary?' (Givat Herzl: Defus Yisrael [Civil Rights League], 1949/50); 11 pp.

77. 'Isaac [Julius] Guttmann, *In Memoriam*', *Iyyun*, 2/1 (1951), 3–10.

78. 'Towards the Basis of Democracy' (Haifa: Beit Sefer Hareali, 1954). [Reprint of II. 38.]

79. Review of S. H. Bergman's *Righteousness in Israel*, *Moznayim*, 18 (1954), 322–3.

80. 'Statecraft and Politics in the Thought of Plato', *Eshkolot*, 1 (1954).

81. Introduction to H. Merhavya's *Freedom and Government* (Jerusalem: Goren, 1945), 5–6.

82. Introduction to the *Collected Works* of Ahad Ha'am (Tel Aviv: Devir; Jerusalem: Hotsa'ah Ivrit, 1947), pp. v–xii; other edns. also published.

83. Introduction to H. H. Ben-Sason's *Dictionary of Political Concepts* (Tel Aviv: M. Neumann, 1950), 5–6.

Index

Printed and bound by CPI Group (UK) Ltd, Croydon, CR0 4YY

13/04/2025

14656576-0001